Llewellyn's
Herbal Almanac
2008

© 2007 Llewellyn Worldwide
Llewellyn is a registered trademark
of Llewellyn Worldwide.
Editing/Design: Ed Day
Interior Art: © Fiona King,
excluding illustrations on pages 2–4,
which are © Mary Azarian
Cover Photos: © Digital Vision, © Brand X,
© Digital Stock, © Photodisc
Cover Design: Kevin R. Brown

You can order annuals and books
from *New Worlds*, Llewellyn's
magazine catalog. To request a free copy
call toll-free: 1-877-NEW WRLD, or visit our
website at http://subscriptions.llewellyn.com.

ISBN 0-7387-0554-3
978-0-7387-0554-5
Llewellyn Worldwide
2143 Wooddale Drive
Woodbury, MN 55125-2989

Table of Contents

Growing and Gathering Herbs

Culinary Herbs

Herbs for Health

Herbs for Beauty

Herb Crafts

Herb History, Myth, and Lore

Introduction to Llewellyn's Herbal Almanac

The herbal landscape is an ever-evolving one. The slow warming of our planet has temperate climates creeping toward the poles, while consumer trends prompt more immediate changes. But through it all, home-grown herbs still make a lasting impact. Llewellyn's 2008 *Herbal Almanac* takes a look at the year-round effects of herbs, re-examining the research on uses of herbs as medicine, as culinary spices, as cosmetics, and more. This year we once again tap into practical, historical, and just plain enjoyable aspects of herbal knowledge—using herbs to address maladies ranging from cradle cap to hypertension; boning up on organic-gardening practices; developing child-friendly crafts; and, of course, trying new recipes for staples such as soy and stew, breakfast delights, and delectable seasoning combinations that enhance your personal favorites. And we bring to these pages some of the most innovative and original thinkers and writers on herbs.

Growing, preparing, and using herbs allows us to focus on the old ways—when men and women around the world knew and understood the power of herbs. Taking a step back to a simpler time is important today as the pace of everyday life quickens and demands more and more of our energy—leaving precious little room for beauty, good food, health, love, and friendship. This state of affairs is perhaps not terribly surprising considering so many of us are out of touch with the beauty, spirituality, and health-giving properties of the natural world. Many of us spend too much of our lives rushing about in a technological bubble. We forget to focus on the parts of life that can bring us back into balance and harmony.

Though it's getting more difficult, you can still find ways to escape the rat race—at least once in a while. People are still striving to make us all more aware of the uplifting, beautiful ways that herbs can affect our lives. In the 2008 edition of the *Herbal Almanac*, the various authors pay tribute to the ideals of beauty and balance in relation to the health-giving and beautifying properties of herbs. Whether it comes in the form of a newfound natural skin cream, a way to ease hot-flash symptoms, another method to create a self-sustaining garden, or a new favorite recipe, herbs can clearly make a positive impact in your life.

Herbs are the perfect complement to the power of the mind, an ancient tool whose time has come back around to help us restore balance in our lives. More and more people are using them, growing and gathering them, and studying them for their enlivening and healing properties. We, the editors and authors of this volume, encourage the treatment of the whole organism—of the person and of the planet—with herbal magic. One person at a time, using ancient wisdom, we can make a new world.

Growing
and
Gathering
Herbs

The Herbal Landscape

ᗧᗧ by Dallas Jennifer Cobb ᗧᗧ

Yards and gardens provide ongoing opportunities for creativity, change, and imagination. They also provide a realm to work with and come to know nature. Landscaping a yard or garden requires knowledge of your climate, growing zone, and soil type in order to work with nature in an efficient and cooperative way.

But regardless of what climate you live in, there are herbs suited to landscaping your garden and yard. Landscaping with herbs provides an opportunity for functional, beautiful, and edible surroundings. Herbs nourish the body, mind, and spirit as food, medicine, and mystical helpers. And because they are hardy, herbs are well suited for landscaping in even the most severe climates.

There are thousands of varieties of herbs, but for the purpose of this article, only the most commonly available and hardy plants are recommended. Let this information interest you, then seek out a greenhouse or landscape specialist in your area to make other recommendations specific to your climate.

A Quick Herbal Primer

Perennials

Perennial herbs are those that come back year after year. They can survive winter with the warmth of mulch gathered around them and a blanketing layer of snow on top. Both these materials help to create air spaces that warm and protect the plant. For a good low-maintenance garden, use mostly perennials, spaced to allow them to grow to their potential.

Tender perennials are those that prefer to be taken inside, into a cool, not cold, environment during winter, and spring back to abundance when they are taken back outdoors in the spring.

Common perennial herbs used in landscaping include catnip, chives, comfrey, coneflower (echinacea), lavender, lemon balm, mint, oregano, sage, thyme, and yarrow. These are widely available at greenhouses or as cuttings from friends and neighbors.

Catnip (*Nepeta cataria*) is part of the mint family and grows wild in much of North America. Growing into a two- to three-foot tall bush, it sports lovely small white flowers on its top. Know for cooling fevers and calming nerves, catnip is also getting attention for its ability to repel mosquitoes. And, of course, our feline friends love it too.

Chives (*Allium sp.*) are an onionlike foliage with hardy purple blossoms that bloom early in the season. Their flavor is more delicate than onions and makes an excellent addition to salads, deviled eggs, and egg salad. A mature plant can create a lovely clump of color and is great as a border plant or visual centerpoint in a garden. The long needlelike foliage can be eaten as well.

Comfrey (*Symphytum officinale*) is a versatile medicinal herb to use in landscaping. It contains allantoin, which helps bones, cartilage, muscles, and skin cells to grow. Comfrey often grows along the banks of streams, and loves moist, clay-rich soil. Because comfrey grows up to four feet tall, it is best at the back of an herb bed. Be sure to tie it so it doesn't droop and overlay other plants. The purple flowering tops attract bees and butterflies.

Purple coneflower (*Echinacea purpurea*) is commonly known as coneflower and is a large daisylike flowering plant with antiviral, antifungal, and antibacterial properties. Coneflower loves the sun and enjoys well-drained, moist soil, and is recommended for USDA zones 4 through 9. Because of its size and abundant flowers, consider coneflower for mass plantings, perennial beds, and mixed borders. Be sure to leave it lots of room.

Lavender (*Lavandula angustifolia*) is a hardy perennial, good in USDA zones 4 through 9. Its tender perennial relative, Spanish lavender, is hardy to USDA zones 7 through 9 only. A most aromatic herb, the fresh flowers of lavender contain up to 0.5 percent volatile oil that is harvested and distilled into essential oil. Lavender is antispasmodic, so it is a common remedy used by menstruating women and headache sufferers. Lavender is also known to soothe frayed nerves. In the house, lavender sachets can be used to keep moths out of clothes and linens.

Lemon balm (*Melissa officinalis*) is said to be good for depression and tension, and aids digestion. Lemon balm is prolific, so it is best contained and deadheaded of seeds so that you don't end up with a lot of plants in your garden. The leaves possess an aromatic lemon scent and are effective insect repellents.

Mints (*Mentha sp.*) come in many varieties. Garden mint is usually spearmint (*Mentha spicata*) or peppermint (*Mentha piperita*). Flavored mints have been produced with tastes such as orange, citrus, and apple. Mint is known for calming upset stomachs, aiding digestion, reducing colic or flatulence, and calming nausea. Mint can also promote sweating and reduce a fever.

Oregano (*Origanum vulgare*) is best suited to full sun and dry, well-drained soil that is slightly alkaline. Originally from the Mediterranean region, oregano is a drought-resistant plant with a great taste. Used in Italian and Greek cooking, oregano is bushy and produces small pink and purple flowers from June to October. Oregano is easily grown from seed or cuttings, and a mature plant may be divided. Medicinally, oregano is used to relieve mucous and respiratory constriction.

Sage (*Salvia officinalis*) derives its name from its reputation for restoring failing memory and invoking insight. Sage grows on a woody stem and becomes bushlike after a couple of growing seasons with abundant silvery-green, velvety leaves.

Thyme (*Thymus vulgaris*) is the cultivated form of wild thyme, which grows throughout the Mediterannean region. Creeping plants with small leaves that come in many colors, thyme has been produced in a variety of flavors that add depth to stews, salads, soups, and meats. It is also a useful filler of cracks and holes in edging and borders, or in multilayered rock gardens.

Yarrow (*Achillea millefolium*) is highly valued as a medicinal herb, lowering fevers and blood pressure, aiding digestion, and toning the blood vessels. Yarrow grows up to three feet tall and has clusters of fragrant white flowers atop a stem with fernlike leaves. Yarrow can be used as a foliage in the back of a garden, visually filling in spaces with its abundant dark greenery.

Annuals

Annual herbs are those that die off at the end of the summer growing season. They do not winter over, though many of them will self-seed if not deadheaded, and tender seedlings will emerge in the spring. Annuals are useful for filling in spots between perennials, making distinct borders, and creating containers or baskets. Annuals can be changed from year to year for a variety of color, tastes, scents, and medicinal ingredients.

Some of the most popular annuals used in landscaping are also easy to grow: basil, calendula, dill, garlic, parsley, and rosemary.

Basil (*Ocinum basilicum*) leaves are bright green to purple, smooth or crinkled. Good in salads and tomato dishes, basil is used to make pesto to flavor pasta and pizza. Rubbed on insect bites, the leaves can relive itching and swelling. In landscaping, the abundant ruffled foliage can make a welcome addition to walkways and borders.

Calendula or pot marigold (*Calendula officinalis*) is a happy, bright flower varying in color from bright orange to bright yellow. Individual plants grow to about eight inches tall, ideal for adding color to the landscape. The edible petals look great in salads, and are widely used in skin-care preparations for their antifungal properties. Calendula blooms right up until the first frost kills it off, as long as you diligently deadhead. Seedpods that fall to the ground will self-seed and sprout the following spring.

Dill (*Anethum graveolens*) is commonly used by mothers as a remedy for colic in small children and to stimulate the flow of breast milk while nursing. The bluish-green stems sprout finely divided yellow-green foliage. In cooking, a small pinch of dill will flavor fish or chicken dishes, and it is often used for pickling.

Fennel (*Foeniculum vulgare*) adds lovely yellow flowers to the landscape. You can use fresh fennel leaves in salads to add flavor, or harvest the dried fennel seeds for use in cakes, breads, and fish dishes. Like dill, fennel helps stimulate breast milk and calm babies. It is also used to ease muscular and joint pains.

Garlic (*Allium sativum*) grows from individual garlic cloves separated from a bulb of garlic, and is available at greenhouses or supermarkets. Known as a powerful antimicrobial plant, it acts on bacteria, viruses, and parasites. Garlic also kills off pathogenic organisms in the digestive tract while supporting the growth of natural bacterial flora. Eaten raw or cooked, garlic is an excellent addition to salad dressings, stews, breads, and tomato dishes. In the garden, garlic sends up a tall snape that curls and flowers at the tip, standing up to three feet tall. It is a great focal point for a garden bed, and also deters many common garden pests.

Nasturtium (*Tropaeolum majus*) grows easily in most soils and produces a gorgeous edible flower varying in color from yellow through deep red. Its mild peppery taste is an excellent addition to salads, as well as a colorful food garnish. Nasturtium also seems to repel insects from the garden. A powerful antimicrobial, nasturtium is an excellent local remedy for infection.

Parsley (*Petroselinum crispum*) is widely used in cooking and is an abundant source of vitamin C. Medicinally, parsley is known for easing gas or flatulence, aiding digestion, and helping reduce water retention. Its leaves can be crinkled or smooth and grow to eight inches in height. Bushy, lush foliage makes parsley an excellent edging plant.

Rosemary (*Rosmarinus officinalis*) has green needlelike foliage and looks a bit like a small fir tree. Its piney taste complements poultry dishes and makes wonderful flavored vinegar and breads. Rosemary can also help to ease muscular pain, sciatica, and headaches when used as an essential oil, diluted and rubbed into the affected area.

Sensual Landscaping with Herbs

Don't limit herbs to eating and cooking. Herbs are not just functional, they are beautiful, stimulating many of the senses. In the garden, combine herbs with vegetables or flowers for variation of size, color, and purpose. As companion plants, many herbs have insect-repelling qualities and serve to protect vegetables and fruits from garden pests.

Culinary herbs can be kept in planters, boxes, and baskets near the kitchen, doorstep, or barbecue. For tender perennials and annuals, this method makes it easy to bring them inside as the weather cools. Just move the basket into the kitchen to enjoy fresh herbs throughout the year and brighten your inside space.

Aromatic herbs such as clary sage, lavender, mint, rosemary, and basil have a distinct pleasant smell because their leaves or flowers contain fragrant oils. Many are used to produce perfumes and essential oils used in aromatherapy.

Ornamental herbs usually have brightly colored flowers and foliage, and are often used dried in wreaths, potpourri, and dried-flower arrangements. Many have white or light-colored flowers that retain their color better when dried. Variegated thyme, mint, lavender, and chives produce colorful foliage and flowers widely used in dried ornamental arrangements.

Textures vary among herbs. Planting a garden with a variety of herbs means you can enjoy the sensual pleasure of different textures. Wooly thyme is soft and cozy, the velvety texture inspiring feelings of wealth and luxury. Sage has a rough raspy leaf that stimulates the tactile sense, and who can resist the silky feeling of calendula petals, which inspire fingers to stroke and caress.

Xeriscaping with Herbs

What is xeriscaping? Derived from the Greek word "xeros," meaning dry, and "scape," meaning a view or scene, *xeriscape* means "dry view." In landscaping, xeriscaping means establishing drought-tolerant plants that grow slowly and conserve water.

Xeriscapes also require fewer nutrients, so fewer compost or fertilizer applications are necessary. Pruning and maintenance are also kept to a minimum. When it comes to disease and pest resistance, xeriscape herbs are hardy and often insect repellents. With a large variety of drought-resistant plants available, there are many beautiful planting options.

Try to choose plants indigenous to your area, suited to the water and temperature climates. Native herbs are recommended, supplemented with drought-tolerant herbs originating in the Mediterranean, southern Europe, and Australia.

Herbs Commonly Used in Xeriscaping

Yarrow grows up to three feet tall and blooms abundantly and continuously throughout the summer. Russian sage grows as a small shrub with silvery feather-shaped leaves and showy purple-spike flowers. It grows up to eighteen inches tall, though flower spikes may reach higher as they seek more sunlight.

Lavender, with its tender spikes of dark purple flowers and enticing scent, loves a dry hotspot, and tolerates little water.

Furthermore, all the herbs with a Mediterranean origin, including oregano, parsley, and sage, work well in a xeriscape. Rosemary, especially the creeping varieties, are very drought-resistant. Finally, most varieties of thyme, especially lemon thyme and silver thyme, love the heat.

These herbs do well in dry conditions, can handle the heat, and require little water. They are great for xeriscaping and for low-maintenance gardens. Their foliage and flowers don't wilt or shrivel, and they look good throughout the dry season. When summer is over, make herbal wreaths for Thanksgiving or Christmas. They look wonderful, smell great, and you can pinch off little bits to use in your cooking.

Low-Maintenance Landscapes

Ideally, gardens provide us with an abundance of food, beauty, and pleasure. Designing a low-maintenance garden maximizes the abundance and minimizes the intense work. Whether you are aging, have limited time, or prefer to admire rather than perspire in the garden, then low-maintenance designs are for you.

Allow yourself to be a lazy gardener, knowing that nature has her own cycles and wisdom. Learn about the local climate and soil, and work with them rather than struggle against them.

Consider your lifestyle needs and how your landscape can support them. Many people think lawns are high maintenance and look for other options, converting small lawn spaces into patios or outdoor living areas. Larger lawns can be planted with ground covers or turned into wildflower gardens that attract hummingbirds, bees, and butterflies.

If you want to establish a garden over an area that has been lawn, forget about digging a garden bed. Try the lasagna layering method of composting instead. Mow the grass as low as you can, then cover the area with thick layers of newspaper or a single layer of corrugated cardboard (preferably brown, unbleached cardboard). On top of the paper, apply a thick layer of organic mulch—wood chip and straw work well. Leave the area alone for a few months until the grass underneath dies, composts, and turns into rich, healthy soil.

Look under the mulch and you will discover that the newspaper and grass are gone, and fertile soil remains. I suggest adding more organic composted material to the specific sites where you will locate your plants, and till the soil only in those immediate areas. Fill in around the plant with soil, and heap more mulch around the base. Mulch suppresses most weed growth and conserves moisture in the soil

Choose low-maintenance plants for your landscape, those that require little water or fertilizer, and minimal deadheading and pruning. Hardy herbs are ideal because they require minimal upkeep and are less likely to die from neglect. Organic-gardening techniques are ideal for herbs because they are so disease and pest resistant. There is little need for pesticides.

For long-term garden care, plan on applying a good layer of compost and mulch in the spring and an insulating layer of mulch in the fall to protect the plants over the winter months.

Primarily choose perennials, which will come back year after year, and supplement them with a small selection of annuals. If you gather seeds from your annuals, you can grow them each year from seed and save yourself from purchasing new seedlings. If you are really a lazy gardener like me, you can let the annuals self-seed, and see what sprouts up the following spring.

Build your flowerbeds up over time, through the regular application of compost and mulch. Raised beds are easier to tend because you don't have to stoop so low to weed or plant, and they have better drainage. In the early spring, raised beds are dry and ready to plant while the remainder of the garden is still muddy.

Keep your garden areas small to limit the time you spend in upkeep and maintenance. A narrow garden lets you reach easily into all areas of the garden. Several small, planned garden spaces can be easier to take care of than one larger space.

Minimize your potential plant problems by choosing disease-resistant plants and those suited to your climate, soil, and space.

Many people like to edge their gardens, which can be done with coiled plastic edging, wood, rocks, or natural landscaping. If you live near a beach, stream, or quarry, make a point of bringing home a rock or two to add to the edging on the raised beds.

Landscaping Design

Think of each bed as a comprehensive whole, tied together by theme, color, or purpose. Be sure to give each herb enough space so it isn't overcrowded or stressed by its companions. A stressed plant is a weakened plant, susceptible to disease or infestation. You might design a small kitchen garden for all your favorite cooking herbs, a distant butterfly garden full of bee balm and coneflower, or a hidden spirit garden with sweet grass and sage.

Start with a small sketch of the area. Consider the natural features including rocks, trees, gravel, and water. Sketch in your constructed features such as fences, sheds, or decks.

With open spaces, think first about their functional use. Will that area be one of high traffic, with kids and dogs playing there, or one of no traffic, far off, a distant view.

Good landscapes are designed in layers. Envision your beds from a distance, and see the creeping herbs and ground covers in the front of the bed where they fill in cracks in the borders and soften the edges. Standing toward the front of the beds are smaller plants, perennials and annuals interspersed. Toward the middle and back of the bed, plant size increases, with the tallest plants and shrubs in the rear. Don't let them overshadow smaller plants, block the sun, or obstruct your view.

Be sure to make boundaries between gardens distinct so that the eye is drawn to the garden. Let your eyes wander, envision what your garden and yard can be, and then get to work. This is your space to be creative and have fun in.

Endangered Herbs

≫ by Patti Wigington ≪

For many of us, herbs are a part of day-to-day life. We use them for cooking, skin care, and in ritual and ceremony. We place them around our homes to brighten our environment and enhance our lives. The majority of people—Pagans and non-Pagans alike—purchase herbs commercially rather than grow their own. Because of this consumer trend, the days of a simple country woman going out and wildcrafting—gathering herbs in the wild—have vanished. Instead, the herb business has blossomed into a multi-billion dollar industry.

Where previously we could only pick up a package of comfrey at the local Wiccan shop—or if we were lucky, the health food store—now grocery stores stock herbal products on their shelves right beside the soup and the potato chips. Dozens of mail-order companies sell herbs, a business that has increased exponentially as the world gets connected online.

The increasing demand for herbal products—not just from consumers but from big pharmaceutical companies as well—has led to an alarming drift. The demand is beginning to outweigh the supply. As if that wasn't problematic enough, as society expands and housing developments and shopping malls are built, civilization itself is encroaching on the natural habitat of the plants upon which so many of us rely. Many herbs we've taken for granted are at risk of becoming endangered or extinct.

We know that care for the Earth and its resources is paramount. Yet many of us are actually contributing to the problem by using plants that are at risk, either for magical or mundane purposes. A wildlife trade monitoring group, TRAFFIC Network, has estimated that nearly one-third of the 16,000 species of plants growing in North America today could be extinct within a few generations.

Popular and At-Risk Herbs

Ginseng

Ginseng is one of the most widely recognized at-risk plants. Although it enjoyed popularity in Asia for centuries as a treatment for a number of ailments, once China's supply was depleted, American ginseng began to be harvested for shipment to the Far East. Recently, Western society discovered the benefits of ginseng, and now it's available in every health-food store across the nation. Ginseng is a very slow-growing plant, which creates a problem for harvesters. The plant must be left alone until it is at least five years old before it can reproduce at a sustainable level. According to the United States Department of Agriculture, there is a trend toward harvesting immature roots, and now the environmental repercussions of gathering ginseng are being felt too soon.

Echinacea

Echinacea shot to popularity in the past few years as an all-purpose cold remedy and immune system stimulant. The most common commercially harvested variety, *Echinacea purpurea*, grows easily, but wild species have been decimated thanks to commercial and residential development.

Sandalwood

Sandalwood, which is often found in rituals dealing with protection, healing, and spirituality, has faced a tremendous decline in recent years due to overharvesting and deforestation. India, once the home of most of the world's sandalwood commerce, has been unable to put an end to illegal harvesting. As such, it is becoming increasingly more difficult to find a stand of mature sandalwood in forests where they were plentiful just a generation ago.

Goldenseal

Goldenseal, a low-growing woodland plant believed by some to help fight off colds and infections, is also used in healing-related magic. It too has been added to the list of at-risk herbs. The early Native American tribes saw it as an all-purpose medicinal herb, and used it in the treatment of everything from cancerous tumors to digestive disorders to fever. When white settlers arrived in the Ohio Valley, goldenseal's main growing area, they learned quickly about the value of this small plant, which was recognized as a powerful healing herb. As demand increased, the supply dwindled.

What Can We Do?

Sadly, the plight of these plants is not uncommon. More and more species are added to the at-risk category each year. If we have pledged to protect and honor our planet, how can we do so in a way that will allow us to use the herbs we need and sustain them at the same time?

For starters, try to use nonendangered substitutions wherever possible. If you're looking for herbs from a medicinal perspective, many plants out there have similar properties. For example, if you are considering purchasing some ladyslipper, which is used for relaxation and calming the nerves, try valerian instead. The two have a similar genetic make-up and have the same effect, yet valerian is not considered at risk for extinction. Ladyslipper is referred to in some areas as "American valerian," despite the fact that they are two different species.

Goldenseal, the healing herb, can often be replaced with Yerba Mansa, barberry, and Oregon grape root. All three contain medicinal quantities of berberine—the chemical that gives goldenseal its healing properties—and yet none of the three are even at risk for extinction.

When it comes to the magical properties of herbs, you have even more leeway. Any reputable book on magical herbalism will offer a list of correspondences, and you'll find that substitutions are often easy once you've put a bit of thought into your goals. Ginseng is popular to include in spells for love—why not replace it with another love-oriented plant, such as jasmine, hibiscus, or even the common rose? Slippery elm bark is the perfect herb for a spell of persuasion, yet its population is dropping because of the invasion of the deadly Dutch elm disease. Instead, substitute marshmallow root, which contains not only the same medicinal properties as slippery elm bark, but the same magical ones as well.

We can also help replenish supplies by growing our own herb gardens. If you find that you use certain herbs more than others—and nearly all Wiccans and Pagans do—why not grow them yourself? Herbs don't require a lot of space, and can flourish under some pretty unpleasant climate conditions. A few even seem to thrive on neglect, so if you don't have a green thumb, don't worry. If you've never gardened before, start small. Mark out a place in your yard that gets at least six hours of direct sunlight each day, and plan ahead of time which herbs you want to grow there. An herb garden is not just a great source of renewable resources; it's also a spot where you can spend time relaxing and meditating.

If you don't have a lot of land, or if you're living in a shared space such as an apartment building or dormitory, never fear. Container gardens are simple and cost-effective. The best part about planting herbs in a pot or container is that you can move them indoors when the weather becomes inclement and you'll have fresh herbs at your fingertips all year. Culinary herbs can be kept on a windowsill near your cooking area, so that whenever you need a bit of thyme, sage, or rosemary, they're right there waiting. Growing your own herbs is also far more cost-effective than purchasing them commercially, so it's worth the time and effort if you have an interest in doing so.

Finally, be an educated and responsible consumer. Make yourself aware of which herbs are endangered, and then refuse to buy them or any products in which they are used as ingredients. Several years ago, a group of herbalists formed United Plant Savers (UPS) to help protect endangered plants. According to UPS, some of the plants currently on the at-risk list are black cohosh, blue cohosh, American ginseng, false unicorn root, eyebright, peyote, trillium, and Virginia snakeroot.

If you must purchase herbs commercially—let's face it, there are some things you just can't grow in your backyard—try to obtain them from an organic grower. Buying herbs that are certified as organic ensures that the plant has been cultivated rather than wildcrafted. While there are many large commercial herb farms growing plants for resale, you may be surprised to find smaller-scale herb growers in your own town. After all, it doesn't take a lot of space to grow herbs, and buying herbs locally is a good way to know where the plants came from. Not only that, it helps support small farmers who may be supplementing their regular crops with herb sales.

The idea that someday, possibly within just a few generations, we may have driven some of our herb supplies to extinction is a frightening one. The sad truth is that unless we change the way we look at herbs—not just as a supply or tool, but as a valuable natural resource—this is precisely what will happen. Stands of sandalwood trees will be gone forever. Patches of goldenseal will never again be found in the forests. Countless other plants that we tend to take for granted will be unavailable.

By growing our own supplies when possible, and becoming responsible and educated consumers, hopefully we can stave off this trend. Perhaps we will be able to look back at our lives and know that when we pledged to protect the Earth and its resources, we really did what we said we would do. We will be able to look at our children and grandchildren one day and say to them with pride, "Guess what? I left you something!"

Marvelous Mints

by Magenta Griffith

Mint is a marvelous plant in many ways. The first is how it grows; it spreads so well it can take over a garden, flourishing in sun or shade. Another is its numerous medicinal uses. A third is its intense flavor: one pound of mint oil can flavor 135,000 sticks of gum.

Two mints, peppermint (*Mentha piperita*) and spearmint (*Mentha viridis*), are the best known and most widely cultivated. Spearmint is distinguishable from peppermint by the absence of a leafstalk. Its flavor is milder than peppermint. These perennial herbs originated in the Mediterranean region, and were introduced into Britain by the Romans.

They now grow all over the world. Lesser-known varieties also prosper for arcane reasons that go beyond flavor.

Pennyroyal (*Mentha pulegium*) is also a true mint and a perennial, but it is only used medicinally because the flavor is unpleasant. The species name *pulegium* is Latin for fleabane, after the plant's property of driving away fleas. Pennyroyal is still used today as an herbal insect repellent. Also, rats and mice are said to be so averse to the smell of any mint—fresh or dried—that they will leave food alone where mint is scattered.

Other mints grow wild, and most are considered weeds. Water mint (*Mentha aquatica)* and curled mint (*Mentha acrispa*) grow in most of northern Europe, as does corn mint (*Mentha arvensis*). None of these have as pleasant a flavor as peppermint or spearmint. Bergamot is considered to be a mint by some botanists, under the name *Mentha citrata*. It is used for perfumes and is the essential ingredient in Earl Grey tea. Horsemint (*Mentha sylvestris)* is found mostly in swampy areas and has very weak flavor compared to peppermint.

The Latin word for mint, *Mentha*, comes from the name of the nymph Menthe. According to one classical writer, Menthe was a nymph of Kokytos who lay with Aidoneus (another name for the lord of the underworld). When he raped Persephone, Menthe complained loudly, raving with jealousy. Menthe boasted that she was nobler of form and more beautiful than Persephone, claiming that Aidoneus would return to her and would banish Persephone from his domain. In anger, Persephone's mother, Demeter, trampled Menthe and destroyed her. From the earth where she was trampled sprang the herb that bears her name.

Mint is not grown from seeds. To grow mint, take a clipping from another mint plant and place it in water—a drinking glass will do. Let it grow for at least a couple of weeks until the white root sprouts are at least three inches long. Place it in soil, either in a pot or in your garden. Once started, mint will grow in almost any soil, though it does best in cool and damp surroundings. Because it spreads so easily, many people prefer to grow mint where its expansion will be limited. For example, you can sink a large flowerpot in the ground and plant mint in it. When harvesting mint, try taking sprigs with big leaves so smaller leaves get more light. Harvest before it has come into full flower for best results. Taking away sprigs from time to time will encourage the plant to keep growing. You can continue to harvest mint until first frost. Be sure not to pull hard on the plant; if you don't disturb the roots, it will keep growing for years. Remove any discolored or insect-eaten leaves, tie the stems loosely into bunches, and hang to dry on strings in the usual manner directed for bunched herbs. Or you can pick the leaves individually and dry them in a dark place. Kept in an airtight container, dried mint will keep a long time.

Mints have been used medicinally for hundreds, perhaps thousands, of years. There is evidence that *M. piperita* was cultivated by the Egyptians. Pliny tells us that the Greeks and Romans wore crowns of peppermint at feasts and decorated their tables with sprigs of mint. They also used it to flavor sauces and wine. Mint is mentioned in the *Icelandic Pharmacopoeias* of the thirteenth century. In the fourteenth century, mint was used for whitening the teeth. Dr. Westmacott, the author of a work on plants published in 1694 that mentions the different kinds of mint, states that they are well known to herbalists and apothecaries.

Mint tea is a traditional remedy for stomach trouble. Renowned seventeeth-century herbalist Nicholas Culpeper gives nearly forty distinct maladies for which mint is "singularly good." The application of a strong decoction of spearmint is said to cure chapped hands. The bruised fresh leaves of the mint plant are said to relieve local pains and headache.

Mint is a local anesthetic and helps relieve itching, and, because it imparts a tingling sensation to the skin, it is used in after-shave lotions and skin fresheners. Due to its anesthetic effect, it can be used to prevent seasickness.

Several studies have shown that irritable-bowel syndrome sufferers who took peppermint oil capsules reduced their symptoms significantly compared to patients who took a placebo. Researchers believe the oil relaxes the smooth muscle in the lining of the intestine, which reduces muscle spasms. The recommended dose is 90 milligrams three times per day, preferably with a meal. Because peppermint oil can trigger acid reflux, make sure that you take the coated-capsule form. This will reduce your chances of getting heartburn.

Peppermint and spearmint are used in candy, chewing gum, coffee, cocoa, and various baked goods. They are used to flavor toothpaste and mouthwash, as well as to perfume soap. The oil extracted from mint through steam distillation is highly concentrated. Chewing gum companies blend mint oils to maintain a consistent and specific flavor. It takes an acre of mint to produce thirty pounds of mint oil. Originally, mint oils were used mainly for medicinal purposes, but the popularity of both chewing gum and toothpaste in the early twentieth century provided a new market. Today 70 percent of U.S.–produced mint oil is used in the United States; 40 percent of that goes to flavor gum and 30 percent to flavor toothpaste and mouthwash.

Many people think of mint only in connection to sweets like hard candies and gum. But because mint aids the digestion, it is also used in many savory dishes. In Europe, fresh mint sprigs are used to flavor green peas and new potatoes, and the powdered leaves are used with pea soup. In Germany, powdered, dried mint is often used in pea and bean purées, as well as in gravies. In Wales, it is not unusual to boil mint with cabbage. Mint jelly, traditionally served with lamb, can be made by steeping mint leaves in apple jelly, or in one of the various kinds of commercial gelatin. In the Middle East, mint is used extensively in savory foods. Authentic tabbouleh will contain chopped mint.

The most unusual use I know is that plumbers use peppermint oil to test the tightness of pipe joints. Because it's very volatile and has a pungent odor, it can be used to check for leaks. Mint truly is a very versatile herb.

A Garden Spot Made in the Glade

✿ by Suzanne Ress ✿

If you own, or have owner's permission and access to, a plot of wooded land, whether it be half an acre or many, an enchanting way to become familiar with the woods and all of its occupants is to make a glade garden and a system of paths leading to it.

A glade garden can be used during every season, under sunlight and moonlight, for solitary meditation, intimate picnics, group meetings, and more. If you make and take care of it yourself, the ongoing process is extremely rewarding and bound to become an important facet of your life.

The best time of year to start is early spring, after the snow has melted, but before you can see any new plant growth on the trees or underfoot. You must first decide where to set up your glade garden, and the only way to do this is to don a pair of sturdy boots,

and, with a long ribbon or strip of rag in tow, wander through the underbrush of old vines, molding leaves, fallen branches, and whatever else may be there, until you find a spot that feels right. This could be because of a particularly friendly tree, a natural spring, unusual plant growth, or for no easily identifiable reason at all!

In my case, the right spot was marked by an abandoned game bird shelter that was made of wood with a terra cotta tile roof, which I thought would be perfect as a storehouse for candles and well-wrapped incense. When I stood in front of the small shelter, I was facing west and looking toward a view of the alps on the horizon. After standing a little longer, I could see there was a natural circle of strong old oak and chestnut trees just downhill, and behind me to the north, a grove of beautiful white-barked birch trees, which I now think of as "the white ladies." Within the circle of oaks there were four or five small dead locust trees that, as I leaned against them, fell over and were shortly cleared away and made into firewood.

What's important is that you find a place that is already naturally open at least three or four yards around, or that can easily be opened by removing dead wood. Eventually, you may need to cut away a few very small sapling trees. Although in general it is best not to kill any living thing, sometimes clearing away too-crowded growth allows more established trees to become healthier.

A glade garden does not need to be very large. In fact, much larger than six yards in diameter would make your woodland hideaway feel less secret and intimate.

Once you have found the right spot, in order to find it again you should mark it by tying your ribbon or rag around the trunk or in a low branch of a highly visible tree. Soon enough you will get to know each tree as an individual.

Clearing a path to the glade garden, whether it diverges from an existing path or is the very first path in an "unused" woods, is started by walking from the desired entrance to the glade to wherever the path must start.

If your path is very long, or your visual memory not so strong, bring enough strips of rag or ribbon to mark a trail, tying pieces to trees and plants every so often as you walk. Walk slowly, and put your feet down firmly. Carefully observe trees, fallen trunks, rocks, and anything else you pass. Is the route you are walking the best, or is there a less steep, less cluttered, or more picturesque detour you could take? Remember that you will have to clear whatever is in the way, so try to take the path of least resistance. Sometimes you may feel attracted to a certain tree or shrub. Make your path pass by it, even if it means having to clear a few extra yards. A winding path seems mystical and merry, but, as a breather for the spirit, make some sections straight, too.

As soon as you come to where your path begins, turn around and walk back again to your glade garden entrance, trying to follow the exact same route. Do this at least twice, and more if possible, as this is how the path begins to take shape.

When you are ready to start clearing your first path and glade, you will need garden gloves, clippers, sharp long-handled pruning sheers, a rake, and the good sense to know when you are tired and need to take a rest! It's easy to get overenthusiastic and want to finish all the clearing and set up the garden as soon as possible, but try to take your time—it's much more enjoyable to work with a clear mind and rested body. And, unless you find yourself in a very well-kept woods, you will probably have to put in several days hard work clearing away undergrowth.

Pay close attention to what is growing naturally! If you don't already know the names, habits, and uses of the plants native to your area, this is a good "hands-on" way to learn. There are many excellent gardening and plant identification books you can borrow or buy, as well as detailed botanical sites on the Web. Knowing the plants (including trees) that already grow on your land will give you a clue as to what type of soil you are dealing with, which will be important if you want to plant new trees, shrubs, flowers, or greenery. Many wild plants can be culti-vated by carefully transplanting them from one spot to another, grouping more of them together, protecting them from invaders, and, if necessary, adding organic compost and insect repellents. In my case I found and transplanted primrose, lily of the valley, periwinkle, ferns, jack-in-the-pulpit, violets, and ground ivy.

If your path is on hilly land, start at the top and work your way down. The first time through, use your long-handled pruning sheers to cut any small trees and thick-stemmed leaves and vines as close to the ground as possible, then throw them to the sides where they will naturally compost over time. Pulling up masses of vines, like brambles and honeysuckle, is easiest to do by hand, but make sure to wear long sleeves and gloves. Toss masses of vines into the woods where they will dry up and gradually be transformed into soil.

Once you have removed the larger and more difficult growth, rake the path of all dead leaves. Finally, pull up or cut off at ground level anything that remains, unless you have decided to keep or transplant it.

Fallen branches can be dragged and piled to the side of the path, in a convenient place for later use as firewood. Sometimes, before trees get their leaves, it is difficult to tell which ones might be dead. If you think a small tree (no bigger than a ten-inch diameter) is dead, lean against it with all of your weight and push. If it's dead, its roots will not hold and the tree will lean with you, and, with further pushing and rocking, will fall. You are acting as a strong wind does, clearing away what needs to be cleared.

When the footpath is cleared, walk it with your pruning sheers and cut any low tree branches that get in your face. Pruning a tree, like trimming your hair, makes it grow stronger, so don't hesitate to cut what's in your way. As you prune, think about who will be walking the path—someone taller than yourself? Someone on horseback? Consider height as well as width.

If your path is very long, or if you make additional paths, you might wish to select a resting place along the way under an inviting tree or next to a mossy bank where you could place a bench, log, or large rock to sit on. Prepackaged benches can be bought in boxes at do-it-yourself centers, dragged (or pushed in a wheelbarrow) to your chosen location, and assembled on-site.

As you begin clearing your glade, every so often sit down and observe your space. Listen, breathe, and look all around you, including up. If you start in March, before the trees have begun sprouting their new leaves, you might not realize how shady your garden might be in July, so keep this in mind if you intend to plant anything that requires a lot of sun. Spring bulbs have been a great boon to my garden—daffodils, crocus, and hyacinth—as they bloom before the garden gets shady, and create a burst of color and scent in the woods when nature is just getting out of bed.

When you have finished clearing your space, look at it and meditate a while. What will you be using your garden for? What features must it have? Consider all senses and angles—how do you want the garden to look when you approach it from the path? Mysterious, with a narrow entrance obscured by plants, or inviting with a view of bright flowers? If your glade contains a natural brook or spring, it will be blessed with the sound of moving water, but if not, you could hang a wind chime from a low branch. For nighttime use, you will want a source of light. Inexpensive garden hurricane lamps on stakes are pretty and make a soft, warm light. Solar lights will not work in the woods unless your glade is exceptionally sunny. White stones used as borders soak up light during the day and glow at night.

Where in your garden will you sit, and will other people be sitting with you? A tree stump, log, or large rock makes a simple and free seat, or perhaps you'd like to put in a more comfortable bench or two, or a hammock. If you are going to hold ceremonies in your garden, where will your altar or magic circle be, and what will it be made of? Do you want to plant flowers, greenery, or shrubs? Consider not only what these plants will give to you, but what you must promise to them—water, protection from invading plants and insects, and enough light.

The hardest work is now done, but your job as caretaker will go on and on, season after season. In this capacity, you can truly get to know and enjoy your glade garden and woods paths.

If your garden is ready by May, Beltane is an enchanting time to celebrate in a glade. In my garden, white petals of locust flowers flutter to the ground throughout the woods in May, making it easy to walk the paths by moonlight. Weave flowers into your friend's or lover's hair by Moon and lantern light, and make a special potion containing edible flowers. Nature's juices are really flowing now, so you'll have to patrol your paths and garden at least two or three times a week for marauding weeds.

Summer Solstice is traditionally a day of magic power for herbs, plants, and trees. If there is an oak tree in your glade, place your left hand on its trunk at midday of the Solstice to bring about a year of good health, happiness, and luck. Have a midnight picnic, bring sleeping bags, and spend the shortest night of the year under the stars.

When leaves begin to change and fall, enjoy their multicolored hues on your paths and garden before getting out your rake. Take photographs late in the afternoon when the Sun is orangey-red and low. Raking paths and glades is much easier than a lawn—just rake all the leaves over to the sides to decompose. But absolutely make sure to rake, at least every ten days or so, or you'll find a lot of new trees growing on your path next spring.

As days grow cooler and nights longer, roast chestnuts in a safely located fire pit or grill. And remember to plant bulbs for next spring!

Once the ground freezes you won't have much work to do. In my garden there is a little holly tree I like to decorate for the birds at Yule time, stringing dried bread cubes and bits of dried fruit and hanging little orange kumquats from its branches.

Whatever season it is, walk your paths often, and take time out from your busy daily life to enjoy your glade garden. It will give back to you many times over what you have given to it!

Shadowplay: Herbs for the Shady Garden

❧ by Elizabeth Barrette ❧

Too often, gardeners look at shade as a problem rather than an asset. This happens often in herbalism because many well-known plants come from the Mediterranean and grow in full sunlight. However, many herbs thrive in lower light conditions, and some need protection from fierce sun, particularly in hot climates.

Also, most yard and garden spaces have a mix of different light availability. My two-acre yard runs the complete spectrum from sunny meadows to dappled lawn under trees to a few corners that are quite dark. A small yard may have a sunny patch, but almost always has sections overshadowed by the house or some trees. When you want to grow herbs, you work with the space you have and plant a diversity of species accordingly.

Types of Shade

All shady gardens are not created equal. The density and duration of light vs. darkness influence what kinds of plants can grow in a given place. The amount of available water also plays a vital role: damp or wet shade is much more hospitable than dry shade. Sometimes you can modify the type of shade to make it a little darker by erecting an arbor, or a little brighter through replacing a brick wall with a lattice fence. Use the guide below to help determine what kind of light conditions you have available.

Full sun – For comparison, this space receives direct sunlight for at least six hours a day, usually including the brilliant midday sun. Unless the soil is very heavy, it dries out fast after a rain. Plants that prefer full sun tend to dwindle in the shade; plants that prefer shade often wilt in full sun. Note that in heavily overcast climates, a garden right out in the open may not get enough light to qualify as full sun! You may then do better planting species that do well in partial or dappled shade.

Partial shade – The area receives several hours of direct sun per day, and shade at other times. Often the location gets only morning sun or only evening sun. For instance, a garden on the eastern side of a house may get direct sun in the morning, but open or deep shade in the afternoon. Other times, a garden may get morning and evening sun. If it lies under a solitary tree, slanting light will reach the garden, but the canopy will block overhead rays. This is useful for plants that can't tolerate the intensity of noon sun, especially in hot or drought-prone environments.

Dappled shade – This creates a pattern of equally mixed sun and shade, which travels across the area over the course of the day. Fine-leaved trees such as birch, honeylocust, or goldenrain create this type of shade under their canopies.

Open shade – Here we see fragmented direct sunlight, but bright indirect light. Large trees with dense canopies, such as oak and maple, cast this kind of shade when they are spaced some distance apart, as in parks and yards. Their high branches block most of the direct light, but allow ambient light to get underneath, reflected from the ground or other nearby objects. A garden near a wall or building may also be in open shade. If not watered, open shade gardens are often a bit dry.

Deep shade – This space receives little or no direct sunlight, and has moderate ambient light. The understory of a forest typically falls into this category; the light is absorbed by successive layers of foliage so that only an occasional sunbeam reaches the ground. Even in daylight it has a slightly dusky tone. Woodland gardens tend to be moist. Certain wildflowers and herbs belong to such habitats, and languish elsewhere. Few other plants do well here. A walled garden, or the space near a building with an overhang, can also qualify as deep shade. These tend to be dry, and may need extra watering.

Full shade – The area receives no direct sunlight and little ambient light. It always looks rather dark. Rock overhangs, wall corners and crevasses, decks and boardwalks, canyon bottoms, and the undersides of dense trees such as pines and spruces can all create this type of shade. If the ground stays dry, little or nothing will grow there. But in wet areas, such as a hidden spring or a water garden, a thriving colony of mosses, lichens, liverworts, and ferns may emerge: a miniature enchanted forest that will grow nowhere else.

Shade-Loving Herbs

Angelica (*Angelica archangelica*) can grow in full sun in cool climates, but requires protection from summer sun in warmer climates. This statuesque plant reaches up to five feet tall and prefers rich, moist, well-drained soil. It makes an ideal background for a woodland garden or shady border. Candied, the stems make an excellent garnish for sweets.

Borage (*Borago officinalis*) prefers partial shade, growing about eighteen inches high. It has large oval leaves covered in hairs, and star-shaped blue flowers. Candy the flowers for a garnish or dry them for use in herbal crafts. The leaves are rich in potassium and calcium.

Chameleon plant (*Houttuynia cordata*, 'Chameleon'), also known as 'Hot Tuna,' thrives in shady, wet areas. In fact, it will grow in water, at pond edges. However, some of mine have run rampant along the partly shady and rather dry eastern wall of our house, and from there spread to the openly shady and considerably dryer northern wall. This herb has a hot spicy flavor. Its heart-shaped leaves are a dramatic blend of green, yellow, cream, and hot pink.

Chervil (*Anthriscus cerefolium*) prefers cool, partial, or dappled shade especially in summer or hot climates. It does better in spring or fall plantings, and needs rich moist soil. Chervil reaches up to twenty inches in height. Its ferny leaves are rich in carotene, iron, and magnesium; use them in salads.

Comfrey (*Symphytum officinalis*) thrives in shade but tolerates some sun, so dappled, partial, or open shade all work. Large hairy leaves rise eighteen inches from a central crown, and blue bell-shaped flowers appear on taller stalks.

Corsican mint (*Mentha requienii*) is among the most delicate varieties of mint. Its tiny, low-growing leaves exude a sweet and creamy mint odor. It needs dappled to dense shade, and rich, moist soil. If protected from more aggressive plants, it spreads to make a nice ground cover, especially in a woodland garden or around a water garden.

Creeping thyme (*Thymus serpyllum*) likes partial shade, grows well in borders and containers, and makes an excellent ground cover. This herb reaches three to six inches tall, but will trail farther down if planted in a hanging basket or by the edge of a wall. In cooking, the tiny leaves go well with robust meats such as beef, pork, and lamb.

Ferns (*Matteucia struthiopteris*, lady fern *Athyrium filix-femina*, *pteridum acquilinum*, etc.) come in many varieties, which all require considerable shade. Do not expose ferns to more than dappled sunlight. Some species live in full shade, such as wet cave mouths. Amphibians love to seek shelter under fern leaves.

Foxglove (*Digitalis purpurea*) tolerates partial, dappled, or open shade in cool areas, but this forest plant really prefers the deep shade and moist rich soil of its understory home. Oblong leaves form a low rosette surmounted by a dramatic flower spike reaching three to six feet high.

Ginger (*Zingiber officinale*) needs rich, moist soil and open or deep shade. Indirect sunlight is okay. It does well in woodland gardens, but also in containers.

Jupiter's beard (*Centranthus ruber*) grows in partial or dappled shade. Bushy clumps of lance-shaped leaves reach up to three feet and produce clusters of tiny pinkish to red flowers.

Lemon balm (*Melissa officinalis*) tolerates partial, dappled, or open shade. It grows well in borders and containers, reaching three feet in height. Its leaves complement fish and chicken, and make a delicious tangy tea. Use them fresh or frozen, as the oils dissipate when dried.

Lily of the valley (*Convallaria majalis*) prefers dappled or open shade. It grows well under trees, in borders, and in pots. Magically, it promotes peace, harmony, and love.

Lovage (*Levisticum officinale*) grows in partial, dappled, or open shade, towering up to six feet tall. Plant in backgrounds or along walls; water thoroughly to encourage deep root development. Its celerylike flavor makes lovage popular in soups and stocks. In bath water, the leaves are deodorizing and antiseptic.

Mandrake (*Mandragora officinarum*) prefers partial shade. It needs a light, deep soil. The leaves first grow upright to about a foot high, then spread out to lie flat on the ground.

Moss (*Thuidium, Leucobryum, Polytrichum, Dicranum*, etc.) may tolerate dappled or open shade, but thrives with deep to full shade. It prefers acidic soil relatively poor in nutrients, and abundant moisture. Northern or eastern wooded slopes are ideal.

Patchouli (*Pogostemon cablin*) grows well in moist, shady sites so it's a good choice for a woodland garden. The bushy plant reaches three to four feet tall, nice as a middle planting in front of foxglove or angelica.

Peppermint (*Mentha spp.*) likes partial shade and rich, moist, well-drained soil. It reaches up to two feet high. Grow in pots to prevent spreading, or allow to ramble as a tall ground cover. It goes well with lamb, fruit, and chocolate. Peppermint makes excellent jelly and the leaves can be candied for garnishes.

Pineapple sage (*Salvia elegans*) requires protection from intense midday and afternoon sun, making it ideal for partially shady gardens with an eastern exposure. It also needs more water than most sage varieties. This herb has a pineapple scent and its bright-red flowers attract hummingbirds.

Roman chamomile (*Chamaemilum nobile*) needs protection from midday sun; grow it in partial or dappled shade. It makes an excellent ground cover, growing only four to twelve inches high. Its feathery leaves and daisylike flowers cheer up a shady garden. Chamomile tea soothes digestion, relaxes the nerves, and brings sleep. It also makes a brightening rinse for blond hair.

Salad burnet (*Poterium sanguisorba*) can tolerate full sun in spring or fall, but tends to suffer sunburn in summer. Protect it from harsh afternoon sun. This herb grows well under deciduous trees or in containers. It can reach up to eighteen inches high, but is best harvested at about four inches because the leaves get bitter with age. Its nutty, cucumber flavor makes it popular in sandwiches, salads, and herbal vinegars.

Sweet woodruff (*Gallium odoratum*) enjoys dappled to deep shade, and a variety of soil conditions. The leaves form rosettes along the stems, and tiny white flowers appear at the stem ends. It often appears as a ground cover in woodland gardens. Sweet woodruff is the crucial ingredient in May Wine.

Violet (*Viola pedata*) enjoys partial to deep shade. Mine grow all over the yard in a variety of conditions. The heart-shaped leaves reach two to five inches high. The flowers may be candied as a garnish, or used to make floral water, perfume, or potpourri.

Wild bergamot (*Monarda fistulosa*) likes partial shade in rich, well-drained soil. The bushy plant reaches three to four feet tall. Its pink to red trumpet-shaped flowers attract bees and hummingbirds. The leaves make excellent hot or cold tea.

Designing a Shady Garden

Shady gardens perform best when planned primarily around the amount of light available in a given location, as that has the strongest influence on what types of plants will thrive. However, you can usually work in a secondary theme, such as the intended use of the plants or their attraction for other creatures.

One popular choice is the woodland garden, which thrives in open to deep shade under trees. A small woodland garden could include angelica, comfrey, foxglove, ginger, lily of the valley, patchouli, sweet woodruff, and violet. A larger woodland garden might add a darker grotto with ferns and moss around a tiny pool. These secluded gardens and their plants attract shy creatures like frogs and snakes.

Another common feature is the shady border, which runs alongside a building or fence. Typically in partial shade, this allows a wide choice of plants that need just a little protection from the Sun. Plant taller ones at the back, shorter ones in front. Good choices include chervil, creeping thyme, lemon balm, peppermint, salad burnet, and wild bergamot. This is ideal as a kitchen garden for tea, salad, and seasoning.

Many yards have a spot between the trees that gets a mix of sun and shade, direct and dappled light. This is a lovely place for flowers that attract hummingbirds and butterflies, a way of brightening up the shadows. Plant such flora as borage, chameleon plant, Jupiter's beard, pineapple sage, and Roman chamomile. Add a gazing ball, birdbath, or white statue to draw the eye.

Shady gardens illustrate two important magical principles on a very practical level. First, they balance light and darkness, thriving in a place of moderation rather than extremes. Second, they make use of the available resources, reminding us to cherish what we have and make the best of it. Shade-loving herbs allow us to grow a garden even if we don't have a bright sunny lawn. Shady places allow us to grow herbs that can't survive hot sun. They give us a serene refuge from the harsh light of day. Find a place to create such a garden where you live, and you too can discover the joys of shadowplay.

For Further Reading

Bremness, Lesley. *Herbs: The Visual Guide to More Than 700 Plant Species From Around the World*. New York: DK Publishing, 1994.

Hodgson, Larry. *Making the Most of Shade: How to Plan, Plant, and Grow a Fabulous Garden that Lightens up the Shadows*. Emmaus, PA: Rodale Books, 2005.

Kowalchik, Claire, and William H. Hylton, eds. *Rodale's Illustrated Encyclopedia of Herbs*. Emmaus, PA: Rodale Press, 1987.

Schmid, George, W. *Pocket Guide to Shade Perennials*. Portland, OR: Timber Press, 2004.

Comfrey: Gardener's Best Friend

❧ By Chandra Moira Beal ❧

C omfrey is a useful herbaceous perennial that every gardener should have at hand. Easy to grow and harvest, it produces large quantities of nutrient-rich leaves that make an excellent fertilizer and compost activator.

Why Use Comfrey?

Comfrey leaves are rich in nitrogen, phosphorus, and potassium, which are readily released as the leaves decay. All plants need nitrogen for healthy leaf growth, and potassium is necessary for producing healthy flowers, seeds, and fruit. In fact, comfrey leaves contain two to three times more potassium than farmyard manure, and their low carbon to nitrogen ratio means there is no risk of nitrogen robbery when comfrey leaves are dug into the soil.

Because they have a low fiber content, the leaves decompose rapidly into a thick, dark liquid, making the nutrients available immediately to growing plants.

Anyone can grow comfrey. The plants are easy to propagate and establish, and they grow well in most soil conditions. Comfrey rarely suffers from pest or disease problems. You can harvest the leaves several times a year, and a single plant can yield four to five pounds each time time you cut, for a harvest of about twenty to twenty-five pounds each season.

Getting Started

Comfrey has large, hairy leaves and tubular purple flowers borne on tall stems. Plants may grow to three feet, with the taproot growing to depths of almost ten feet!

Before introducing comfrey to your garden, decide on a permanent site. Comfrey can live twenty years or more and needs a place where it can grow undisturbed and establish a deep root system. Don't plant it as part of crop rotation because roots left in the soil will continue to grow, thereby causing a weed problem. It's also too vigorous to grow in a pot.

Consider the size of your plot, what you want to use the comfrey for, and how well it will grow on your site before deciding on a number of plants. A small bed in the corner of your garden with just four to eight plants can be harvested several times a year, providing prolific amounts of leaf material. If you later decide you need more plants, you can always propagate them after their first year of growth.

Spring is the best time to plant comfrey. Plants started between March and May will have a full season to settle in before cutting the following year. However, you can plant as late as September, while the soil is still warm but before the plant goes dormant for the winter. No matter when you plant, do not harvest until the following spring.

Comfrey is most easily grown from root offsets. Each root segment has a growing point that will sprout once the plant takes root. Offsets can be obtained by mail order, or you might be offered plants by other gardeners or neighbors. Of the different types, the best one for producing fertilizer is Russian comfrey (*Symphytum x uplandicum*), particularly the 'Bocking 14' cultivar, because it produces fewer seeds.

Plant the offsets about two to three feet apart. In poor soil where the plants may not be as vigorous, you can plant them closer together. Place the offsets with the growing points just below the soil surface.

Once the plants get rooted and are growing well, comfrey is fairly low maintenance. Regular weeding will help remove competition for nutrients. Remove any flowering stems that form in the first season to gain maximum leaf growth the next year. Be sure to keep it well watered and cut it regularly to harvest the leaves and prevent flowering.

To get maximum leaf growth and a good harvest while still harvesting four to five times per season, plants need extra feeding. They will grow without feeding, but the yields will be lower. Use manure, compost, grass clippings, or fertilizer to feed, and stop feeding at the end of summer as the plant growth slows down.

To conserve moisture and add more organic matter to the soil, keep the bed covered with mulch such as hay, leaf mold, or straw. These can go over the top of any other manure or compost used to feed.

Harvesting

After two growing seasons, the plants will achieve maximum leaf production, and you can begin harvesting three to five times in a year. Make the first cut in April when the plants are about two feet high, but before the flowering stems develop. Use shears or a sickle to cut off the leaves about two inches above the soil. Wear gloves, as the leaves and stems are covered in stiff hairs that can irritate the skin.

Allow the plants to grow back to about two feet. This may take four to five weeks. Don't cut any more after September, even though the plants may continue to grow into November. This helps the plants build up their reserves for winter. As the leaves die back, nutrients return to the roots and are stored up for the next year.

Propagation

Increasing your comfrey stock is simple, as the pieces of root regrow readily. The best time to propagate is between March and May, though it can be done any time of year except December and January, when the plant goes dormant.

In the spring, remove the crown of a mature plant by driving a spade through it about three inches below the soil surface. Split this into offsets, with each piece having its own growing point. Cover the remaining root surfaces with soil so it can regrow.

You could also dig up the entire plant, remove and use the crown as above, then chop up the taproot into one or two-inch lengths. Plant these segments two inches deep in their permanent site, or in pots to start them.

Using Comfrey

One of the most popular ways of using comfrey is to make a liquid fertilizer to use on house plants, on hanging baskets, and on greenhouse and potted plants.

There are two main methods for making the fertilizer. One makes a ready-to-use feed and the other makes a concentrate that can be stored and diluted for later use.

Ready-To-Use

Fill a lidded container with water and add about two pounds of leaves per three gallons of water. Cover with the lid to keep the smell in and the flies out. The leaves will decompose to a smelly brown liquid that can be drawn off and used undiluted as a plant food after four to six weeks. You can top off the container with leaves during the season or make new batches after each harvest.

Concentrate

Place the leaves in a lidded container as above, then simply let the leaves decompose to a black liquid that is collected from the bottom. Strain off the liquid and store this concentrate in a loosely covered bottle in a cool, dark place. It can be used immediately or stored up to one year. Always dilute before using. As a general rule, when the concentrate is thick and black, mix with twenty parts water before use; when it's thin and brown, dilute to a 10:1 ratio.

Other Uses for Comfrey

You can use wilted comfrey leaves in planting holes when putting in potatoes, beans, and tomatoes. Just place the wilted leaves in the bottom of the hole, cover with a thin layer of soil, fill in with the plant or seeds, and fill the hole with soil. The leaves break down readily for instant fertilizer.

You can also place a layer of comfrey leaves around plants on top of the soil. These will slowly rot down to release nutrients. An extra layer of grass clippings on top can be effective at controlling weeds and will help speed up decay. Do not use this mulch around acid-loving plants because the leaves produce an alkaline residue as they decompose, which increases the pH of the soil.

When building a compost heap, add a two- or three-inch deep layer of comfrey leaves between layers of other garden waste. The decomposing leaves encourage bacterial action, causing the heap to heat up and speeding the breakdown process.

Surround crops with a ring of comfrey leaves to prevent slugs. Renew the leaves weekly, more often in dry weather, removing slugs at the same time.

Comfrey can accelerate the production of leaf mold, which can then be used in seed and potting compost. Fill a trash can or black polythene sack with alternating layers of two- or three-year-old leaf mold and wilted, chopped comfrey leaves. Tamp the mixture down and add moisture if the leaves are dry. If it's wet, turn it out to dry for a few days before making up the mixture. The resulting compost is ready to use in two to five months, or when the comfrey leaves have virtually disappeared. Use it as a general potting compost or adjust it to use as a seed compost by adding 25 percent sharp sand. The pH of this is usually between 5.8 and 6.2 so if you need it more alkaline, add lime.

Comfrey is a gardener's friend and deserves a place in every plot. With minimal effort it will produce abundant results and give your gardens a welcome boost, making it one of nature's best loved herbs.

Organic Gardening Practices

❧ By Lynn Smythe ❧

Before a garden can be enjoyed for its beauty alone, much hard work must be accomplished. Before his garden can be filled with pleasure-giving plants, the gardener must know his craft.
—Anthony Huxley,
An Illustrated History of Gardening

There are myriad reasons to practice organic gardening techniques. According to Patricia S. Michalak in the book *Rodale's Successful Organic Gardening Herbs*, "the goal of the organic gardener is to keep all the natural cycles in balance." Organic gardening works in harmony with Mother Nature and her natural gifts of health-providing plants. Chemically laden fertilizers end up polluting our rivers, streams, lakes, and other ground water resources. Practicing organic gardening methods is essential for growing items such as herbs, vegetables, and fruits that are going to be consumed as part of your diet. This article describes a variety of organic techniques such as composting, natural fertilizers (and mulching guidelines), natural pest controls, and watering techniques that can be used in your own garden.

Composting

Compost is more than a fertilizer or a healing agent for the soils' wounds. It is a symbol of continuing life.
—Rodale's Encyclopedia of Organic Gardening

Composting is easy. Keep two small plastic buckets with tight-fitting lids under the kitchen sink. Place all kitchen scraps into these buckets. When the buckets are full, take them outside and stir the contents into compost bins. I purchased my two compost bins from my local solid waste authority (SWA). Once a month, the SWA travels to one or more of the county libraries in my area where they sell recycling bin holders along with composting bins. The compost bins cost ten dollars each and come with an under-sink compost bucket and a ninety-six page guide on how to start, maintain, and use your finished compost.

The perfect mixture to maintain in your compost pile or bin, in order for it to decompose in an efficient and timely manner, is three parts brown matter to one part green matter. Examples of brown matter, which is high in carbon content, include dry leaves, hay, sawdust, shredded newsprint, and wood chips. Examples of green matter, which is high in nitrogen content, include grass clippings, kitchen scraps, nondiseased yard trimmings, and certain animal manures.

Properly prepared, finished compost does not smell bad. When your compost is crumbly, dark brown, and has a sweet, earthy smell, it is ready to be used. I like to fill a wheelbarrow with compost to take to the area of my garden where it is needed. Then I break up any large clumps of compost with a small shovel or trowel before adding it to my garden beds.

Reasons to Compost

1. Compost makes a fantastic soil amendment.
2. Compost helps clay soil drain better.
3. Compost helps sandy soil retain moisture longer.
4. Up to 30 percent of a family's garbage consists of organic matter. Adding this organic matter to your compost bins and piles is a great way to recycle garbage that would otherwise end up in a landfill.
5. Compost increases the organic matter content of your garden soil.
6. Compost attracts beneficial organisms such as earthworms to your garden.
7. Compost makes a natural fertilizer to add to your garden plants, vegetables, and herbs.
8. Compost can be used as a mulch.

What to Compost

Common everyday items can fill your compost bin rather quickly. Here are some kitchen and house scraps you can use.

- coffee grounds and filters
- tea bags and loose tea leaves
- vegetable and fruit scraps
- pet hair and most vacuum cleaner bag contents
- lint from your dryer
- black/white newspaper (do not use the colored inserts)

Avoid recycling meat, fat, and bone scraps, as they will not properly break down in your compost bin and will only serve to attract scavenging wildlife such as raccoons and rats.

Add Yard Waste to Compost Pile

If you have a yard, summer and fall are great times to stock up on compost materials. Just outside your door, you likely have access to fallen leaves, pine needles, nondiseased yard trimmings, and grass clippings. You can even compost small amounts of wood ash from a fire pit, campfire, or charcoal grill.

Do not add large chunks of material to your compost bins or piles—shred them into smaller pieces first. Also, remember to check your compost bins at least once a week to make sure they are moist enough. Compost piles should be as wet as a damp sponge. Add water if your pile is too dry. I also stir the contents of my compost bins at least once a week using a compost turner, but a small pitchfork or garden shovel would work too.

Keep quality in mind when adding compost material. Avoid adding weeds or any other type of yard waste that produces lots of seeds. My bins never get hot enough to kill off all the seeds. The first time I used my dark and rich homemade compost, I ended up with unwanted tomato seedlings and purslane plants all over my garden. Learn from my mistakes! Diseased plant material may survive the composting process and end up spreading the disease wherever the compost is used in your garden, so I do not recommend adding diseased plant material to my bins.

Charge and Accelerate Your Compost

Adding certain items will help speed up the decomposition process of your compost bins and piles while also increasing the nutrient content of your finished compost.

A scoop or two of garden soil or finished compost will help start the composting process. Bone meal and blood meal bolster the concentration of nutrients. Finally, the manure and bedding from rabbits, cows, horses, goats, sheep, or guinea pigs will also enhance your compost. (Do not use other types of animal manure. Worms and other parasites in cat and dog droppings— among other animals—can be spread to humans.)

Natural Fertilizers

Only after the last tree has been cut down.
Only after the last river has been poisoned.
Only after the last fish has been caught.
Only then will you find that money cannot be eaten.
—Cree Indian Prophecy

Some of the organic fertilizers that you can add to your garden include the following:

- bone meal (adds phosphorus and calcium)
- blood meal (adds nitrogen)
- compost (adds micronutrients, improves soil texture)
- fish emulsion (adds nitrogen)
- greensand (adds potassium and micronutrients)
- seaweed emulsion (adds potassium, micronutrients)
- earthworm castings (adds micronutrients, improves soil texture)
- dirty water from your freshwater aquarium

I add one tablespoon of fish or seaweed emulsion to my garden sprayer along with one gallon of water. I use this mixture to spray onto the leaves of my fruits, vegetables, herbs, and flowers. This is a foliar type of fertilizer; it is milder than commercially made inorganic fertilizers and can be used more frequently. Sometimes I add a teaspoon of liquid dish soap to the mixture to help the spray stick to the leaves better. Do not use this type of spray right before it rains or it will all be washed off your plants. Also, do not use it on a very hot or sunny day, as the presence of the spray on your leaves along with the heat of the sun can cause them to burn.

Bone meal and blood meal can be purchased in small bags from your local home-improvement store in the garden section. Follow the directions on the bag to mix into your soil.

Compost Tea

Here is an easy method for making an inexpensive organic fertilizer. Fill a one gallon bucket one-third of the way with finished compost. Add water to the top of the bucket and let the mixture steep for three to four days. Strain out the liquid through cheesecloth. Dilute the strained liquid with enough water to turn it the color of weak tea. Use the compost tea to water your plants. After draining off the liquid, add any remaining solids back to your compost pile.

Mulching Guidelines

The unmulched garden looks to me like some naked thing which for one reason or another would be better off with a few clothes on.
> —Ruth Stout, *The Ruth Stout No-Work Garden Book*

My husband uses a mulching lawn mower to cut our grass. The fine grass clippings that remain on your lawn act as a natural mulch, which helps retain moisture in the soil while and also acts as a natural fertilizer. We rarely water or fertilize our grass, and we have one of the healthiest looking lawns in our neighborhood. This lawn mower also has a basket attachment that collects the grass for you. Occasionally, I have my husband use the basket attachment and the clippings then go into my two compost bins whenever they need a shot of green stuff to give the composting process a boost of energy.

Besides being a great natural fertilizer, mulch reduces evaporation of soil moisture, suppresses weed growth, prevents erosion of soil from heavy winds and rain, keeps soil from overheating in the summer, keeps soil warmer in the winter, and prevents soil from being splashed onto your plants every time it rains or whenever you water your garden.

Keep in mind that your mulch does not have to be limited to lawn clippings. Shredded pine needles, shredded bark (eucalyptus, cedar, cypress), pine bark nuggets, cocoa bean hulls, finished compost, and dried and shredded leaves can be added to the mix. Use your lawn mower to chop pine needles and leaves into smaller pieces before using them as mulch or adding them to your compost piles.

Mulches To Carefully Consider

Straw may have been sprayed with harmful herbicides that can leach into your soil anytime it rains. Straw can safely be used on ornamental plants, but I would be wary of using it on any plants meant for consumption, such as culinary herbs and vegetables.

Hay may contain too many weed seeds, which could germinate after being added to your garden. However, one of my country gardening magazines mentions alfalfa hay as working very well for gardening purposes.

Natural Pest Controls

The more we pour the big machines, the fuel, the pesticides, the herbicides, the fertilizer and chemicals into farming, the more we knock out the mechanism that made it all work in the first place.
        —David Bower, Environmentalist, 1912–2000

The organic gardener should try to encourage beneficial creatures to come into the yard. They will eat a variety of harmful pests that may infest your garden from time to time. Ladybugs love to feast on aphids and mealy bugs, for example. And utilizing natural pest controls may lessen or even eliminate your need to use harmful chemical-based pesticides. Common beneficial creatures that should be welcomed into your yard include green lacewings, ladybugs, tachinid flies, parasitic wasps, syrphid flies, spiders, lizards, snakes, birds, and toads.

Certain garden-supply companies sell beneficial insects, such as ladybugs and green lacewings, which can be released into your garden when needed. Instructions for utilizing these organic pest controls are included with your shipment of beneficial insects. Organic-based insecticides, such as cayenne pepper spray and insecticidal soap, can be purchased at garden-supply stores. Do-it-yourselfers can concoct a similar spray from garlic oil. Other tried-and-true natural methods include:

Dusting diatomaceous earth on plants to kill pests such as cutworms and hornworms. Use this material with caution, as it will also kill beneficial critters such as caterpillars or butterflies. As an avid butterfly gardener, I have stopped using diatomaceous earth in my garden and prefer to hand-pick the larger pests from my plants.

Placing a ring of wood ash around the base of plants that are bothered by soft-bodied pests such as snails, slugs, cutworms, and cabbage maggots. The sharp edges of the material discourages these pests from crawling to your plants and doing their damage.

Hand-picking bugs and larger pests off your plants, which is one of the easiest methods of natural pest control.

Blasting water from your garden hose, which can help to wash off pests such as aphids and spider mites from the undersides of the leaves of affected plants.

Homemade Fungicide

1 tablespoon baking soda
1 gallon water

Add the baking soda to a garden sprayer and fill with the water. Spray this mixture all over the foliage of any plants that seem to be attacked by fungal diseases such as powdery mildew. I water my plants in the late morning or early afternoon to make sure the foliage has plenty of time to dry off before the sun sets. Watering late in the day is not a wise idea because wet foliage is more susceptible to being attacked by fungal and other diseases.

If you suffer from slug infestations, old stale beer in a container is supposed to attract them away from your plants. One year I tried this when I thought I might have a slug problem. I went out at midnight with my flashlight to check the slug traps, but there were none to be found. The pests turned out to be cutworms, but I had a couple of very happy toads slurping down the beer. My neighbors probably got a kick out of seeing my daughter and I poking around the garden in our pajamas and slippers! The toads haven't left my yard since that night—they must be thinking, "When's that crazy garden lady going to get us another beer?"

Homegrown Insect Repellents

Certain plants are thought to have insect-repelling properties. You may want to add one or more of these plants to your garden as a form of natural pest control.

Herb	Pests it repels
Coriander	Spider mites
Feverfew	Moth repellent, general insecticide
Garlic	Aphids, Japanese beetle
Marigold	Aphids, nematodes, cucumber beetle
Nasturtium	Aphids, squash bug, whiteflies
Pennyroyal	Ants, fleas, mice
Rue	Cucumber beetle, flea beetle
Tansy	Ants, flea beetle, Japanese beetle, squash bug
Wormwood	Ants, flea beetle, mice, whitefly

Watering Techniques

To waste, to destroy, our natural resources, to skin and exhaust the land instead of using it so as to increase its usefulness, will result in undermining in the days of our children the very property which we ought by right to hand down to them amplified and developed.

—Theodore Roosevelt

The methods mentioned below are all earth-friendly ways of providing adequate moisture to your plants without excessively taxing our precious natural resource of water.

Rain Barrel

Rain barrels can be set up underneath your rain gutters and are used to collect water any time it rains. A spigot can be added toward the bottom of the barrel to dispense the water into a watering can and then used as needed to water individual plants. Rainwater doesn't cost anything and is free of chemicals.

Drip Irrigation and/or Soaker Hoses

These systems provide water directly to the root system of your plants without getting the foliage wet. Mulch can be used to cover the soaker hoses and the mini-irrigation lines of the drip systems to further conserve moisture. At our last house, my husband installed drip irrigation systems for two of my raised garden beds. These beds contained the majority of my vegetables and culinary herbs and required more water than the rest of my garden. At our current home I have opted to use soaker hoses in all my herb and vegetable beds. The materials necessary to install either system can be purchased at home-improvement centers.

Quick-Connect Systems

At our last house, my husband placed a quick-connect hose system at the end of each of my six raised planting beds. I simply took a piece of fifteen-foot hose with a watering wand attached to one end to whichever bed needed supplemental watering between rainstorms. This is a lot easier than having to drag a giant hose all over the yard. This method of watering is much more efficient than irrigation systems that water the entire yard, or overhead sprinklers that often end up spraying water on areas such as nonporous, impermeable driveways and sidewalks.

My Water Log

As my south Florida gardening experience has increased, I have tried to focus on planting herbs and vegetables that can survive the heat without much supplemental watering. Keeping a gardening journal of which plants do well and which do not in various growing conditions has been helpful. I currently garden in subtropical USDA Zone 10, but have recently purchased property in the mountains of western North Carolina, USDA Zone 7. I look forward to discovering which plants do well while learning how to garden in this new type of environment when we retire there in a few years. My garden journal will serve as a reference to my organic gardening successes and failures.

Culinary
Herbs

Feasting on Rosemary

by Anne Sala

F ew culinary herbs thrive so happily in the environment that shaped rosemary, a native of the hot lands surrounding the Mediterranean. For thousands of years, its spiked, waxy leaves have been used to commune with the gods and to flavor a variety of foods, both sweet and savory.

As travelers began to expand their knowledge of the world, they carried rosemary with them. Now it grows naturally wherever the winters are warm and the climate dry.

Traditionally, rosemary is paired with rich foods such as pork and lamb, because it is said to help with the diges- tion of fat. It also has antiseptic quali- ties, making it an indispensable herb in pre-refrigeration days. Even today, its strong pinelike flavor can hide the fact that a cut of meat is past its prime.

Rosemary

For most cooks in the United States, rosemary recipes end with savory dishes. In other cultures, however, its unique flavor has been used to enhance everything from fruits to dessert—beyond the realm of savories. In fact, rosemary could really be put to the test and challenged to appear in every course of a dinner menu, including the after dinner pick-me-up. This is only advised if all guests at the table are fans of the flavor.

There is just one species of *Rosmarinus officinalis*, so all cultivars can be eaten. Medicinally, rosemary has been used to quell upset stomachs and to bring on menstruation. For that reason, pregnant women ought to keep their intake of the herb to a minimum. Some parts of this rosemary-themed menu should be started the day before. Try to start the sorbet two days ahead.

Appetizer: Grilled Shrimp with Rosemary
(Serves 4)

A friend told me a hip culinary use for rosemary is to showcase its aroma only. The resinous taste can be overpowering when combined with delicate foodstuffs such as shrimp. If you have a vigorous plant growing on your property, ask your guests to snip off a branch to sniff between bites of shrimp throughout this course. Otherwise, fresh rosemary sprigs can be found in the produce section of most supermarkets.

If grilling the shrimp outdoors, toss a few branches of rosemary on the coals to scent the yard and set the party's mood. Inside, burn sprigs as incense.

12 shrimp, shelled, deveined, tails intact

¼ cup olive oil

Juice of 1 lemon or ½ cup white wine

3 green onions, sliced (both the white and green parts), or a handful of snipped chives

1 teaspoon pepper

4 branches of fresh rosemary

1. Place the shrimp and next four ingredients into a nonreactive bowl or resealable bag and refrigerate for 30 to 90 minutes.

2. If you are using wooden skewers, soak them for about 30 minutes before grilling. You may also broil the shrimp in the oven, with or without the skewers.

3. Start the grill so the coals will be white when you are ready to cook, or preheat the broiler.

4. Remove shrimp from marinade and discard the marinade. Thread 3 shrimp on each skewer. To prevent shrimp from wobbling while flipping on the grill, use 2 skewers per bunch.

5. Grill—or broil on a broiler pan—for 1 or 2 minutes per side, or until cooked through.

6. Serve immediately with a rosemary sprig. Encourage your guests to inhale the aroma throughout the course.

For future reference, or for a more pronounced flavor, sturdy rosemary branches—stripped of leaves—can be used as skewers. Be sure to soak them before introducing them to the fire.

First Course: Mushroom and White Bean Melange (Serves 4)

Mushrooms and white bean melange can also be mashed up or pureed and made into a savory spread. This dish could also serve as a meatless main course if accompanied by a green salad (use rosemary in the vinaigrette, of course).

1 tablespoon butter

1 tablespoon olive oil (or 2 tablespoons if no butter)

1 small white onion, chopped

8 ounces button mushrooms, wiped clean with a damp paper towel and roughly chopped

½ cup white wine or white wine vinegar (or any mild vinegar), or vegetable stock

1 tablespoon fresh rosemary, chopped, or 2 teaspoons dry, crumbled

1   teaspoon thyme, fresh or dry
1   15-ounce can white beans, such as cannellini or
navy, rinsed and drained
Salt and pepper
1   lemon cut into wedges

1. Place large skillet over medium heat and melt butter with the olive oil. Do not let butter turn brown.

2. Once the butter is melted, or the olive oil slides easily across the pan when tilted, add the onion and sauté until translucent.

3. Add mushrooms and gently stir until they give up their juices and reduce in size.

4. After most of the mushroom's liquid has disappeared, pour in the white wine, vinegar, or vegetable stock, to deglaze the pan. Add rosemary and thyme.

5. Stir in the beans and simmer for 5 to 8 minutes until they are cooked through. If there is still a lot of liquid, continue cooking until it is mostly gone. Add salt and pepper to taste.

6. Serve warm and with lemon wedges. The juice brightens the flavors.

Main Course (Serves 4)

Chicken with Rosemary and Dijon
Side: Roasted Sweet Potatoes and Pear
Palate Cleanser: Rosemary Wine Sorbet

Rosemary is such a versatile herb. The main course and side dish are mere examples of how rosemary can be used to enhance meat and potatoes. Instead of chicken, try lamb. Since lamb is such a sweet meat, substitute green apple for the pear, to create a more perky pairing. The recipe is written so that you can cook both parts of the course simultaneously.

The sorbet is simply a way to add a bit of coolness to the meal. It is particularly welcome if you serve this meal in summer.

For the Main Course:

4	boneless, skinless chicken breasts, pounded flat
¼	cup fresh rosemary, minced
1	tablespoon salt
1	tablespoon pepper
2	cups bread crumbs
1	cup Dijon mustard
½	cup olive oil
3	tablespoons butter

For the Side Dish:

2	large sweet potatoes, peeled
3–4	pears, such as Bosc or d'Anjou, peeled and cored
2	garlic cloves, crushed then sliced
¼	cup fresh rosemary
½	tablespoon salt
¼	cup olive oil

1. In a bowl, combine the rosemary, salt, and pepper. Next to it, place the breadcrumbs in another bowl. Lastly, put the mustard in a bowl nearby.

2. Use your fingers to sprinkle the one side of the chicken with the rosemary mixture. Then, using a spoon, slather the same side with mustard.

3. Set the breast, mustard-side down, into the breadcrumbs. Move it around so that side is completely covered.

4. Keep the breast in the breadcrumbs and repeat step two on the second side. Then dredge that side in the breadcrumbs.

5. Repeat this procedure with the three other chicken breasts.

6. Cover the breasts and refrigerate for at least 10 minutes, allowing the breadcrumbs to set.

7. Preheat oven to 425 degrees F.

8. While oven preheats, chop the sweet potatoes into ½-inch chunks and slice the pears.

9. Spread the potatoes and pears in a roasting pan, trying to get as thin a layer as possible. You might need to use two pans.

10. Sprinkle the garlic pieces, rosemary, and salt over the contents, then drizzle with olive oil. Carefully toss until all potato and pear pieces are glistening. You can include the rosemary stems if you like.

11. Place roasting pan(s) in the oven and cook for 40 minutes, stirring occasionally until sweet potatoes are somewhat brown and pears are very soft.

12. Once the side dish has been placed in the oven, remove chicken from refrigerator.

13. Heat skillet over medium-high heat and add olive oil and butter.

14. When the oil begins to sizzle, place one or two breasts into the skillet. Sauté for at least 8 minutes on the first side before flipping. Sauté until the interior is no longer pink.

15. Keep the cooked breasts warm while you sauté the remaining chicken.

16. Depending on how thick the mustard layer, the breading may come off in some spots. Do not let it burn. Let it brown and then remove to use as a crispy topping.

Palate Cleanser

Rosemary Wine Sorbet

Sorbets are so simple to assemble. They are just flavoring, water, and sugar that you pop in the freezer until they're frozen. It is easy to go wild with the flavorings, but the end result will be milder than you expect, due to the freezing. I strongly suggest starting this component of the main course two days ahead.

As a palate cleanser when the two other courses are so sweet, the sorbet is made with less sugar than usually recommended. Use a crisp wine that you would enjoy drinking—perhaps even the same one you are serving with your dinner—because its flavor will be in the forefront. If you would rather make the sorbet without wine, use an unsweetened white grape juice or a sparkling white grape juice. Or, add more lemon and water.

2½ cups water

½ cup sugar

¼ cup fresh rosemary

¼ cup fresh peppermint, or peppermint and lemon balm combined

1 cup dry white wine

Juice of ½ a lemon

1. Pour the water and sugar into a saucepan set over high heat. Stir to begin dissolving the sugar. Add the herbs and continue stirring occasionally.

2. Bring to a boil, then reduce heat to simmer for 5 minutes.

3. Remove from heat and let cool.

4. Pour into a nonreactive container, cover, and refrigerate overnight.

5. The next day, strain the herbs from the sugar syrup.

6. Combine the syrup with the wine and lemon juice.

7. Place the container (plastic might be best) in the freezer.

8. After an hour, check on the sorbet. Use a fork or spoon to roughly chop up the ice that has formed.

9. Continue checking on the sorbet about once every hour for the next 4 to 6 hours, breaking up the ice crystals with a fork. The more often you break up the ice, the smaller the crystals will be, making for a smoother sorbet.

10. Serve small shavings on the plate, or set each person's portion in a separate bowl.

Dessert

Rosemary Scented Sugar Cookies

After so many strong flavors bombarding your guests' senses, a simple sugar cookie is a nice way to wrap up the meal.

½   cup butter, softened

⅔   cup granulated sugar

2   eggs

1   teaspoon vanilla extract

2   teaspoons baking powder

2½   cups flour

¼   cup fresh rosemary, chopped

¼   cup sugar for decoration

1. Cream the butter in a mixing bowl.

2. Add the sugar slowly, and cream with the butter until the mixture gets light and fluffy.

3. Add the eggs one at a time, beating the first one thoroughly into the mixture before adding the second.

4. Mix in the vanilla.

5. Sift in the baking powder and flour. Mix well.

6. Cover the bowl and chill in the refrigerator for at least 1 hour.

7. Preheat oven to 350 degrees F.

8. Grease two cookie sheets with butter or shortening.

9. Roll out the dough with a floured rolling pin. Divide the dough into more manageable sizes, if necessary. Leave the unused portions in the refrigerator until you are ready to roll them out.

10. Cut the dough into shapes, using cookie cutters or cardboard patterns.

11. Pour the sugar for decorating onto a plate and sprinkle with the rosemary. Take each cookie and press one side into the mixture. Just a few pieces of herb will scent the whole cookie.

12. Place the cookies on the baking sheets (sugar and rosemary side up) and bake for about 10 minutes. They are done when the edges begin to brown.

13. Cool on wire racks. Makes about 30 cookies.

Rosemary Tisane
(Serves 4)

As your guests begin to push away their dessert dishes, offer them a last bit of rosemary before they leave. This tea is said to prevent hangovers and nightmares, so tell them it is for their own good. Just this once, another herb is at the forefront, but rosemary certainly is in there.

4 cups water

½ cup fresh thyme, or 3 tablespoons dried

2 tablespoons fresh rosemary (or 1 dried)

2 tablespoons fresh spearmint (or 1 dried)

Bring four cups water to a rolling boil. Place herbs in a teapot. Pour water over herbs and let steep for 3 to 5 minutes. Strain into four teacups. Serve with lemon and sugar or honey on the side.

Then, send your guests on their merry way to dream rosemary-scented dreams.

For Further Reading

Gardner, Jo Ann. *Living with Herbs: A Treasury of Useful Plants for the Home and Garden*. Woodstock, VT: The Countryman Press, 1997.

Hollis, Sarah. *The Country Diary Herbal*. New York: Henry Holt and Company, 1990.

Marcin, Marietta Marshall. *The Herbal Tea Garden: Planning, Planting, Harvesting & Brewing*. Pownal, VT: Storey Communications, Inc., 1993.

Norwak, Mary. *East Anglian Recipes: 300 Years of Housewife's Choice*. Dereham, England: Larks Press, 1996.

Rockwell, Anne. *The Mother Goose Cookie-Candy Book*. New York: Random House, 1983.

Tolley, Emily. *Herbs: Gardens, Decorations, and Recipes*. New York: Clarkson N. Potter, Inc., 1985

Traunfeld, Jerry. *The Herb Farm Cookbook*. New York: Scribner, 2000.

Soy and Tofu Tucker

~ by Zaeda Yin ~

Tofu is made from soybeans and is the Japanese word for bean curd. The meat substitute originated in China over 2,000 years ago and is one of the protein mainstays of Asian diets. Consumption of bean curd and associated soy products spread from China to Japan, Taiwan, Korea, and Southeast Asia, where it also became localized. When the written word came into being in China, much honor was accorded the humble tofu in poems, proverbs, recipe books, and in the odd medical tome that described it as "meat of the fields" and "meat without a bone." In Asian communities, tofu is indispensable because of its nutritional properties and suitability for all seasons and climates.

Bean curd is important to Asian cookery, but Japan's "traditional tofu masters" have turned tofu into an art form. Until a long sojourn in Japan introduced me to the versatile and nutritious aspects of tofu and soybean foods, like most people in the West I saw it as bland, limp, and boring. Japanese "tofu masters" in different locations have their respective methods for manufacturing tofu and soy products, which are closely guarded secrets. Families are not short of diverse recipes for tweaking tofu into savory, tasty, sweet, and nutritious culinary delights. In recent times, more types of tofu have been created by commercial manufacturers, gourmet chefs, and cooks motivated by new trends of haute cuisine, now popularly known as "fusion cuisine."

Supermarkets and health stores stock numerous varieties of tofu, tempeh, miso paste, soymilk, tofu-based yogurt, tofu ice cream, and other soy products. The gamut runs from silky to smooth, and soft to hard. Putty in the hands of whoever is preparing the dish, tofu renders itself easily to culinary transformations. Tofu cubes placed in a bubbling earthenware pot with vegetables, peas, corn, beans, or mushrooms make hearty fare that can be added to rice, noodles, and pasta (excellent for cold winters). Deep frying turns tofu golden brown and crispy.

Nutrients

The soybean, and products made from it, is high in protein, low in saturated fats, a good source of calcium, free of cholesterol, and a useful source of vitamin E as well as manganese. Soy is also rich in amino acids, which in some cases cause the body to release the hormone glucagon (an anti-insulin hormone). Glucagon helps mobilize stored carbohydrates from the liver to keep the body supplied with energy, potentially eliminating hunger.

Soyfoods also contain isoflavones, disease-fighting substances known as phytochemicals found only in plants. The two primary isoflavones are daidzein and genistein, with the respective glucosides genistin and daidzin. The ratio of genistein and daidzein varies among different soy products. Although the concentration of isoflavones may differ in various products, most traditional soyfoods, such as tofu, soymilk, tempeh, and miso, are rich sources of isoflavones. The only two soy products that do not contain isoflavones are soy sauce and soy oil.

Soy Health Benefits

Scientific studies show that protein contained in soybeans helps lower cholesterol. Soy is also believed to prevent some cancers and hot flashes in menopausal women. Researchers are still examining the possibility of soybeans being able to protect against breast cancer, prostate cancer, cardiovascular disease, menopausal symptoms, and osteoporosis. More than three decades of research has shown that people who consume a lot of soyfoods and tofu experience some of the following health benefits:

Decreased Risk of Heart Disease

Populations in countries where soy products are eaten daily have less risk of heart disease. Soy decreases both total cholesterol and LDL (or "bad cholesterol") levels. Eating an average of 50 grams of soy each day can lower cholesterol by 9 percent, which, if applied to a nation's popuation, could reduce the number of heart attacks by 20 percent.

Cancer Prevention

In Asian countries where diets are rich in soy, breast cancer is less common. For example, Japanese women have one quarter the rate of breast cancer of American and other Western women.

Reduced Rate of Prostate Cancer

Japanese, Chinese, and other Asian males who consume vast amounts of soy products have a far lower risk of prostate cancer. Soy products, mainly tofu, have been part of the diet in those cultures for many centuries.

Ease Menopausal Symptoms

Soyfoods are known to ease menopausal symptoms such as night sweats and hot flashes. This is due to the isoflavone compounds, which are able to act as estrogen to counteract decreased natural estrogen production during menopause.

Prevent Osteoporosis

Diets rich in soy protein help diminish the rate of bone loss and in some cases may even increase bone density. Apart from isoflavones, some soy products contain more bone-building calcium than others.

Soy Sauces

Many Asian sauces used for cooking are extremely high in sodium. Soy sauce contains about ten times as much sodium as barbeque sauce. However, low-salt soy sauce versions are readily available. Those on low-salt diets for health reasons should avoid any sauces that are high in sodium. A lot of soy sauces also contain wheat, and therefore are not suitable for those with gluten intolerance. Black and yellow sauces made from either salted or fermented soybeans are high in salt and thickened with wheat flour. Be sure to read labels carefully before purchasing.

Curdling Agents

Manufacturers use different types of agents for curdling soymilk, which determines the quality of the tofu you get. The best is the traditional Japanese coagulant "nigari," a mineral-rich gray liquid that drips from hessian bags containing raw sea salt. Calcium sulphate, which occurs naturally as a gypsum, is also widely used because it increases the percentage of calcium in tofu. If you intend to make tofu at home, shop around for the right source—poor-quality calcium sulphate is an industrial by-product.

Tofu or Beancurd

Tofu is a soft, white curd that when pressed resembles fresh cheese. When soaked soybeans are ground with water, cooked, and strained, soymilk is made. By curdling soymilk and separating the resultant whey from the curds, tofu is formed. Hard tofu has a compact texture that will not disintegrate when fried or cooked in soups. Ideally, hard tofu should be used the day of purchase, but can be refrigerated for three to five days.

Soft tofu is called "kinugoshi" in Japan, meaning "silken" tofu. Throughout Southeast Asia, soft tofu is generalized as "tahu-fah." During production, it is not pressed and the curds mingle and set in the whey. Then the whey is carefully scooped off. Soft tofu has a delicate, silken texture, and can be served with ginger tea, tapioca, jelly, puffed barley, and lotus seeds.

Miso

Miso is a paste made with fermented soybeans, cereal grain, and sea salt. Used extensively in Japanese cooking, miso is a hallmark flavor in many guises. Miso paste can be used to make sauces, gravies, dips, custards, milk shakes, stock, and soups. It also gives a distinct but delicious flavor to stews, casseroles, and stir-fried dishes. Miso paste can also be used as a marinade, pickling medium, salad dressing, and even as a nutritious bread spread.

Chinese miso, though a progenitor of the Japanese product, has not entered the Western market to the same extent as Japanese miso. There are more than 250 types of Japanese miso, as each Japanese locality produces different varieties and not all are exported to the West. Miso paste available outside Japan is usually light yellow miso made with polished rice as a major ingredient and is sweeter than darker miso paste. Rice miso is also called "kome" or "shiro."

Darker miso pastes are produced from a combination of soybeans and barley, soy, and brown rice, or simply soy without any cereal. Those made with barley are called "mugi miso," and are deep brown in color with a hearty, semisweet flavor. Brown rice miso, known as "genmai miso," is savory-sweet. It can darken by the month, as well as change from a light flavor to a strong flavor as it "ages" from light brown to almost black. "Hatcho miso" originates from a region renowned for its Samurai warrior ancestors. Containing only soy, this black-brown variety has a totally different flavor from any other Japanese miso.

Soymilk

Supermarkets and health stores carry numerous brands of soymilk, which vary in flavor and texture. Read labels carefully, as some products are loaded with sugar, chemicals, or "soy isolate," which is not the real thing. Genuine soymilk is also kosher. In recent times, some Western communities began making "Toffuti" (soy-based ice cream), which evolved from a New York Jewish cafe. Be wary of commercial advertisements gushing about their brands being natural, having low cholesterol, and containing no dairy products. They make no mention that their products may contain heaps of sugar and chemicals. Be wary of natural-sounding ingredients such as "corn syrup," a chemical sucrose derived from cornstarch by industrial refining.

Tempeh

Tempeh originated in Indonesia and is made of hulled, cooked soybeans that are fermented with a white mold (mycelium) until they form into blocks, slabs, or cakes. It can be marinated, grilled, or added to soups, casseroles, and stews. As raw tempeh soaks up oil very quickly, it is best to brush each piece lightly with oil before browning in a nonstick skillet. Across Indonesia, tempeh is mostly fried or deep fried after being marinated with local sauces. Fried tempeh is called "tempeh goreng." Depending on the additional ingredients combined with soybeans during manufacture, tempeh comes in many varieties. Pure soy tempeh has the strongest taste while other kinds made with grains and seeds have a lighter taste. Due to its texture, flavor, and high protein content, tempeh is the closest thing to meat the vegetable kingdom offers. Condiments that enhance tempeh are chili, coconut milk, cucumber, and raw or blanched vegetables.

Yuba

Yuba is Japanese for dried bean curd "skin," another favorite food consumed daily in many Asian households. It is made by allowing thick soymilk to simmer uncovered at a very low temperature until a "skin" forms on top that quite resembles scalded cream. To eat it at its freshest, insert a chopstick under the "skin" and lift it up. Yuba, widely available at Asian grocery stores in the form of cubes, sheets, and sticks, can be dried and stored for up to six months. Buddhist vegetarian cookery uses a lot of yuba, employing techniques that turn dried bean curd into mock smoked meats, mock chicken slices, mock ham, and other meaty-textured dishes with a wide variety of sauces, marinades, and condiments. In Chinese cooking, the cubes are soaked in water for use as wrappers for stuffing vegetables, fish, and other ingredients. Yuba sheets can be simmered in sauces and soups. The sticks are mainly shredded and used in vegetable stir-fries, soups, stews, and fried noodles. A warm dessert can be derived from an old Chinese folk recipe: Yuba sticks boiled in a sweet broth of barley, lotus seeds, and egg or quails eggs.

Shoyu or Soy Sauce and Tamari

Soy sauce is called "shoyu" in Japanese. Its production involves soaking and cooking soybeans combined with cracked roasted wheat and inoculated with a culture known as "koji." When the wheat and soy are entirely covered by the culture, sea salt and water are added. The mixture is then poured into huge wooden barrels and left to ferment for two to three years. After this period, it is strained to remove wheat-meal, soy, and oil. The liquid substance is then pasteurized and bottled. Another type of soy sauce is known as "tamari," which is similar to shoyu, but contains no wheat. Naturally made shoyu and tamari from Japan are like fine, well-matured wines in epicurean value. Soy sauces from different countries have distinct flavors, colors, and textures. Traditional Chinese sauces differ from Japanese variations as much as Indonesian and Thai varieties do. All soy sauces contain unique local ingredients. They may be produced with wheat flour or soy flour and some even combine oyster sauce and shrimp.

Some Soyfood Recipes

Sweet Simmered Miso or Nerimiso Topping

This basic form of simmered sweet miso is generally prepared in small portions of 1 or 2 cups. It is preserved for use over several weeks as a topping or seasoning for cooked grains, vegetables, potatoes, salads, tempeh, and tofu. Unused portions will retain their flavor for 2 to 4 weeks if refrigerated in sealed containers. The following recipe renders half a cup.

5	tablespoons "red" or barley miso
2–4	tablespoons natural sugar (to taste)
1	tablespoon water
1–2	teaspoons sake (rice wine) or white wine

Combine all ingredients in a small saucepan and simmer for 2 to 3 minutes on low heat. Stir constantly with a wooden spoon until the mixture becomes slightly firmer than regular miso paste. Remove from heat and let contents cool to room temperature before serving. Store extra portions in sealed containers for refrigeration.

Mushroom Miso Saute

Miso saute can be used with vegetables, nuts, and fruits, then served with fried tofu, rice dishes, porridge, noodles, fresh vegetable slices, or steamed vegetable chunks. This recipe makes a bit over half a cup, but a little goes a long way.

2	tablespoons oil
10	mushrooms, thinly sliced

1   tablespoon of the miso paste of your choice

1–2 teaspoons natural sugar

Coat a wok or frying pan with oil and heat it up. Add mushrooms and sauté over medium heat until tender. Reduce heat to low, then add miso and sugar. As the mixture cooks, stir regularly until the mushrooms are evenly coated. Leave the sauté to cool to room temperature and serve.

Soybean Casserole with Tomatoes and Corn

1   cup cooked soybeans

1   cup cooked corn

1   cup cubed tomatoes

¼   teaspoon paprika

¾   teaspoon sea salt

½   teaspoon natural sugar

1   teaspoon minced onion

2   ounces grated vegetarian cheese

¼   cup chopped peanuts

Preheat oven to 350 degrees F. Wash and thoroughly dry a casserole dish before brushing it with oil. Spread the first seven ingredients in the dish, sprinkle cheese and peanuts on top, and bake for 45 minutes to an hour.

Fried Crispy Tofu

12   ounces firm tofu

1   teaspoon sea salt or vegetable salt

5   tablespoons flour

5   tablespoons oil

2   tablespoons shoyu (soy sauce)

Slice tofu lengthwise into halves and then crosswise into thirds, then use a clean cloth to pat each piece dry. Sprinkle with salt and roll tofu pieces in flour. Heat oil in a wok or skillet until quite hot. Add tofu and fry on both sides until golden brown and crispy. Drain oil onto paper towel. Serve with shoyu. Serves two.

Tofu and Miso Stew

1 large onion, thinly sliced

6 mushrooms, cut into halves

1 cup potatoes, cubed small

1 cup pumpkin, cubed in larger pieces

1 small carrot cut into thin rounds

½ cup green peas, corn, or sliced green peppers

3 cups water or stock

½ cup ketchup

2 tablespoons butter

½ cup miso paste of your choice

12 ounces firm tofu, cut into 16 small rectangles

Combine the first seven ingredients in a large pot and bring to a boil over high heat. Reduce heat to low and cover. Let contents simmer for 15 to 25 minutes or until potatoes and pumpkin become soft. Stir in ketchup, butter, and miso. Cover and simmer for another 15 to 25 minutes while regularly monitoring the consistency. This recipe generally makes a brothy stew. For a thicker consistency, add a heaping tablespoon of corn flour to half a cup of water. Mix this well, pour it into the pot, and stir. Add tofu to the simmer and cover for another 5 to 10 minutes. Let sit for 5 minutes before eating. Serves four.

Making Soymilk at Home

Making soymilk to a preferred taste and texture can be time-consuming and messy, but after experimenting a few times, the process should only take an hour. Utensils and implements required are a large pot, a huge heatproof glass bowl or stainless steel container, a blender, a cloth sack or flour bag, and a saucepan. If possible, use high-quality organic soybeans and soak them overnight in lots of water. Strain off the liquid and wash the soybeans the next day. This recipe is for 1 cup of soaked soybeans, so multiply when necessary as you go along. For a thicker and richer flavor, use 2 to 3 cups of soaked soybeans.

Boil 7 to 8 cups of water in a kettle. Pour 5 cups of boiling water into the large pot over high heat. Puree the soybeans in a blender with the remaining 2 to 3 cups of boiling water until well ground and milky. Pour this into the large pot containing the other 5 cups of water and reduce heat to medium. Stir continuously until the mixture is well cooked or until foam rises. Pour contents into a moistened cloth sack set in a large bowl. Strain the liquid by pressing firmly with a large wooden spoon to extract soymilk. Rinse the large pot. Place the cloth sack in 1 cup of hot water in a saucepan and squeeze the bag again to ensure all remaining milk is extracted. Pour all the soymilk back into the pot and bring to a boil with high heat.

Those who like it sweet can add 3 to 5 tablespoons of raw sugar to the boiling soymilk. Stir the mixture very often to prevent the milk from burning. When the milk begins to boil, reduce heat to low and simmer for another 5 minutes before serving. This recipe makes about 4 to 5 cups of soymilk that is similar to that made in Southeast Asian countries like Singapore and Malaysia. (Japanese and Chinese recipes, which have different consistencies and tastes, are more difficult to make).

Leftover soymilk can be poured into a container and refrigerated and served cold or warmed up later.

Tofu Ice Cream

18 ounces tofu, chilled

 3 tablespoons natural honey

¼ teaspoon vanilla extract

⅛ teaspoon salt

1 egg yolk

2 tablespoons chopped almonds

Put 12 ounces tofu, honey, vanilla extract, and salt into a blender and puree for 1 minute. Pour into a container, cover it, and freeze the contents overnight. Next day, take tofu out of the freezer and cut into small chunks. Put these into the blender and puree with the remaining 6 ounces of tofu at high speed. While pureeing, add a few chunks of frozen tofu at a time and blend until contents are smooth. Before finishing the pureeing process, add an egg yolk and 2 tablespoons chopped almonds, some frozen fruits, or shredded coconut. Serves two.

Variation: For a green tea–flavored ice cream, omit vanilla extract and add 1 teaspoon of "powdered green tea" (matcha) and 1 additional teaspoon of honey.

Health note: Consuming untreated raw eggs carries a risk of salmonellosis as a result of the salmonella bacteria. Children, the elderly, pregnant women (the developing fetus), and people with chronic health problems that weaken the immune system or undergoing chemotherapy are most at-risk for food-borne illnesses. If possible, use eggs that have been in-shell pasteurized, which are safe to eat without further cooking.

Stew on This!
A History of Ingredients

≈ by Nancy Bennett ≈

Carrots, onions, potatoes, peas, and barley. The makings of a fine stew, some would say. Add in some lamb and you have a great Irish stew! Something to warm the soul and stick to the ribs, stew is one of the most nourishing meals you can make. But while you're cooking this delectable dish, did you know you are also cooking history?

Carrots

It is generally believed this orange root originated in Afghanistan, though the Greeks brought it into public view. The Greeks called the carrot "Philtron" and used it as aphrodisiac. It was said to make men more eager and women more surrendering.

It never really caught on as a food until the sixteenth century, when the

Germans and French experimented with growing bigger ones of various colors. The Irish loved them, and the sweetness of the carrot was so admired that their writers referred to carrots as "underground honey."

In the Middle Ages, doctors said carrots would cure you of syphilis or the bite of a mad dog. Knowing it to be a favorite food of Queen Elizabeth I, one ardent fan once presented the queen with a wreath of carrots embellished with diamonds with a pot of butter in the middle. Elizabeth is said to have removed the diamonds and sent the rest to the kitchen to be cooked. The end result, of course, was buttered carrots.

Not only the Elizabethans but the Dutch made much of the carrot. In the sixteenth century, Dutch growers, overcome with patriotism, grew the orange vegetable to honor the "House of Orange." Carrots are a versatile food—great to eat raw, steamed and buttered, as a juice, as a flavoring in cakes and puddings, and of course, in stew.

Onions

Sacred enough to make one's eyes water with tears of joy, onions were fed to the workers on the great tombs in Egypt (and buried with the Pharaohs for the coming afterlife).

In Mesopotamia, in the oldest known body of law, the Code of Hammurabi, onions and bread are given to the needy in monthly ration. Romans started their day with a breakfast of raw onions and bread, sure to keep away any door-to-door salesmen. In America, cowboys in the West knew the onion as a "skunk egg," but still used it in their "son-of-a-bitch" stew.

A folk cure for a cold is to eat a whole raw onion. Though I have never done this, there are many who swear by it.

Onions are not technically vegetables but part of the lily family. They have vitamins A and C and also a bacteria-destroying chemical called allyl aldehyde, so onions are great when you are feeling under the weather. What could make you feel better than a nice bowl of stew?

Potatoes

Gardeners in Ireland take spade to ground to plant their spuds on Saint Patrick's Day every year. Why? No one knows, but it is still a tradition. An old Irish saying goes, "If beef's the king of meat, potato's the queen of the garden world." Both the Irish and potatoes were often looked down upon by Englishmen like William Cobbett, who referred to the potato as "Ireland's lazy root."

In South America, it was in the Andean region that potatoes were first reported. The Incas worshiped them, even though their version had purple skins. They called them "Papas," and in this prayer from the sixteenth century AD, they would speak in homage to the spud.

"O Creator! Thou who givest life to all things and hast made men that they may live, and multiply. Multiply also the fruits of the earth, the potatoes and other food that thou hast made, that men may not suffer from hunger and misery." Though the South Americans exalted it, pregnant women were warned not to eat potatoes lest their babies be born with too large a head.

Around this time the first potato made it from the "New" world to the "Old" world (in this case to Spain), and slowly spread from there. Some folks were none too crazy about it, saying it caused leprosy and scrofula.

Eventually, though, potatoes earned a place alongside other starches such as rice and pasta, as a staple "fill you up" food. In 1770, after a disastrous grain crop, potatoes became the food that kept many poor Europeans alive. Today you can find potatoes used in fish and chips. (This traditional dish was discovered by accident when fish was cooked in large oil vats to allow it to be shipped and the spud chips were used to cool the oil down when it got too hot.) Potatoes are also used in breads and breakfast dishes, and if you are a homemade wine maker you can turn them into potato champagne. Of course there is one meal that is synonymous with the potato—that would be stew.

Peas

If an army marches on its stomach, then peas must have their due. Both Greek and Roman soldiers had them as rations. Dried peas were easy to pack and provided good protein for fighting men. Though a great addition to a meal, peas were not favored by the upper classes, who looked upon it as poor folk's food.

Peas were known to the early citizens of India, and have also been found in excavations of Bronze Age men living in Switzerland. Helen of Troy may have eaten them, as they were found in diggings in ancient ruins of that noble race. In Norse myth, Thor sent down those sweet edible peas not as a gift to the humans, but as a curse! Thor had sent his dragons to drop the peas down wells to foul up the water of his ungrateful followers below. But the dragons missed the target, and instead a new food crop was created. The people gave thanks and ate it on Thor's holy day of Thursday.

Peas were not really cultivated in Europe until the eighteenth century, though toward the end of the seventeenth they had become a much-favored delicacy for the upper class. "This subject of peas continues to absorb all others," Madame de Maintenon wrote in 1696. "Some ladies, even after having supped at the Royal Table, and well supped too, returning to their own homes, at the risk of suffering from indigestion, will again eat peas before going to bed. It is both a fashion and a madness."

The French arriving on the shores of Quebec carried the dried pods for starter, and soon everyone was eating and growing peas. In the seventeenth century they made their way from England to the colonies of New England.

"Pease porridge hot, pease porridge cold, pease porridge in the pot nine days old" goes the rhyme. Pease porridge was a porridge made from peas, also known as pease pottage. Back then the poor would often cook one big meal and continue to heat it up every night, not wasting a bit. After nine days, I wouldn't recommend eating it! Though peas do make a great addition to (you guessed it) stew!

Barley

In ancient times, barley was sacred to Demeter, and the secret orgies in honor of this goddess culminated in the unveiling of a spike of perfect grain, most likely barley. Isis also had a hand in bringing it to our wild roots. She discovered it while making sacrifices to the ancestors, and was later known as the Queen of Bread and the Queen of Ale.

As early as 5000 BC, barley was being grown in Egypt, and in 3000 BC it had spread to the eastern Mediterranean area of Mesopotamia. From there it continued to flourish in Europe, China, Norway, India, France, Turkey, and finally North America. But barley can be traced back even further, into prehistoric times.

The grain can be made into flour (the Romans favored barley bread made with honey), soaked and combined with fruit to make a breakfast cereal, turned into fine ale, or added to stews.

Now that I have whetted your appetite, it's time to try a recipe. Cubed meat (lamb for Irish, beef for English) can be added to it. Make sure to dredge the meat in a flour mixture and brown it in advance before adding it to the stew, for a nice taste and texture.

Athens Vegetable Stew

Olive oil

1   onion, chopped

1   clove garlic, chopped

3   carrots, chopped

3   potatoes, chopped

½   cup frozen or fresh peas

½   cup pearl barley

1   teaspoon ground black pepper

1   teaspoon salt

½   teaspoon dried oregano
    Splash of lemon juice
2½ cups water
    Splash of Worcestershire sauce (optional)

In a frying pan, heat olive oil and brown onions and garlic. Drain. In a large pot over medium high heat, combine prepared onions and garlic, carrots, potatoes, peas, barley, pepper, salt, oregano, splash of lemon juice, and water. Bring to a boil and then turn down so that stew is simmering. (An old English saying that "a stew boiled is a stew spoiled" applies here).

Continue simmering, stirring occasionally, until vegetables are tender and barley is cooked, about 50 to 60 minutes, adding more water if necessary. If you want a bit more flavor and a darker tinge, add a splash of Worcestershire sauce before serving.

Breakfast and Brunch Delights

↠ by Lynn Smythe ↞

"When you wake up in the morning, Pooh," said Piglet at last, "what's the first thing you say to yourself?" "What's for breakfast?" said Pooh. "What do you say, Piglet?" "I say, I wonder what's going to happen exciting today?" said Piglet. Pooh nodded thoughtfully. "It's the same thing," he said.

—A. A. Milne,
The House at Pooh Corner, 1928

The ritual of taking a leisurely Sunday breakfast has occurred on a regular basis for many years at my house. It's the one day of the week when we usually aren't all rushing around like crazy people trying to get ready for school and work. There's nothing like waking up to the smell of my husband's freshly brewed coffee as he begins to prepare breakfast for the entire family. We often will serve breakfast for dinner one night of the week if we missed our normal Sunday morning meal due to one of our camping trips or mountain biking expeditions.

Brunch is a combination of traditional breakfast and lunch foods and is usually served between 10 am and 2 pm. A brunch-time feast features a variety of both sweet and savory dishes. This article includes a variety of recipes to feature at your next home-cooked breakfast or brunch celebration.

The Appeal of Herbs

Herbs are the scents of the kitchen, and must be used as subtly as other scents so that each dish retains its particular flavor and character.
—Celestine Eustis, *La Cuisine Creole*, 1903

Fresh herbs are called for in most of these recipes. There is nothing to compare to the flavor of fresh herbs in your cooking. If you don't have these herbs growing in your own garden, most grocery and health food stores sell packages of fresh herbs in their produce sections. You may also want to check your local farmers' market to see if any of the vendors offer fresh herbs for sale.

If you don't have the time to cook all your meals from scratch, simply adding a few fresh herbs to prepackaged foods is a quick way to imbue the healing power of nature into your meals. Herbs such as parsley, chervil, and chives work especially well to add a fresh herb taste to your food without overpowering the other flavors of your meal.

Chervil Vegetable Scramble

Chervil is a very mild-tasting herb with a faint aniselike taste. Its delicate fernlike leaves give it an appearance similar to parsley. (In the Middle Ages it was sometimes referred to as rich man's parsley.) Chervil symbolizes new life and hope. The scientific name for this herb is *Anthriscus cerefolium*, the second part of which derives from the Greek word chairophyllon, which means happy or delightful leaf.

1	tablespoon vegetable oil
½	cup green onions, sliced thin
½	cup red bell pepper, seeded and diced
½	cup mushrooms, chopped
6	eggs
2	tablespoons heavy cream
½	teaspoon salt
¼	teaspoon black pepper
¼	cup fresh chervil leaves, chopped fine
⅓	cup shredded cheese (optional)

In a large frying pan, heat the oil over medium heat. Add the green onions, bell pepper, and mushrooms, and cook for 5 minutes, stirring occasionally. Remove the vegetables to a plate and reserve for later. In a mixing bowl, whisk together the eggs, cream, salt, and pepper. Then stir in the reserved sautéed vegetables and pour into the frying pan. Sprinkle the chervil on top of the egg mixture, then add the shredded cheese if you like. Stir the eggs around until they are firmly cooked. Makes four servings.

Cinnamon Pecan Muffins

Cinnamon was once an exotic and expensive commodity only available from a few spice dealers. In order to keep the price high, disreputable dealers concocted fantastic tales of how they obtained their supply of cinnamon. An incredible story was told that in faraway lands, large birds built huge nests using twigs of cinnamon. In order to collect the cinnamon, which was too high for humans to reach, the collectors would entice the birds with large pieces of meat placed at the base of the nests. The birds would take the meat to their nests, which would quickly become weighed down and cause the nest to come crashing down to the ground. This enabled the collector to easily harvest the cinnamon twigs from the ground.

I am lactose intolerant, so I substitute regular or vanilla soymilk for regular milk in many of my recipes.

1¾ cups all-purpose flour

½ teaspoon salt

3 teaspoons baking powder

½ cup granulated sugar

1 teaspoon cinnamon

6 tablespoons butter, chilled

1 cup vanilla soymilk or milk

½ cup pecans, chopped

Preheat oven to 450 degrees F. Sift the flour, salt, baking powder, sugar, and cinnamon into a large mixing bowl. Add the chilled butter and cut into the dry ingredients using a pastry blender or two knives until it has the appearance of coarse cornmeal. Stir in the soymilk and pecans. Grease a muffin tin and fill each section approximately ⅔ of the way with the dough. Place the pan in the oven and bake for 12 to 15 minutes or until golden brown. Use the icing to frost the rolls. Makes 12 cinnamon rolls.

Icing

1 cup powdered sugar, sifted

1 teaspoon orange extract

1⅓ tablespoons water

Add the powdered sugar to a small bowl. Add the orange extract and just enough water to make a thin frosting. When the cinnamon rolls have been removed from the oven, place them on a large serving platter. Drizzle the icing onto the rolls until all of the icing has been used up. The icing will harden as it cools to room temperature.

Herb and Cheese Biscuits

Parsley seeds were thought to have to go to the devil seven times and back before they would sprout and grow in your garden. Parsley seeds are notoriously difficult to germinate, but you can give them a head start by soaking them in a small container of warm water a few hours before you plant them in your garden.

I prefer to use flat-leaved parsley, also referred to as Italian parsley, in this recipe. But regular curly leaved parsley would work too, as long as you chop it up extra fine.

1¾	cups all-purpose flour
½	teaspoon salt
3	teaspoons baking powder
6	tablespoons butter, chilled
1	cup soymilk or milk
⅓	cup fresh parsley, minced
½	cup shredded mild cheese (Swiss, Monterey Jack)
2	tablespoons melted butter

Preheat your oven to 450 degrees F. Sift the flour, salt, and baking powder into a large mixing bowl. Add the chilled butter and cut into the dry ingredients using a pastry blender or two knives until it has the appearance of coarse cornmeal. Stir in the milk, parsley, and Swiss cheese. Grease a muffin tin and fill each section approximately ¾ of the way with the dough. Pour the melted butter evenly over the top of each portion of biscuit dough. Place the pan in the oven and bake for 12 to 15 minutes or until golden brown. Makes 12 biscuits.

Lemon Basil French Toast

Basil is one of many herbs that can be added and used in love spells, as it is thought to help promote peace and harmony between lovers. A container full of basil placed outside of your window was once a signal that a woman was ready to be courted.

I like to grow containers of the small-leaved spicy-globe basil on my patio. They add a nice decorative element to my home and it's easy for me to pop outside to harvest a bit whenever a recipe calls for basil. If you don't have lemon basil on hand, you can substitute an equal amount of sweet basil.

For the French Toast:

- 4 eggs
- 1 cup vanilla soymilk or milk
- 1 teaspoon lemon extract
- Zest from 1 lemon
- 1 tablespoon fresh lemon basil, minced
- 1–2 tablespoons butter
- 8 slices French bread (1-inch thick, day-old bread)

In a medium size bowl, whisk together the eggs, milk, lemon extract, lemon zest, and lemon basil. Melt the butter in a large frying pan placed over medium heat. You may use nonstick cooking spray instead of the butter to coat the frying pan if desired.

Dip each slice of bread into the batter, being sure to coat each side evenly. Place the bread into the frying pan and cook until well browned on both sides. Add additional butter to the pan if necessary to prevent the French toast from sticking. Serve with the lemon syrup recipe listed below or with maple syrup.

For the Topping:

- ½ cup lemon juice
- ½ cup granulated sugar

In a small bowl, mix together the lemon juice and sugar until all the sugar has been dissolved. Serve this syrup along with the French toast. The syrup also tastes great served on top of waffles or pancakes.

Lovage-Infused Tomato Juice

Sometimes known by the folk-name of love ache, lovage is thought to be a useful ingredient to add to love potions and a range of love spells. Lovage has a faint celerylike taste and aroma, making it a perfect complement for many tomato-based dishes.

The leaves from the heart of celery stems make an acceptable substitute if you don't have lovage growing in your garden. I have also used fresh cilantro leaves mixed into this juice. You can either substitute them in place of the lovage or add a 50/50 mixture of cilantro and lovage.

46 ounces tomato juice

¼ cup lemon juice

½ teaspoon freshly ground black pepper

1 teaspoon hot pepper sauce, to taste

¼ cup lovage leaves, minced

6 lovage stems (optional)

Add the tomato juice, lemon juice, black pepper, hot pepper sauce, and lovage leaves to a large pitcher and mix together. Let chill in the refrigerator for at least 2 hours. To serve, pour into individual glasses and use a lovage stem to garnish each glass of tomato juice if desired. Lovage stems are hollow and the larger ones can be used like a straw. Makes 6 to 8 servings.

Quiche Lorraine with Savory Crust

Winter savory is a perennial plant, while summer savory is an annual plant and must be replanted from seed every year. The small, thymelike leaves of savory can be used to attract fairies to your garden. Most cooks agree that the tender leaves of summer savory have a better flavor than the tougher winter savory leaves. I have used the two varieties interchangeably in my recipes.

For the Crust:

1¾ cups all-purpose flour

½ cup butter, chilled

1 egg

3 tablespoons water

1 tablespoon fresh winter or summer savory, minced

Preheat oven to 375 degrees F. Sift the flour into a mixing bowl. Add the butter and mix into the flour using a pastry knife or two knives until it has the texture of coarse cornmeal. In a small bowl, whisk together the egg, water, and savory, then stir into the flour mixture. Use your hands to thoroughly mix all the ingredients together. Use additional flour if necessary to prevent the dough from sticking to your hands. Press the dough onto the bottom and sides of a greased 10-inch tart pan. Prick the bottom and sides of the crust with a fork. Place in the oven and bake for 15 minutes. Remove the crust from the oven and set aside while you are preparing the filling for the quiche.

For the Filling:

3 eggs

¾ cup milk

¾ cup heavy cream

1 tablespoon fresh chives, snipped with scissors

¼ teaspoon black pepper

1½ cups cheddar cheese, shredded

¾ cup chopped onion

1 package of bacon (6–10 slices), well browned

In a large bowl, whisk together the eggs, milk, cream, chives, and pepper. Stir in the shredded cheese and onions. Crumble and spread half of the bacon onto the bottom of the prepared crust, carefully pour in the egg and cheese filling, then crumble the remaining bacon on top. Bake the quiche for 40 to 50 minutes until the eggs are set and no longer runny. Let the quiche cool for about 5 minutes before serving. Makes 8 servings.

Spiced Coffee with Cinnamon and Cardamom

The spicy seeds of cardamom have reputed aphrodisiac properties and are called grains of paradise in some countries. Cardamom seedpods can be found in the spice aisle of most grocery and health food stores. Be sure to purchase light-green pods, as the light-beige ones have been chemically treated to remove the natural green coloring. To use cardamom, I place a few pods on a wooden cutting board and lightly crush the pods with a rolling pin or the smooth side of a meat mallet. Then I remove the small dark brown seeds from the interior of the pod to use in my recipes. This beverage makes a delightful change from regular coffee.

    6   tablespoons ground coffee beans
    ½   cinnamon stick, broken into pieces
         Seeds from 6 cardamom pods
    8   cups water
         Half and half (if desired)
         Sugar

Grind the cinnamon and cardamom seeds together in a coffee grinder. Place a filter in the basket of your coffee maker. Place the ground coffee, cinnamon, and cardamom into the filter. Brew your coffee as usual. This makes a strong flavored coffee. I like to serve it along with plenty of half and half and sugar. Makes 6 servings.

Vegetable Latkes with Garlic Chives

Chives are thought to be capable of chasing away all diseases and evil entities. Garlic chives are also called Chinese chives or tender-leaved chives. They have a delicate flavor that is like a combination of mild garlic and a bit of onion. Common chives can be used as a substitute in this recipe if necessary. I have found small pots of both garlic and common chives at my local garden center, and in the nursery section of my local home-improvement store, which I take home and transplant into my garden. Chives also make a wonderful plant to grow inside in small containers.

- 1 cup carrots, peeled and shredded
- 1 cup leeks, chopped fine
- 1 cup mushrooms, chopped fine
- 1 cup potatoes, peeled and shredded
- 2 tablespoons garlic chives, chopped fine
- 2 eggs
- 1 teaspoon garlic powder
- 1 teaspoon onion powder
- ½ cup all-purpose flour
- ¼ cup vegetable oil
- Sour cream (optional)
- Salt and pepper (optional)

In a medium bowl, mix together the carrots, leeks, mushrooms, potatoes, and chives. In a small bowl, whisk together the eggs, garlic powder, and onion powder, then stir into the bowl of vegetables. Add the flour and stir until well blended. Heat the oil in a large frying pan over medium heat, adding additional oil if necessary. Make individual latkes by pouring ⅓ heaping cup of the batter into the pan and flattening each one with a spatula. Brown well on both sides, then remove to a paper-towel-lined platter to drain off the excess oil. Serve with sour cream and salt and pepper on the side if desired. Makes approximately nine latkes.

Fashion Your Own Bouquets Garnis

❧ by Chandra Moira Beal ❧

Bouquet garni is French for "garnished bouquet," a small bundle of herbs usually tied together with string and mainly used to flavor soup, stocks, or stews. The classic combination includes a bay leaf with a few sprigs of parsley and thyme, wrapped in a leek leaf or bunched with a piece of celery. The bouquet is simmered alongside other ingredients, but is removed prior to consumption.

Today there are endless variations to the classic combination depending on the results you want to achieve in your dish. Modern cooks continue to use the secured bundles, but have expanded into using combinations of chopped fresh herbs or dried herbs and spices contained in cotton bags or tea strainers for ease of use. The flavors have expanded beyond the original French herbs to include dishes from around the globe.

Herbs here are grouped into two general categories according to flavor and strength, and loosely follow the annual and perennial classification.

Mild herbs combine well with most other herbs and their flavors soften in cooking. They can be used in larger quantities and with more variation than robust herbs, and several of them can be combined if their flavors are complementary. Mild herbs often appear in salads and dishes in which the leaves are used raw or cooked only briefly. Good examples are basil, bay leaf, chervil, dill, marjoram, and parsley.

Robust herbs stand up well to cooking, which makes them suitable for braised or roasted meat, grilled foods, and long-simmered dishes, especially soups and stews. Their flavors are subtly altered during cooking, sometimes muting, sometimes intensifying. With the exception of garlic, they combine well with just a few other robust herbs, and used judiciously they can be used with basil, marjoram, and other mild herbs. Garlic, oregano, rosemary, sage, sorrel, tarragon, and thyme are all robust herbs.

The proportions of herbs in the bouquet garni are important. For the best results don't limit yourself to only one or two herbs per dish; rather, use three or four plus a spice or two. Robust herbs will mask the mild ones if used in equal parts. It's better to use more mild herbs and fewer robust herbs to bring out the flavors.

The aim of making a good bouquet garni is to combine the herbs in a balanced, complex way that makes your diner want to take another bite, but not analyze the dish. The herbs should complement the flavors of the dish, not overpower them.

Fresh herbs will provide maximum flavor. Omit an herb that is not available fresh rather than substitute it with a dried herb.

Experiment with lots of different combinations to find the blend you like best!

Complementary Flavor Families

Classic: basil, bay, oregano, and parsley

Herbal: basil, marjoram, rosemary, and thyme

Hot: chili peppers, cilantro, cumin, and garlic

Pungent: celery, chili peppers, cumin, curry, ginger, and whole black pepper

Sweet: allspice, anise, cinnamon, cloves, and nutmeg

Mediterranean: rosemary, sage, and savory

Italian: oregano, marjoram, thyme, savory, basil, rosemary, and sage

Traditional Preparation Method

The traditional way to prepare a bouquet garni is to tie the fresh ingredients together with a piece of string. Leave the twine six to twelve inches long so you can attach it to the pot handle, making it easier to retrieve. (Dental floss may be used if kitchen twine is not available, but make sure it is unwaxed and unflavored.)

If you are using fresh herbs along with dried or powdered herbs or spices that won't hold together well, place them inside cotton muslin drawstring bags, a square of cheesecloth secured with a string, or even a tea strainer.

Manufactured garni bags are available in grocery and specialty stores. Similar to tea bags, they contain preselected herbal ingredients and are sealed in paper steeping bags.

If you have a bounty of fresh herbs, bouquets garnis can be made ahead and frozen. Just place them inside a bit of plastic wrap or waxed paper and seal them first.

Any bouquet garni can be infused in vinegar or olive oil, as well, and make popular gifts. Just drop the tied bundle into the bottle with the vinegar or oil to infuse, and seal.

Recipes for Fresh Herbs

Traditional Bouquet Garni

3 stalks parsley	1 sprig thyme
1 bay leaf	1 stalk celery or leek

Tie the herbs onto the celery or leek. Add the bouquet garni to any stew, sauce, or casserole, and remove it before serving. To add a bit more zest to this basic bouquet garni, tie a twist of lemon peel to the bundle.

Herbes de Provence

1 sprig oregano	1 sprig savory
1 sprig thyme	1 sprig marjoram
1 sprig rosemary	

Tie the herbs together into a small posey and add to the cooking pot. This bouquet garni will add a touch of French flavor to any Provençal dish, but can also be used to complement salads, vegetables, meat dishes, and even hot desserts.

English Mixed Herbs

1 sprig Italian parsley	1 sprig chives
1 sprig thyme	1 sprig tarragon

This is the English version of Herbes de Provence and a wonderful complement for lamb, pork, or stuffing. Rosemary, sage, and marjoram can be used in addition or as substitutes.

Fines Herbes

This garnish is simply 1 tablespoon each of finely chopped tarragon, parsley, chervil, and chives. Although the blend is sometimes used dried, none of the herbs have much flavor in the dried form. Fines herbes should be added to cooked dishes at the end of the cooking period, as the herbs, with the exception of tarragon, do not stand up well to heat. For the best results, sprinkle the mixture over dishes as a garnish or place it in a bowl to pass around the table.

Fines herbes are excellent when sprinkled over green salads, and also work quite well with egg dishes, especially omelets. Use to garnish light vegetable or simple cream-based soups. Fines herbes are excellent with simple fish dishes, and can turn steamed vegetables such as beans, marrow, and broccoli into a delicacy.

Mild Bouquet Garni

1	sprig basil	1	sprig cilantro
1	sprig lemon thyme	1	sprig marjoram

Robust Bouquet Garni

1	sprig oregano	1	sprig sage
1	sprig thyme	1	sprig winter savory
1	sprig rosemary	1	sprig spearmint

Recipes for Dried Herbs

Garam Masala

This blend is mild and dominated by the scent of cardamom. It is ideal for meat curries.

20	green cardamom pods	3	cinnamon sticks
4	dried bay leaves	4	teaspoons cumin seeds
2	teaspoons whole cloves		
2	teaspoons freshly grated nutmeg		
2	tablespoons black peppercorns		

Split the cardamom pods with a sharp knife and remove the dark brown seeds. Discard the pods and crush the seeds in a mortar and pestle.

Break the cinnamon sticks into fairly small lengths. Crumble the dried bay leaf into several small pieces.

Put all the pieces, except the nutmeg, into a heavy frying pan. Dry-fry over medium heat for 2 to 3 minutes. Remove the pan from heat and put the spices into a small bowl. Allow to cool and stir in the grated nutmeg. Grind the spices in small batches to a fine powder. Pack into sterilized jars, seal, decorate, and label.

Five-Spice Powder

This blend is a harmonious mix of bitter, sweet, sour, and salty. Its pungent taste lends itself to Chinese and Vietnamese dishes.

2	cassia sticks	6	star anise
1	tablespoon whole cloves	1	tablespoon fennel seeds
1	tablespoon anise seeds (or whole black peppercorns)		

Break the cassia sticks into several pieces. Put all the spices into an electric grinder and grind to a fine powder. Pack into sterilized jars, seal, decorate, and label.

Pickling Spice

This popular mix is used to enliven the flavor of chutneys, pickles, and vinegars. Start with 4 blades mace, 2 cinnamon sticks, 2 small dried red chilies, and 2 pieces of dried ginger root. You'll also need 2 tablespoons each of the following:

allspice berries	whole cloves
coriander seeds	mustard seeds
whole black peppercorns	

Break the mace blades, cinnamon sticks, and chilies into pieces. Chop the ginger root. Mix together with the remaining ingredients. Place everything on a square of muslin and tie up tightly with a long piece of string. Add to the recipe when specified. Remove the bag after pickling

Seven Seas Spice Mix

This fragrant mix is perfect for Asian dishes.

15	green cardamom pods	1	cinnamon stick
2	teaspoons whole cloves	2	dried red chilies
1	tablespoon cumin seeds	2	teaspoons celery seeds
2	tablespoons coriander seeds		

Remove the seeds from the cardamom pods and crush them in a mortar and pestle. Break the cinnamon stick into several pieces. Put all the spices into an electric grinder and grind to a fine powder. Pack into sterilized jars, seal, decorate, and label.

Herbs
for
Health

Natural Cold and Flu Remedies

❧ by Karen Creel ❧

We've all experienced it: runny nose, sneezing, itchy, watery eyes, cough, congestion, and sore throat. Add a fever, a few muscular aches and pains, and you guessed it . . . the cold and flu season. In fact, in the United States alone, people suffer about one billion colds a year. Beginning in the fall, the rates of colds increase and remain high until about March or April.

More than two hundred different, highly contagious viruses cause both the common cold and the flu. Distinguishing the two may be difficult. The flu usually has a rapid onset, produces a fever (102 to 104 degrees F), and is associated with severe headaches, fatigue, muscular aches and pains, and a dry hacking cough. Left alone, most people recover from the symptoms of cold and flu within a week, but symptoms can last up to fourteen days. While our supermarket shelves are lined with over-the-counter and prescription medications, a cure for the cold has eluded us for centuries. Today's "modern medicines" are designed to provide temporary relief of symptoms. These medications, unfortunately, may generate their own set of problems. Drowsiness, restlessness, and dry mouth are often associated with decongestants, and those with other health problems such as high-blood pressure are warned not to use certain cold and flu preparations. Antibiotics will not cure, prevent, or help treat the symptoms of a cold, and the overuse and misuse of antibiotics has resulted in a host of antibiotic-resistant bacteria.

Herbal Alternatives

Herbal remedies, used throughout the ages, offer an alternative for those who want to reacquaint themselves with the healing power of plants. A number of herbs are known to effectively boost the body's immunity, soothe cold and flu symptoms, and shorten the length of our suffering. The following herbs are not all-inclusive, but are good for beginners, and may be more readily available in local health food and herb stores.

"An ounce of prevention is worth a pound of cure."
The best defense against a cold and the flu is to stop them before they strike.

Astragalus (*Astragalus membranaceus*): A member of the pea family native to northeast China, astragalus is the root of *Astragalus membranaceus*. Known for its antibacterial, antiviral, and immune-boosting action, it can be found in American herb and health food stores in the form of powdered root, teas, tinctures, capsules, tablets, and extracts. Astragalus has no reported side effects or contraindications.

Recommended dosage: Capsules 1 to 3 (440 mg) daily. To make a tea, steep 1 to 2 teaspoons in a cup of boiling water.

Echinacea (*Echinacea augustifolia, E pallida, E purpurea*): Known as purple coneflower, echinacea enhances the immune system by stimulating the production of white blood cells. It is believed to shorten the duration of colds and flu, and to reduce the severity of symptoms. It is most effective when taken in the early stages of symptoms. Echinacea can be purchased as a capsule, tincture, or liquid extract. Recommended dosage is 900 milligrams of echinacea a day. If you already have cold symptoms, you should take ½ to 1 dropper full (30 to 50 drops) of echinacea liquid extract every two hours. Echinacea should only be taken for about two weeks, then allow a resting period of one week.

Caution: People who are allergic to flowers in the aster family may also be allergic to echinacea. If you have an impaired immune response due to tuberculosis, multiple sclerosis, or HIV, you should not take echinacea.

Soothe a Sore Throat

Slippery elm (*Ulmus rubra*): Slippery elm is the inner bark of a tree in the elm family. It soothes irritated mucous membranes, especially in the lining of the respiratory and digestive tract. Slippery elm lozenges are available in herb and health food stores, or a hot tea may be made of ½ teaspoon of the powdered bark steeped in a cup of hot water. Drink the tea 2 to 3 times a day. There are no side effects or special precautions associated with slippery elm.

Sage (*Salvia officinalis*), thyme, and sweet marjoram have traditionally been used in herbal medicine to soothe a sore throat. You can make a tea for gargling with any one of the herbs. Use 1 teaspoon dried, or 2 teaspoons fresh herbs, in a cup of boiling water. Cover, and let steep for 10 minutes. When cooled to a lukewarm temperature, gargle. Do not swallow. Use 3 to 4 times a day. Store unused tea in the refrigerator and use within 24 to 48 hours. If you prefer to drink a tea, add 1 teaspoon honey to each cup and drink 2 to 3 times day.

Open the Airways

A stuffy head and nose can make you miserable during the cold and flu season. Chest rubs, teas, herbal steams, and inhalations are great ways to ease breathing and open up the nasal passages. Peppermint, eucalyptus, and rosemary are three herbs often used to bring some relief in breathing due their menthol properties.

Try putting a couple of drops of peppermint or eucalyptus essential oil on a cotton ball and place it on your nightstand to breath the vapor. (Do not rub the oil on your mucous membranes or get it in your eyes, and never use it on or around the nose of an infant or child, as it has been reported to cause respiratory arrest.)

Make a steam to inhale: Boil a quart of water. Lower the heat and add a ½ cup dried or 1 cup fresh peppermint to the pot. Remove the pot and allow the herbs to steep uncovered for about 5 minutes. Take off the lid and lean over to check the temperature. If the temperature is comfortable, drape a towel over your head and breathe in through your nose. You may also use essential oils in the water instead. Add 3 to 6 drops of rosemary, peppermint, or eucalyptus as directed above.

You can make an inhaler by adding the essential oils in a small vial or bottle. Put 1 tablespoon of rock salt in a small vial or tincture bottle. Mix 2 drops of eucalyptus oil, 2 drops of rosemary oil, and 1 drop of peppermint oil and add to the salt.

A simple massage oil or lotion can be made to help ease congestion. Add 15 to 20 drops of eucalyptus oil to 1 to 2 ounces of unscented lotion or olive oil. Rub on chest, back, and feet. Never use eucalyptus oil undiluted or internally.

Calm a Cough

Herbs for calming a cough include mullein (*Verbascum thapsus*), thyme (*Thymus vulgaris*), and horehound (*Marrubium vulgare*). Cough drops or hard candy help stop the tickle and moisten the throat.

Horehound Cough Drops

8   cups boiling water

½   cup horehound leaves

4   cups sugar

1¼   cups dark cane sugar

1   tablespoon butter

1   teaspoon cream of tartar

Bring water to a boil and remove pan from heat. Add the horehound and set aside to let steep for 20 minutes. Strain, discarding the horehound. To 8 cups of this liquid, add 4 cups sugar, 1¼ cups syrup, 1 tablespoon butter, and 1 teaspoon cream of tartar. Cook these ingredients until the liquid reaches the hard-crack stage (300 degrees F on a candy thermometer). Immediately pour into a well-buttered cookie pan or any shallow pan with low sides, 10 × 15 inches or larger. As the candy begins to cool, quickly score into pieces by running a buttered knife through the warm candy. Depending on the room's temperature, the candy will set up faster or slower, but it should be hard enough to break in 5 minutes or less. After breaking it on the score lines, put candy, still warm, into a plastic bag with 1 cup of sugar and coat the candy. This keeps the candy from sticking together. Store in an airtight bag or container. Use like candy, or for coughing.

Teas to Soothe Coughs and also Act as an Expectorant

Thyme tea: Use 1 tablespoon dry or 2 tablespoons fresh thyme to 1 cup boiling water. Steep covered, for 10 minutes. Strain, and drink the tea hot.

Mullein tea: Use 1 to 2 teaspoons dried leaves or flowers to one cup boiling water. Let steep, covered for 10 to 15 minutes. Strain, and drink hot. Drink 2 to 3 cups per day.

Honey may be added to the tea for extra flavor.

In addition to the natural remedies suggested here, there are some things you can do to prevent reinfection or spreading the virus to others. Disinfect the phone, remote control, computer keyboard, sink handles, etc., to keep from infecting others. Throw your toothbrush away and purchase a new one. Change your bed linens frequently, use paper towels in the kitchen and bathrooms, and wash your hands frequently.

Although herbs are "natural," do not take lightly their medicinal power. If you have existing medical conditions such as high blood pressure, thyroid disorders, or heart disease, be especially cautious with herbs, as with any pharmaceutical medication. Educate yourself on the properties and uses of the herbs, as well as any cautions. If you are pregnant, or thinking of becoming pregnant, now is not the time to start experimenting with herbs. The dosages given here are intended for adults. Use the dosage directions of purchased herbs, tinctures, or capsules and consult a health care professional if your symptoms persist.

For Further Reading

Byers, Dorie. *Herbal Remedy Gardens: 38 Plans for Your Health and Well-Being*. North Adams, MA: Storey Publishing, 1999;

Foster, Steven. *Herbs for Your Health*. Loveland, CO: Interweave Press, 1996.

Gagnon, Daniel. "Herbal Care for Colds and Flu." *Herbs for Health*, September/October 1996.

Long, Jim. *Great Herb Mixes You Can Make*, Blue Eye, MO: Long Creek Herbs Publishing, 2003.

White, Linda B., M.D. "Cold Busters, Herbs to the Rescue," *Herbs for Health*, September/October 1998.

Hypertension:
A Distressing Disease

↠ By Leeda Alleyn Pacotti ↞

If the truth about hypertension were more widely publicized, the United States would be known as a nation at risk. An insidious, intense disorder, high blood pressure robs its victims of sound mind, sound body, hopes and dreams, recreational pursuits, and strength of purpose. If the nation were under siege from an external foe, this would be war!

Generally accepted solutions mean only to keep this ailment at bay, leaving casualties of hypertension to wonder about resuming a normal or desired life. However, naturopathy and lifestyle changes can minimize and even deter this looming beast of illness.

What is Hypertension?

Interestingly, whether you know this systemic ailment as hypertension or

as high blood pressure, both names are appropriate. Thinking in terms of physical stress, hypertension is an excessive tension or pressure against the walls of arteries, veins, and the heart. Although physical stress on bones or muscles can be easily felt, the sense of pressure throughout the circulatory system is indiscernible until serious consequential problems arise, such as heart damage or an arterial or venous rupture. By then, the problem of hypertension has become life-threatening.

Currently, health science delineates hypertension as two types, essential (primary), and secondary. Essential hypertension is the most common and more mysterious of the two, with no known or detectable physical cause. Secondary hypertension is actually a consequence arising from damage to the kidneys or an endocrine dysfunction, particularly the adrenal glands.

In determining high blood pressure, a simple measurement with an inflated cuff on the arm produces a reading of two numbers, the larger of the two reported "over" the lesser. The greater number is the systolic, the maximum pressure when the heart contracts and pushes blood into circulation. The lesser number is the diastolic, the minimum pressure while the heart relaxes between maximum pressure contractions, allowing a flow of blood from one heart chamber to the other.

A normal blood pressure reading in a healthy young man or woman is considered 120/70. Sometimes, an average taken between the two numbers produces the measurement of mean blood pressure. In this case, the mean is 85. A mean greater than 100 is considered above normal or high.

Whether the blood pressure measurement is taken by a professional or as part of personal health care, the procedure is quick and easy.

A Nation Out-of-Sorts

The prevalence of hypertension staggers the imagination. One in six Americans currently has high blood pressure. Of the 300 million residents in the United States, 50 million people suffer this crippling circulatory discomfort, often not knowing they have it. Among these 50 million instances, 90 percent (45 million) of those afflicted have essential hypertension, indicating underlying problems in American attitudes and lifestyle. Were hypertension communicable or contagious, this health condition would be looked upon as an epidemic.

Without regard for socioeconomic status, race, age, or religion, hypertension can take hold. Although many people assume high blood pressure and its companion complications are conditions of age, usually discovered first in older adults, the truth is aging does not increase susceptibility. To the surprise of those who hold mistaken ideas, hypertension strikes children, teens, young adults, pregnant women, midlifers, and seniors. Hypertension is a silent killer without bias.

Causes of Hypertension

As previously explained, the lesser incidences of secondary hypertension arise from previously occurring conditions affecting the kidneys or endocrine system. When these conditions are known, the health provider will already be monitoring blood pressure for abnormalities.

The causes and contributing factors toward essential hypertension are another matter entirely. These particulars appear to be hidden and mysterious, but they are usually personal, idiosyncratic habituations. Consequently, they cannot be easily typed as an identifiable cause until a person is able to recognize and disclose them.

These causes are varied, sometimes observable and sometimes accepted as a part of life. Generally, the reasons for hypertension coexist, often reinforcing each other. Whether they are lifestyle or mindset, the toll of their effect is a hindrance on anyone with dreams, plans, or activities.

Starting with lifestyle, most hypertensive sufferers have one or more of the following common habits. They are often overweight, getting little or no exercise. Their diet is disproportionate, with a higher intake of fatty foods, excess salt and sodium, and insufficient calcium. As well, they may be exposed to cadmium from industrial pollutants, coastal or farm-raised seafood, or cigarette smoke.

When hypertension is detected, these individuals find it more difficult to exercise in an overweight condition or they want to eat more comfort foods such as ice cream, butter, and cheese. In the case of smokers, anxiety over high blood pressure increases the frequency of the smoking habit. Those who have a high salt or sodium diet increase the high blood pressure by creating cellular edema, in which all cells in the body retain fluids, increasing pressure in and against the circulatory walls.

Dietary imbalances of fatty foods lead to atherosclerosis, a form of arteriosclerosis, in which deposits of fats collect against the circulatory walls and on heart muscles, narrowing the channels of arteries and veins and the chambers of the heart. While insufficient calcium contributes to hypertension, high levels of this mineral creates the condition of arteriosclerosis. The American diet of high sodium, high fat, high dairy, and high protein frequently produces a simultaneous presence of these two conditions, from which the combined accumulations of fat and the calcium mineral create a thick plaque, similar to a cement, coating the interior walls of the bloodstream and the delicate linings and valves of the heart. Not only does the circulatory system lose its flexibility, but the delivery of nutrients to organs and tissues is seriously curtailed, causing a degenerating malnourishment throughout the body.

The Mind Over Matters

Attitude plays a noticeable part in the presence of hypertension, which can be found in persons of normal weight. Into play here are psychological personality type, preconceived notions, and emotional habits.

Long identified is the Type A personality, the controller and worrier. This person attempts to control events beyond his or her personal management and can be described as "playing god" or "being a control freak." This person can be very active and frequently has higher levels of adrenaline in the bloodstream, which causes faster and stronger heart action, eventually deteriorating the heart musculature.

Preconceived notions include assumptions about the necessities of life and job. Often, these revolve around symbols of status and success, with financial worries abounding. Some hypertension sufferers are induced into their condition by purchasing homes, vehicles, and possessions that outpace their incomes. Others will work excessive hours on the job or at home, to demonstrate their dependability, responsibility, or authority.

In either case, a repetitious internal pressuring forces these people to prove themselves to someone else they believe they can please, whether that person is present or not. These individuals either do not know—or have forgotten—the difference between comfortable and wealthy, or have not developed a balance between the needs for productivity and relaxation.

As mentioned before, anxiety is a definite emotional factor toward a hypertensive condition. Although other emotional displays figure in as well, such as anger, a person with high blood pressure usually has overemotional or melodramatic behavior. Without a middle ground or balance, the emotional response is either excessive or inappropriate to circumstances. Such emotional behaviors have their basis in the continual reliving of emotional situations, which stimulate memory of unresolved psychic wounds. This emotional condition is a mainstream form of post-traumatic stress syndrome, spawned from mentally dwelling negatively on personal inabilities, past failures, and distrust of specific types of people. The person with hypertension finds repetitious and disastrous manifestations of inability, failure, and opponents cropping up more frequently and overwhelmingly in life experiences.

In studies of individuals with hypertension, the personal habit of talking too fast dramatically increases and maintains high blood pressure. When subjects were forced to talk more slowly, their blood pressure demonstrably decreased.

Interestingly, laughter temporarily increases blood pressure, although this disruption and release from other problems is probably well worth the risk.

Finally, a recent observation is the fleeting and peculiar "White Coat Hypertension." Individuals who experience this phenomenon become worried and anxious when entering a health office, usually in fear of receiving bad news. White coat hypertension occurs when the blood pressure measurement is taken, which can rise as much as 20 to 50 points higher than normal, for both the systolic and diastolic readings.

Symptoms and Consequences

The condition of high blood pressure cannot be felt. However, some telltale indications, occurring separately or concurrently over a period of time between health visits, raise suspicion of a change in the circulatory system.

Physical symptoms include breathing difficulties, dizziness, edema (water retention), fatigue, headache, insomnia, intestinal problems, migraines upon waking, nosebleeds, and tinnitus (ringing in the ears). Emotional symptoms manifest as anger, anxiety, competitiveness, fear, stress, and worry. Of these symptomatic guides, the emotional conditions have greater influence in perpetuating increased blood pressure, as well as producing the physical symptom portraits. Therefore, emotional strains must be resolved and neutralized before nutritional or other biological treatments to alter the condition can be effective.

If hypertension goes undetected, untreated, or unmanaged, the deteriorating health consequences are severe and potentially life-threatening. Working the heart too hard damages heart muscles by thickening the muscular wall and not allowing enough blood to be pumped. Both insufficient and excess calcium create an imbalance of fluids in the body, causing more mineral excretions through the kidneys, more frequent urination, and possible urinary stone formations. Both the brain and eyes need a high flow of oxygenated blood. Without this flow, eyesight dims and cataracts form, while the brain can develop vascular lesions.

Although arteriosclerosis can lead to hypertension, high blood pressure can also produce arteriosclerosis, with calcium deposits hardening and rupturing circulatory walls, which can result in cerebral hemorrhage or stroke. In a progressed stage, this plaque build-up works its way into the heart, producing a heart attack.

All of these consequences seemingly happen unexpectedly, because changes in blood pressure cannot be felt!

Help Your Body and Yourself

Hypertension is a conspiratorial ailment, creating mental and physical fatigue that make changes to thinking and lifestyle difficult. Once the condition is known, the strongest weapon is the determined attitude to regain strong health, which will come.

Personal lifestyle changes are recommended for anyone who has habits inimical to health. Giving up some things are definitely helpful: alcohol, caffeine, fried foods, salt, smoking, and excess weight. Specific herbs to avoid, because they elevate blood pressure, are ephedra (*Ma huang*), ginger, licorice, nutmeg, and pepper spices. Foods to eliminate from the daily diet include aged cheeses, cured meats, pancake and other cake mixes, canned soups, soy sauce, canned tuna, and TV dinners. Besides chemical preservatives, most of these foodstuffs are overly salted to improve their taste.

While high blood pressure is a problem, the daily salt limit is three grams. Although the body needs some salt, its requirement is met quickly in prepared foods. Read the nutritional disclosures on the labels of any foods purchased, even when those are marked as low in sodium. For instance, six tablespoons of "lite "sodium" soy sauce fulfills the three-gram maximum, as does one cup of onion soup, prepared from a package mix.

Naturally low-sodium, high-potassium foods make the best diet to reduce high blood pressure. Buckwheat, raw fruit (especially watermelon), millet, oats, rice, seeds, nuts, and vegetables (especially the leafy green ones) are principal foods, which also create weight loss and help maintain energy levels. To make some of these foods more palatable, flavor them with cayenne pepper, fennel, garlic, parsley, and rosemary. Hops or valerian root tea will help soothe the nerves, with valerian producing muscle relaxation. To calm the heart, drink a tea from hawthorn berries.

To bring blood pressure down quickly and stabilize it, eat watermelon only for up to one week or fast with juices (raw fruit or vegetable purees) for three or four weeks. Thereafter, keep to the foods and herbs specifically indicated for lowering high blood pressure.

In several studies conducted in Russia, both garlic and buckwheat were shown to reduce blood pressure. By consistently eating a raw garlic clove three or four times a day, your blood pressure will likely reduce 10 to 20 points in subsequent readings.

Mineralized waters are of no help, especially if arteriosclerosis or atherosclerosis are present. Drink only steam-distilled water, and use it in making teas and cooking. Lacking minerals, distilled water binds to minerals in the bloodstream and on the circulatory walls, gradually softening the plaque deposits, which eventually will be sloughed off.

Because stress is frequently a factor in hypertension, a B-vitamin complex and a calcium/magnesium mineral complex in a 2:1 ratio help soothe nerves and produce relaxation. The B-vitamin complex should be taken at the beginning of the day, and the calcium/magnesium complex, which produces drowsiness, should be taken about an hour before retiring for bed.

To some extent, these dietary changes will cause weight loss, which has a profound impact on hypertension. An overweight condition is 20 percent over ideal weight. From an ideal weight of 100 pounds, overweight is 120; an ideal of 150 pounds is over-weight at 180; and an ideal of 200 is overweight at 240.

Controlled studies of individuals overweight and suffering high blood pressure show that, for every two pounds of weight shed, the blood pressure reduces one number on both the sys-tolic and diastolic readings. Also, 25 percent of individuals who are overweight with mildly high blood pressure, when the sys-tolic number is 140 or slightly above, will reach normal readings by losing 10 to 15 pounds.

Once some weight comes off, most people begin to feel energized and rejuvenated. Even if the weight loss is slow, moderate exercise helps tone the muscles, relax the nerves, and improve circulation. A 30-minute program of an easy walk and moderate exercise, coupled with deep breathing, is the best way to start, gradually increasing the length of the walk and exercise. The best walking environment is in greenery and cool air.

While blood pressure is elevated, exercising seems tiresome. However, exercise reduces stress-related chemicals, usually adrenaline derived, in the bloodstream, which constrict arteries and veins. Furthermore, exercise produces endorphin, which relaxes the body and reduces blood pressure. Increased circula-tion from exercise moves more HDL cholesterol from the liver, which flushes the LDL cholesterol from circulatory walls. As a bonus, all these effects of reduced blood pressure, reduced LDL cholesterol, reduced stress, and increased relaxation remain a constant, even if no weight loss is realized!

When exercising with high blood pressure, a cardiologic rule-of-thumb is important in preventing a worsened hyperten-sive condition. Exercise at 60 percent of your maximum heart rate, which is determined by subtracting your age from 220 and multiplying the result by 0.85. A 30-year-old has a maximum heart rate of 162 and a high blood pressure exercise heart rate of 97. At age 45, the maximum heart rate is 149 and the exercise heart rate is 89. At age 70, the maximum heart rate is 128 and the exercise heart rate is 77. Anyone over age 40 with high blood pressure, however, needs to coordinate the exercise program with a health provider.

Ultimately, the inner life needs as much change as the physical. When negative thoughts of consequences and outcomes well up, think the opposite to produce positive results. Dwell on self-recognition rather than self-deprecation; acknowledge the good qualities of others and their abilities to achieve happiness rather than feeling responsible for them or distrusting them.

Instituting meditation periods, especially in closing the day, create thought habits of peace, calm, and security. Return to loving experiences of childhood, activities of sheer enjoyment, and secure memories of parents and relatives. For as long as meditation or relaxation techniques are used, these procedures will help maintain a lower blood pressure. Unfortunately, if these techniques are stopped and not resumed, blood pressure will gradually rise to unhealthy levels.

Sleep rejuvenates the body after a day of wearing down physical resources and strength. Learn to sleep for a longer period, preferable eight or nine hours, by going to bed earlier and not using an alarm clock.

Remove constant blood pressure elevators from your daily environment, especially at home. Stop any jarring or jangling noises, alarms, engines, loud televisions, and loud music. Recurrent effects from upsetting noises keep blood pressure elevated one month or longer.

Change the colors around you, both at home and at work, if possible. Blue lowers blood pressure and creates calm, green soothes the mind, and violet both creates peace and suppresses the appetite.

If your home life permits, add a pet. Studies linking pets and high blood pressure show that the mere presence of pets reduces hypertension measurements by 12 to 15 percent. Stroking, petting, and attending a pet disrupts worry patterns of thought and redirects the mind to a need outside oneself.

With modern emphasis on self-monitoring, keeping track of blood pressure is no longer a mysterious procedure of the health giver's office. Because the unhealthy condition of hypertension ranges widely throughout the population, monitoring devices are now easy and common to find in drugstores, wholesale membership outlets, and catalogs. Blood pressure equipment can be minimal—the classic squeeze pump and inflatable cuff is priced at about $30, while various types of electronic memory units cost between $35 and $75. Because the population of hypertension sufferers tends to overweight conditions, most manufacturers will offer a larger arm cuff for free with proof of purchase or at a minimal cost. The overall goal is to be cognizant of blood pressure abnormalities.

Being affordable, these devices are invaluable in keeping track of triggers that spike blood pressure and provide an inexpensive form of instant biofeedback. In taking blood pressure, be sure to sit quietly for 10 minutes before the reading. Observe your thoughts during those 10 minutes. Are they filled with simmering anger toward someone? Have molehills of slight hurts become mountains of injury? Are the plans of the next workday, workweek, or workmonth uppermost? If yes, the blood pressure reading will most likely be elevated over the usual.

Changing thoughts intentionally after the reading for another 10 minutes will produce a reverse effect. Think love instead of anger and shift to love thoughts about someone you genuinely want to have happiness. Think fondly of a pet, or, better still, talk to and touch the pet. Skip thoughts of work accomplishments and mentally go fishing. When the next reading is taken, the measurements can dramatically drop as much as 20 points for both systolic and diastolic.

Not only is this exercise an excellent mental management tool to uncover runaway emotional triggers, it is also proof that thoughts of love and kindness cure!

Treatments of Conventional Medicine

Some individuals have persistent or morbid hypertension, which may be genetic or heavily anchored in a difficult lifestyle. For them, blood pressure readings can be as high as 300 for the systolic and 200 for the diastolic. These readings indicate an immediate threat to life and cannot be prolonged. In these cases, two primary types of pharmaceutical medications may be utilized to bring the blood pressure to a manageable level.

Beta blockers prevent the effects of endogenous catecholamines, epinephrine (adrenaline), and norepinephrine (noradrenaline) on the heart and other organs. These chemicals are released as part of the "flight or fight" defensive response of the human organism. Individuals stuck in this defense have persistent high blood pressure, compounded by the other physical factors described earlier. Common side effects of this medication include drowsiness, fuzzy mindedness, and slowed physical reactions.

The second possible prescription is an ACE inhibitor, which relaxes circulatory walls, lowering the resistance of the blood flow and increasing veinal capacities. The problem of rigidity in the circulatory walls may be genetic. The principal side effect is an increased excretion of sodium in the urine. This medication needs to be monitored carefully with blood tests to maintain the potassium/sodium ratio in the bloodstream.

After allopathic intervention is given to save a life, consider talking with the health care provider about changes in lifestyle, diet, and attitude, with an eye toward eventually reducing or eliminating the prescription.

Spiritual, Physical Herbal Healing

❧ by Alice DeVille ❧

Down through the ages, individuals have relied on herbs and plants to replenish energy, cure ailments, and nourish the body and soul. Every culture discovered and used herbs for their aromatic, cosmetic, culinary, mystical, and healing properties. The oldest systems of medicine in the world came from China, India, and ancient Egypt. The roots of the medicine that flourished from the Roman Empire until the Middle Ages have Greek origins. After the Crusades, Arabian physicians shared their plant and herb expertise with Europeans. Arab businessmen opened the first herb shops. Another Arabic contribution to medicine was the use of astrology to help select appropriate medicines and herbs.

In medieval Europe, monasteries were constructed on plots of land that included pleasure gardens comprised of expanses of lawn with low borders of sweet-smelling herbs surrounded by taller shrubs and fruit or shade trees. The Great Age of Herbals started in Germany around 1530, spread throughout renaissance Europe, and continued well into the mid-eighteenth century. In the peak era of herbal healing, colonists of the New World brought their herbal lore and gardening styles to the Americas. Simultaneously, scientific advances disrupted the prominence of herbal medicine, replacing it with more "orthodox" practices—synthetic additives and patent medicine. A resurgence of interest in herbal medicine unfolded in the nineteenth century that continues to this day.

Herbal Medical Origins

Laurel wreaths of victory, made from the leaves of the bay tree held in esteem by Greeks and Romans, crowned the heads of kings, priests, prophets, poets, and victorious soldiers. The ancients believed a plant of such power also had to be good medicinally, and used it to treat snakebites, wasp and bee stings, urinary problems, and bruises and scrapes. Early Egyptians used chamomile to cure fevers and malarial chills that plagued their population. Ancient Hebrews selected coriander as one of the bitter herbs featured in the ritual of Passover, while Romans prized it as a spice and added it to a vinegar stock used to preserve meat.

The aborigines of Australia discovered that eucalyptus held water in the roots and used it to quench their thirst. They also learned that eucalyptus oil worked effectively in medicinal applications as a component of antiseptics and poultices for skin ailments. Ginger, a balm for indigestion and a mild stimulant, originated in the Orient nearly 4,500 years ago. Early Greeks traded with the Far East and made gingerbread from the herb. Spaniards started growing ginger in the sixteenth century. Later, the Spanish conquerors introduced this spicy root to occupants of the New World. Because of its pungent aroma, ginger has also been used in rituals to drive away evil spirits. The Dutch bred the first juniper evergreens to make gin, a popular alcoholic beverage. Native Americans found other uses for this plant that are medicinal, involving the use of juniper ointments. They also applied steaming bundles of the boughs directly to the skin to relieve arthritis, bruises, and wounds.

Licorice is native to Mediterranean and Asian countries, where it was used to soothe throats, open respiratory passages, quench thirst in the arid regions, and provide nourishment when eaten fresh. Today we still eat licorice candy and find it in cough drops or cough syrups. The considerable medicinal components of licorice help ulcer patients find relief from pain. Greek physicians like Hippocrates and Dioscorides used seeds of the wild-growing marsh mallow herb to make a paste and treat wounds and stings. Renaissance herbalists found marsh mallow helpful for internal ingestion to soothe stomach problems, sore throats, and constipation. They made a vinegar-based gargle from the herb for throat infections and toothaches.

Pennyroyal came into use in the eighteenth century on both the European and North American continents as a repellent whose leaves could be crushed and rubbed into the skin to keep away flies, mosquitoes, gnats, and other outdoor pests. Many commercial sprays and lotions contain the minty pennyroyal oil to this day. Native American folk healers favored both topical application and the use of teas made from the herb to treat colds and flu. The oil was more commonly used in high doses to induce abortion or expel the afterbirth of a stillborn child. While teas made from brews using pennyroyal were once recommended for relief from cramps and colic, this plant has been considered unsafe for internal consumption by the Food and Drug Administration since the latter half of twentieth century.

Experts claim that at least 25 percent of prescriptions dispensed today contain active ingredients from plants. The more you know about herbs, the more you'll understand the treasure trove of rewards you'll reap by using them to enhance your health, your home, and your inner harmony.

Energizing Your Diet

Many factors can zap your energy reserves, including physical and emotional illness, lack of sleep, and poor diet. You can improve your energy level by reviewing what you eat and adding important herbs to your diet. Consumers value natural foods for their healing properties and abilities to improve certain ailments and conditions. As the basis of a well-balanced diet, herbs can be the key to good health and greater inner harmony. See what happens when you include some of these tasty species on your menu.

Basil is one of the most popular herbs in the mint family. It aids digestion and helps relieve nausea, bloating, and other gastrointestinal maladies. You can grow it in your own garden or buy dried basil in jars. This pungent herb freezes well. Fresh basil leaves are one of the best flavor enhancers for fish, beans, and veal, and in tomato and pesto sauces.

Fennel is a great detoxifier and internal cleanser. Considered by individuals as far back as the seventeenth century to be an appetite suppressant, fennel has properties and a taste similar to anise. The seeds and fresh leaves add flavor to breads, meat dishes, sauces, and soups. Although considered an acquired taste, you can eat the sweet fennel stalks and bulbs like celery. Americans season food with the seeds while natives of Mediterranean countries prefer the fresh shoots, often serving fennel as a palate cleanser between courses.

Flaxseed: There is no better source of omega-3 fatty acids, vitamin E, iron, calcium, potassium, and magnesium than this medically touted herb. Most hearty-grain breads contain flaxseeds, also known as linseeds. Sprinkle them over salads or add them to your breakfast cereal. Flaxseed adds protection from heart disease and breast cancer.

Garlic stimulates the growth of beneficial bacteria in the stomach. Considered a wonder food with antiviral, anticancer, and antifungal qualities, garlic also protects your heart and reduces blood cholesterol and blood pressure levels. Two cloves a day clear the sinuses and ward off chest colds and flu. Along with onions, garlic fights candida, a yeast organism that lives in your body. It can also help diabetics by reducing blood-sugar levels. Cooks from every culture flavor their savory cuisines with cloves from the garlic bulb, also known as the "stinking rose." Treat your taste buds by blending minced garlic into a mouth-watering cheese spread and serve it with crackers.

Parsley: You can chew on a sprig after eating garlic to clear your breath. This mild herb has so many essential vitamins (A, B, C, and iron) that eating it is like taking another multivitamin tablet. Parsley is also a beneficial calcium source. Use it in meal preparation to blend the flavors of other herbs and spices in cooked dishes and salads. Flat-leaf Italian-style parsley has more flavor than the traditional curly-leaf variety. Check the herb bundle carefully when you buy it at the market—it looks a lot like the more pungent coriander, called cilantro at many grocery stores.

Rosemary: As a seasoning, sprigs of rosemary harmonize beautifully with every type of roasted meat as well as vegetables, breads, cheese, and egg dishes. Its piney, somewhat minty flavor complements other key spices in soups, marinades, and dressings. Rosemary has some antioxidant properties that enhance prepared foods, but its oil is very strong and cannot be consumed in large quantities. As an aromatic or cosmetic component, the oil of this perennial plant works effectively to refresh your skin, to enhance the sachets lining your dresser drawers, or to give shine to your brunette hair as an after-shampoo rinse.

Thyme is one of the fines herbes of French cuisine used in the bouquets garnis that enrich the flavors of chowders, soups, stocks, vegetable dishes, poultry stuffing, and just about every meat or fish course in the culinary lineup. Artichoke hearts marinated with thyme, olive oil, and lemon juice make a mouth-watering appetizer. Add some grated parmegiano reggiano cheese to the mix, put it in a blender, and you have a tasty spread for French bread. All you need is a bottle of wine. Leaves, sprigs, and ground thyme give your taste buds a workout when added to braised or slow-cooking foods—reducing the need to add salt. After dinner, you'll find that thyme squelches the belches and calms the gastrointestinal juices so you can relax and let your evening unfold in a metaphysical partnership with your soul.

For Your Spiritual and Emotional Health

Use of herbs, both flowers and roots, plays a part in rituals to open the senses and help you with the body-mind connection. Meditation rooms take on the serenity and calmness necessary to let go of daily stress.

Ignatia imara or **St. Ignatius bean:** When your body experiences shock or trauma, including grief, sad events, irritability, sleeplessness, or disappointment, this herb helps alleviate the conditions. You will find it sold as a homeopathic remedy in vials of tiny pellets that you place under your tongue.

Lavender: Widely cultivated worldwide, this herb has many healing properties and appears in many lotions, massage oils, perfumes, and topical remedies. Potpourris frequently include this herb. To freshen a bathroom, just saturate cotton and leave it in a dish. Rooms scented with lavender help quiet your mood, calm your nerves, and set the tone for meditation and reflection.

Mugwort: Want to remember your dreams? Placing mugwort in a handkerchief under your pillow helps stimulate the senses, open your Third Eye, and induce vivid dreams, some of which may be precognitive.

Scented geranium: An amazing number of delicious scents describe this herb of South African origin, not to be confused with the ornamental geraniums most widely cultivated in western gardens. Look for the species *Pelargoniums* at the nursery if you want to grow them in your flower boxes. Then harvest your own apple, coconut, lemon, and strawberry varieties for use as aromatics in your spiritual development and meditation rituals.

St. John's wort: This balsam-scented herb has ingredients comprised of oil, resin, tannin, and dye. In earlier centuries, this attractive perennial had affiliations with both religion and witchcraft—practitioners believed it drove out evil spirits. Today the dye is a main part of tablets used to treat mild depression.

Individuals new to meditation and going within to find answers complain that they cannot relax. Perhaps setting the mood with a few of these herbs will change the dynamic.

Improving Your Physical Space

Nothing benefits your body and soul more than living or working in an invigorating environment. Certain spaces seem to lack life or the air is stale and tired. The room may be too dark, too intense, too cramped, or too airy. Furniture could be hogging all the wall space or be improperly arranged. A huge culprit is the collection of junk and clutter you accumulate. You leave no breathing space for the positive energy called chi to circulate and clear the air. During feng shui consultations, I have visited homes where shelves adjacent to the bed held piles of journals in which the occupant unloaded years of life's angst. Can you guess why the prevailing complaint was, "I can't get any sleep in this room?" Remember to shred or burn those corner-clogging dissertations when you have moved past the issues. Your heirs will thank you.

In other dwellings, an argument may have taken place in a room or building before you arrived, yet the remnants of negative energy remain in the air. It's not enough to simply wash away the painful exchanges while you do the dishes. Entering rooms like this make you feel ill-at-ease or tired. Maybe your home has a few toxic spaces that could use a lift. Once you remove some of the physical clutter, try a few of these herbal remedies.

Cinnamon bark burned as incense raises the vibration of any room. Herbalists will tell you to watch the money and good luck roll in when you use it. Romantic partners credit cinnamon with helping the flames of passion burn brightly. Sprinkling cinnamon in water and simmering it on the stove has similar properties, a technique Realtors recommend to create an inviting aroma for potential buyers who visit the home.

Flaxseed: Aside from the nutritional value noted earlier, this herb fills additional roles. Need help in settling arguments? Sprinkle some seeds around you and others who are causing trouble. The doorways to main entrances may be brushed with flaxseed oil to promote harmony and understanding among residents and their guests. I have known a few wise souls who would arrive early for business meetings to dab the doorways or meeting tables with flax oil, with the intention of minimizing tension and getting quick consensus on agenda items.

Peppermint: If you are feeling the blahs and indoor spaces reflect it, dab peppermint aromatherapy oil on candles or on strategic places in your rooms. Light the candles and let the crisp-smelling scent freshen the air. This herb gives an uplifting feeling when you feel tired. Just open the bottle and smell it to clear your head. Note the number of available cleaning products that contain mint-based solutions for cleaning your home.

Sage is a multifunctional and multispecies herb. Aside from its culinary and ornamental properties, sage is an active ingredient in perfumes, soaps, candles, and cosmetics that are mixed with other herbs like lavender. Lotion manufacturers use sage for its astringent properties because it perks up the skin. As a main ingredient of herbal baths, sage stimulates energy, heals aching joints, and soothes tired feet. While its fragrance induces sleep, it is also used in smudge sticks to cleanse toxic spaces and provide protection from negative energy.

Use of herbs opens up a world of comfort, healing, and relaxation. Culinary herbs offer nutritious additions and zest to your diet. If for no other reason than appreciating their essences, grow herbs in your indoor and outdoor gardens. Consult your favorite gardening store for information about growing conditions and planting seasons.

Soothing Herbal Remedies for Your Baby

❧ by Michelle Skye ❧

There's nothing worse than seeing your infant in pain or discomfort. As a parent, you want to help and heal your child, but the products on the market can be overwhelming. Most commercial brands are filled with chemicals and additives that you'd really rather not expose your child to. All-natural choices are expensive and, often, not easily obtained. (And, to be perfectly frank, the store seems so very far away when you've only had two hours of sleep!) Yet, thankfully, there is an alternative—make your own oils and salves with herbs and essential oils of your choosing.

Creating herbal oil is actually much easier than most people believe. You will be amazed by the ease and simplicity of this process and, once you've mastered oil-making, you can move into salve and lotion-making with little

difficulty! The following two recipes (one oil and one salve) were created out of necessity in order to heal my daughter, Neisa, who suffered from cradle cap and (as is common with babies wearing diapers) diaper rash. By researching various herbs and through trial and error, I found two recipes that worked for her. Feel free to use these recipes as a starting place in creating your own, personalized recipes for your own children. Every child is different and you will find that your child responds to some herbs better than others. As a note of caution, be aware that your child could be allergic to any of these herbs. It is best to use a test patch first when applying the oil or salve to the skin. If you see any redness or any bumps, discontinue use immediately. (Incidentally, my daughter has very sensitive skin and did not have a negative reaction to either of these recipes; however, it is still wise to use a test patch.)

Before beginning your foray into creating your own herbal pharmacy, you will need a few items. These can be bought at any specialty kitchen store and at higher-end department stores. You might even be able to purchase them at your grocery store, if it's one of the bigger, all-inclusive chains. None of these items are very expensive so don't worry about having to dip into your retirement account for the money! You will need a small funnel made of plastic or metal, a fine-mesh strainer or cheesecloth, and a double-boiler. If you don't have a double-boiler, you can use two same-sized kitchen pots and put one on top of the other. You will also need several small glass bottles or jars (baby food jars work very well) and extra virgin or virgin olive oil. I use olive oil because it is very moisturizing, easy to find, and not too expensive. However, feel free to use jojoba oil, which absorbs into the skin easily, or apricot kernel oil, which absorbs into the skin very fast. (**Note:** Some studies have shown that olive oil helps to accelerate the growth of a type of skin yeast known as malassezia. Some doctors preclude the use of olive oil for cradle cap for this reason.)

Once you've purchased the equipment to make your herbal remedies, you have to decide on which herbs to use. It is important to do research on this topic as well as to follow your intuition. Try to purchase herbs from a reputable herbal shop, either near your home or online. These places will offer the freshest dried herbs and will be able to answer all of your questions. My recipes include herbs that are traditionally used for skin irritations, as well as others that I added for various reasons, oftentimes using my intuition or whatever I had around the house.

Cradle Cap Oil

Gather together equal parts of nettle, comfrey, chamomile, and white willow bark. I use the "wild woman" way of measuring herbs for my recipes, preferring to give you general amounts so you can make as little or as much as you need. You decide what 1 part equals, whether it's ½ ounce, 1 ounce, or 2 ounces, and then you do the math at home. (For instance, if you decide that 1 part is equal to ½ ounce and the recipe calls for 1 part calendula and 2 parts comfrey then you would add ½ ounce of calendula and 1 ounce of comfrey to your herbal preparation.)

Before you take your cooking utensils out of the cupboard, here is a brief rundown of the properties of your ingredients.

Nettle is generally used internally as a wonderful tonic herb rich in calcium, plant iron, and vitamins A and K. It is commonly taken to relieve PMS or menopause symptoms, to increase milk production in new mothers, and to stop hemorrhaging during childbirth. Nettles have also been shown to alleviate the pain and inflammation of rheumatism, gout, and arthritis when applied externally. European folk medicine suggests using nettles for seborrhea of the scalp, the "adult" name for cradle cap.

Comfrey has been the healing plant of choice for centuries, especially in relationship to cuts, scrapes, broken bones, and bruises. It helps to stimulate cell growth and connective tissue and has been used to treat ulcers. It contains vitamin A, B vitamins, calcium, iron, and protein.

Chamomile is a calming and soothing herb that is great for easing tension, anxiety, or worry. It helps heal digestive problems, feminine irregularities, and nervous disorders. Chamomile is also highly anti-inflammatory and antibacterial, which will help to protect your child in case open sores develop.

White willow bark is traditionally used internally as a pain and fever reducer. The synthetic compound that works in aspirin is found naturally in white willow bark. It is used to alleviate any type of pain, but especially headache, toothache, and back ache. As with aspirin, it is inadvisable to internally administer white willow bark to a child under sixteen years old with a fever or flu-like symptoms. However, since our oil will be applied topically, there is no cause for concern.

Place equal amounts of the herbs in the top of your double-boiler and cover them with the oil of your choice. Make sure that all the herbs are soaking in the oil. Fill the bottom of the double-boiler a little over halfway with water. Put the top on top of the bottom and heat over the stove. Once the water is boiling, turn the heat down very low so that the water is bubbling but not boiling over. The oil should not be bubbling at all. Cover the pot with the oil in it and allow the double-boiler to heat on the stove for six to eight hours, remembering to replenish the water every couple of hours. (You don't want to burn your pot!) If you don't want to heat the herbs over the stove, you can fill a canning jar with the herbs and oil and put it in the sunlight for two weeks.

Once the eight hours (or two weeks) is up, take the oil out of the heat and strain out the plant parts using the fine-mesh strainer or the cheesecloth. I find cheesecloth to be slightly messier, but more effective in straining out tiny particles. However, if small bits of herbs don't bother you, the strainer is very efficient. Allow the oil to cool before adding your essential oil to the herbal oil mixture. The essential oil helps to preserve the herbal oil so that it can be stored at room temperature. Add at least 15 drops of essential oil, more if you love the scent. I suggest lavender essential oil, as it is well-known for its calming qualities and its promotion of relaxation. Now that your oil is complete, pour it into your glass containers using the funnel, cap it, and store it at room temperature.

Diaper Rash Healing Salve

You will need equal parts comfrey, calendula, and plantain herbs, as well as several ounces of beeswax and an essential oil of your choice. You can also use vitamin E in place of the essential oil to preserve your salve. I prefer the scent of the essential oils, but some people choose vitamin E for its moisturizing properties. As I have already highlighted the values of comfrey, I will not repeat them here, focusing instead on the other two herbs.

Calendula (a large marigold) is a wonderful herb for skin irritations and infections. It is anti-inflammatory and antibacterial so it can heal a variety of pesky skin problems. It has been known to kill the staph germ, hydrate skin (including stimulating the production of collagen), relieve pain and itching in the genitals, and prevent skin damage due to bug bites or sunburn.

Plantain (not to be confused with the bananalike vegetable of the same name) is traditionally used for wounds, coughs, and all types of skin irritations. The leaves can be placed directly on the skin for bug bites and stings, eczema, and small cuts. It has also been known (in historic tomes) to remove poison from the system when applied externally, although I don't know if I'd want to chance it!

Prepare an herbal oil of equal parts comfrey, calendula, and plantain as described above. After the oil has been infused with the herbs for eight hours, strain out the plant parts and place the herb-infused oil in another pot. (I usually use the bottom section of the double-boiler, since it only contained water, but you can use another similarly sized pot.) Put the oil over very low heat and begin to add beeswax. It is best to cut your beeswax into very small pieces as they will melt faster and will give you greater flexibility in determining the consistency of your salve. Stir the beeswax and oil combination to help speed the melting time.

The amount of beeswax used depends on your salve consistency preference. Some people like their salves very hard, and thus will use more beeswax than those who like their salves softer. To test the consistency of your salve, dip your spoon into the beeswax and oil mixture and allow a small amount to pool in the well of the spoon. Then place the spoon in your freezer for a minute or so. When you remove the spoon, the salve will have hardened, giving you an idea of its density. You can then add more beeswax or more oil to your salve in order to achieve the texture of your choice.

Once you are satisfied with the consistency of your salve, take the pot off the stove and pour it into your sterilized glass containers, using the funnel. Wait for your salve to cool down for a minute or so and then add your essential oil or vitamin E. I usually add 5 drops of essential oil to each baby food jar. When using vitamin E, I open 4 capsules and share them between five jars. Keep the jars open until the salve has completely cooled and hardened, then cap them, and store them at room temperature.

When you are creating your herbal recipes try to attune yourself to the energy of the herbs. Working with plant matter can be very fulfilling and rewarding. There is something to be said for working with the natural product that the earth provides for us. Herbs start out as tiny seeds and flourish into wonderfully heavy leaves and scented flowers that can heal and protect us. They truly are a miracle and their inherent powers can help heal your little miracle. What a great way to recycle and reuse the Earth's bounty!

Lighten up to Beat the Winter Blues

≫ by Chandra Moira Beal ≪

When winter brings shorter days and colder temperatures, bears turn to hibernation and sheep grow a fleecier coat, but humans just get depressed. Most people find they eat and sleep slightly more in winter and dislike the dark mornings and shorter days. But for some people, the winter blues are severe enough to disrupt their lives and cause considerable distress. These people are suffering from Seasonal Affective Disorder, or SAD.

Animals react to the passage of seasons with changes in mood and behavior, and human beings are no exception. As seasons change, there is a shift in our internal biological clocks, or circadian rhythm, partly due to changes in sunlight patterns. These changes cause our biological clocks to

be out of step with our daily schedules. Anyone affected by SAD knows that this depressive disorder can make you feel as if winter will never end, and you feel inclined to stay in bed with a hot water bottle, a warm drink, and a pile of good books.

The farther you live from the equator, the worse the condition (except where there is snow on the ground, which reflects light). Women are twice as likely to suffer from SAD as men, and children and adolescents are also vulnerable.

What Are the Symptoms?

SAD has a wide range of symptoms including depression (some experts contend that SAD is essentially seasonal depression), mood swings, irritability, lethargy, cravings for sweet foods, and a general feeling of being down in the dumps.

Many suffer from sleep problems—oversleeping, waking up groggy, or needing a nap in the afternoon. Others tend to overeat, especially carbohydrates that lead to weight gain.

These symptoms are compounded by feelings of despair, misery, guilt, or anxiety, and simple everyday tasks become frustratingly difficult. Family and social life can suffer, as SAD victims tend to avoid company and experience loss of libido. SAD can even manifest in physical symptoms, often as joint pain, stomach problems, and lowered resistance to infection.

The initial diagnosis of SAD can be difficult because the sufferer does not know what is causing the symptoms. While even children can experience SAD, the symptoms usually arise during the late teens or early twenties. As with depression, the mood swings, irritability, difficulty concentrating, and feelings of isolation associated with SAD are often (and sometimes correctly) attributed to the physical, social, and emotional changes inherent to young adulthood: growth spurts and the accompanying hormonal changes; a transition from life at home to college and/or the workplace; romantic relationships that may be blossoming or bursting. So consult a medical doctor to examine all possible causes. For example, hypoglycemia has similar symptoms.

What Causes SAD?

The problem stems from the lack of bright light in winter. Researchers have proven that bright light makes a difference in brain chemistry, although the exact means by which sufferers are affected is not yet known. The nerve centers in our brains controlling our daily rhythms and moods are stimulated by the amount of light entering the eyes. During the night, the pineal gland produces melatonin, which makes us drowsy. At daybreak, the bright light causes the gland to stop producing melatonin. But on dull winter days, especially indoors, not enough light is received to trigger this waking-up process.

More recently, good evidence has linked exposure to bright light with the increased production of serotonin, another brain chemical that produces happy feelings.

Remedies for SAD

Herbal Supplements

Herbal supplements are an easy and inexpensive way to tackle SAD symptoms. **St. John's wort** (*Hypericum*) is well known for its mood-lifting properties. Taking 15 drops (0.6 ml) of tincture two to three times a day can help you cope with the bleak midwinter. Start taking it a few weeks before SAD symptoms really set in to you to allow it time to begin working.

Passionflower (*Passiflora*) is another helpful herb that has been described as a "hug in a bottle." Its gentle sedative action on the central nervous system helps alleviate nervous tension, depression, and anxiety.

Oats (*Avena sativa*) are rich in B vitamins that are essential for a healthy nervous system, and have a calming and restorative effect. You can often find oats and passionflower combined in an effective complex. Taking 20 drops twice a day can be a real boon to SAD sufferers.

In the Middle East, **basil** is made into a tea that is taken to relieve mild depression. It has a long history in Ayurvedic medicine as a good herb for the treatment of nervous disorders and anxiety and, in aromatherapy, the essential oil can even have a mildly sedative effect.

Some people swear by **yellow dock** to treat seasonal affective disorder. The idea is that the cells of the yellow dock plant are similar to the cells of the pineal gland, so the yellow dock feeds the pineal gland through its similar cellular structure.

Feverfew and **licorice** can help regulate blood sugar and even out your levels of energy, and therefore your moods. Both are tasty brewed up in an herbal tea.

Siberian ginseng (*Eleutherococcus senticosus*) and **Cordyceps** (*Cordyceps sinensis*) are great for increasing energy and reducing the winter blues. You can often find these herbs together in the same formula designed for high-performance athletes, but they can also give a boost to most people if taken on a regular basis.

Vitamin D is another important supplement, but most of our body's vitamin D is produced by the action of sunlight on the skin, which is lacking during winter. Vitamin D supplements are safe and can help adjust your body's levels as they drop during the winter months.

Diet and Exercise

Diet is another aspect to consider. Avoid stimulants such as coffee, tea, and other caffeinated drinks as these can tax your adrenal glands, which you need to cope with stress. For the same reasons, avoid sugary and refined foods that lack nutritional value.

Add foods to your diet that are rich in omega-3 essential fatty acids such as fish or, for vegetarians and vegans, flaxseeds. Avocados, beans, bananas, wheat germ, oats, brown rice, and whole grain pasta will help increase serotonin. Also, be sure to stay hydrated with plenty of water. It's just as important in the winter as in the summer!

Exercise is vital, too. Go for a bracing walk to get much-needed oxygen and produce endorphins, those wonderful feel-good chemicals. With so many modern people working indoors in artificial light, getting out for a walk even if it looks gloomy will help because there will be more light than indoors.

Light Therapy

Since the cause of SAD is lack of bright light, the best treatment is to be in bright light every day. Light therapy, designed to replicate natural sunlight, has been used to treat SAD with good results, proving effective in 85 percent of diagnosed cases. Of course, spending the winter in a brightly lit climate, whether skiing or somewhere hot and sunny, is indeed a cure, but not always an option.

Light boxes and body clocks work by using your body's natural response to sunrise and sunset to help synchronize your sleep/wake pattern. The light must be suitably bright, at least 2,500 lux (lux is the technical measure of brightness), which is five times brighter than a well-lit office (a normal living room might be as low as 100 lux); brighter lights up to 10,000 lux work faster. The light does not need to be special daylight, color matching, or full spectrum light; simply changing the lamps in a room to these special types might not produce sufficient light—remember, the brightness of the light is the most critical factor.

Most SAD sufferers use light therapy almost every day. Some people can skip two or three days while others notice symptoms creeping back even after one day.

There can also be days when there is bright sunshine outside, even in winter and especially in the southern climate. If you can get out and make the most of it, you might not need extra light therapy that day.

Dawn simulators, or body clocks, don't provide lots of light; they simulate a natural sunrise by gradually increasing the light at your wake-up time to give you a head start. These simulators work well for milder symptoms, especially if your main problem is getting yourself going in the morning. Dawn simulators can also be used in addition to light boxes.

Health insurers will often pay for a light box, as SAD is a clinical depressive disorder. It's worth asking your doctor about it. Expect to spend $200 to $500, depending on the intensity and style of the light.

You don't have to feel blue during the winter months. Just turn to Mother Nature and you could be feeling in the pink before you know it!

Hot Flash Herbs

≈ by Dallas Jennifer Cobb ≈

I always thought hot flashes were a joke until a close friend had one while we were out for a walk. "I've gotta sit down," she said. "I'm having a hot flash." And while I was ready to make a joke, I saw the deep red flush on her face and her drawn features. There was nothing funny about it; she was in considerable discomfort. After handing her my bottle of water, I sat on the bench next to her and could literally feel the heat radiating off of her. I no longer make light of hot flashes. There is nothing to laugh at.

In my mid-40s, with menopause on my near horizon, I started to research hot flashes, their cause, and how I could ease myself through that enormous life and body transition, moving from the archetypal mother to crone. Much of my research has focused on

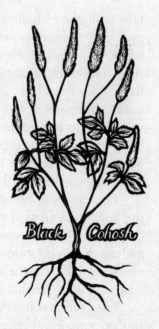

Black Cohosh

natural remedies and practices that could help to relieve the symptoms. These include herbs, diet, and exercise.

Maybe you know someone who is already having hot flashes. Hot flashes are one of the most prevalent—and bothersome—symptoms of menopause. However, the ferocity of hot flashes varies greatly from woman to woman, and culture to culture.

There are many herbs and herbal remedies that aid the body's transition through menopause, reducing the incidence and severity of hot flashes. Many can also help reduce the effect of other menopausal complaints, such as the increased risk of osteoporosis and changes in sexual energy and function. And these benefits are not just health food store rumors, the efficacy of herbs is being researched by the National Center for Complementary and Alternative Medicine (NCCAM), where scientists are examining the ability of herbs to reduce the effects of hot flashes.

What Is a Hot Flash?

Hot flashes are often described as a hot wave that sweeps over the body, sometimes accompanied by nausea, dizziness, headaches, heart palpitations, and anxiety. The outer signs may be reddening or blotching of the skin and heavy perspiring. These flashes can be as brief as thirty seconds, or persist for up to an hour. Most women report feeling helpless or a loss of control, which results in heightened anxiety, and for some, depression.

Hot flashes that occur during sleep are called night sweats, because of the profuse perspiring that accompanies them. Not everyone who has hot flashes experiences night sweats.

The causes of hot flashes are not fully understood. While the body does all of these things normally to cool down when overheated—blood vessels near the skin dilate to release heat, and the person perspires—a hot flash is a sudden, intense version unconnected to overheating. The cooling effect following a hot flash is so effective that many women get the chills.

The National Institutes of Health classifies a hot flash as a sudden temporary onset of body warmth, flushing, and sweating.

Technically named vasomotor flushes, hot flashes are common in 75 to 80 percent of menopausal women in North America, and were initially thought to be stimulated by a drop in circulating estrogen levels as ovarian function declined with age.

However, the estrogen-drop theory has been questioned because other research has confirmed that some women with low estrogen levels never have hot flashes, while others with excess estrogen have hot flash symptoms. Studies researching the effect of estrogen replacement on menopausal women were inconclusive, recording a 30 percent reduction in hot flash severity and occurrence in women who were given a placebo.

Because of the inconclusive results, researchers continue to search for the origins and causes of hot flashes. The research has spread in a number of interesting directions.

One theory suggests that hot flashes are triggered by a sudden change in the body's internal temperature. Because estrogen and progesterone play a role in temperature regulation, the theory is that a change in the levels of these two hormones triggers a change in temperature, which subsequently triggers a hot flash as a response from the system trying to maintain homeostasis.

Other research is examining how the declining levels of estrogen and progesterone trigger a withdrawal of naturally occurring opiates. The opiate withdrawal impacts mood, pain control, and hormone modulation, making women more susceptible to even small shifts in temperature or sensation. Perhaps the body doesn't really get hotter, it just feels hotter.

There is also a lot of research focusing on the acid/alkaline balance of the blood and the connection to hot flashes. This research postulates that an overly acidic environment is more prone to hot flashes, whereas an alkalized system is not.

Who Doesn't Get Hot Flashes

While hot flashes occur in 75 to 80 percent of menopausal women in North America, the occurrence isn't as high for women living elsewhere. Studies have shown that less than 10 percent of menopausal women in Japan, Korea, and Southeast Asia experience hot flashes. Research from Mexico also indicates a much lower incidence of hot flashes.

So what is different about these women or their lifestyle that makes for such a marked difference in hot flash occurrence? Research shows that Asian women have lower natural estrogen levels than occidental women, so they would experience less of a drop in estrogen levels, and fewer side effects. But what explains the lower incidence of hot flashes for women in Mexico?

When the different cultures were studied for lifestyle similarities it was discovered that each consumed a high-fiber, low-fat diet with a high dietary intake of bean products. In Asia the soybean is widely used, and in Mexico black beans, fava beans, and broad beans are a large part of the staple diet.

Beans contain phyto-estrogens, plant hormones with estrogenlike effects. Soy, the most versatile bean, is a complete protein, and is made into a variety of food products common to the Asian diet: soymilk, soy cream, tofu, tempeh, miso, and soy sauce.

Researchers have noted that the cultural reliance on bean-based foods corresponds to the reduced incidence of hot flashes, and think it is because the diets high in phyto-estrogens supplement estrogen levels in the body. In North America, the common diet trends toward the opposite—animal rich and reliant on high-fat, low-fiber foods.

Common Triggers for Hot Flashes

While the research is still inconclusive, many women agree that specific circumstances can trigger hot flashes. While many causes are diet related, some are due to emotional and lifestyle conditions. To reduce the incidence of hot flashes, try to limit:

- spicy foods with cayenne, ginger, pepper, and curry;
- caffeine in any form, including chocolate and soda;
- alcohol of any sort, including wine and beer;
- stress and intense emotions, especially anger;

- highly refined foods such as white sugar, white flour, and white bread;
- exposure to hot weather, hot tubs, and saunas;
- tobacco, marijuana, and other recreational drugs;
- acidic foods such as pickles, vinegar, and tomatoes; and
- hydrogenated or saturated fats, including meat, margarine, and many snack foods.

Whether these foods overstimulate the system and increase the tendency to overheat, or acidify the system which increases the incidence of hot flashes, is not clearly known. But those who believe in the acid/alkaline theory swear that foods that acidify the body are to be avoided. These include dairy products, refined foods, animal products, sodas, sweets, baked goods, and empty carbohydrates. By alkalizing the system through consumption of a diet based primarily on fruits, vegetables, legumes (beans), nuts, and seeds, one could reduce the occurrence of hot flashes.

Lifestyle Changes

Because the low incidence of hot flashes in Asia is attributed to dietary differences, many North American women have considered diet as a factor, and lots of them swear they have lowered their incidence of hot flashes by making dietary changes. Research from varied sources seems to substantiate their claim.

To reduce hot flashes, the ideal diet is one that is vegetarian-based, high in fiber, and low in fat. Consume lots of fresh fruits and vegetables and lots of beans, especially soybeans, which contain the phyto-estrogens genistein and daidzein. Hot flashes are also reduced by foods rich in calcium, magnesium, and vitamin E, all common in dark leafy greens, nuts, and seeds. Fiber and minerals also help to diminish hot flashes, so include lots of whole grains, fruit, and sea vegetables.

Drinking lots of water helps eliminate waste products and replenishes the fluids that you lose through perspiration during hot flashes and night sweats. Most sources recommend at least two liters (eight glasses) of good-quality spring water a day.

While diet and herbs can help relieve the symptoms of menopause, exercise also reduces the severity of symptoms and aids bone and cardiovascular health. A half-hour of exercise daily can help reduce hot flashes by raising endorphins and decreasing the amount of two pituitary hormones that regulate progesteron and estrogen levels in your system—luteinizing hormone (LH) and follicle stimulating hormone (FSH).

The best exercise I can recommend is to take a brisk walk, with arms swinging by your side. A weight-bearing but low-impact activity, walking elevates the heart rate, stimulates cardiovascular health, and helps maintain bone density.

Herbs for Hot Flashes

If after making some lifestyle changes you still have hot flashes, why not find a herbal practitioner to help you explore herbs that help hot flashes? Many herbs generally have a cooling effect on the system, nourish or increase oxygen use in the liver, or are rich in phytosterols.

Traditionally, North American herbs have been used successfully, but this article will also cover some common herbs used in traditional Chinese medicine that have proven effective in reducing the incidence and severity of hot flashes.

North American Herbs

When I say North American, I mean herbs that grow in North America and are relatively easy to find in your neighborhood health food store or at your local herbalist. Indigenous cultures and early settlers have used these herbs for generations. Their medicinal and curative properties have been tried, tested, documented, and, of late, backed up by scientific research.

Herbs are powerful allies, but must be used responsibly. The information provided here is only intended to help you explore alternatives and is not to be taken as medical advice. Always consult an herbalist to help you determine what herbs to use and the proper dosages. My personal preference is to consume herbs in their natural forms, taken as teas or tinctures. While many herbs come in convenient pill form, you really don't need all that extra stuff in your diet. A good herbalist should suggest loose herbs and carefully teach you how to prepare them.

The most common herbs recommended for menopausal women have gained a reputation as a female tonic: black cohosh (*Cimicifugae racemosae rhizoma*), chaste tree berry (*Vitex angus-castus*), dandelion (*Taraxacum officinale*), licorice root (*Glycyrrhiza glabra*), motherwort (*Leonurus cardiaca*), nettle (*Urtica dioica*), and oatstraw (*Avena sativa*).

Many of these contain phyto-estrogrens—plant-based properties that mimic estrogen. Others cleanse and nourish the liver, kidneys, and endocrine glands. The varied research indicates that a combination of these qualities is the most effective treatment for reducing the frequency, severity, and duration of hot flashes.

Black Cohosh (Cimicifugae racemosae rhizoma)

Black cohosh was used traditionally by indigenous cultures and early settlers to relieve menstrual cramps and symptoms of menopause, including hot flashes and depression. Recent research in Germany indicates that black cohosh has proven so successful in the treatment of hot flashes, vaginal atrophy, and emotional and nervous conditions associated with menopause that the German government has officially approved it for use.

Because black cohosh contains phyto-estrogens, it has a significant estrogenic effect that reduces luteinizing hormone (LH) levels. Black cohosh also has digestive properties that, if taken with meals, reduce the nausea for some menopausal women.

Women who take synthetic estrogen-replacement therapy should not take black cohosh because of the estrogenic effects.

Chaste Tree or Chaste Berry (Vitex angus-castus)

While chaste tree doesn't grow in North America, it is part of our herbal repertoire because it grows and is widely used in

Europe and the Mediterranean regions. Chaste tree affects the two pituitary hormones, FSH and LH, which regulate progesterone and estrogen levels. It is effective in treating hot flashes and dizziness, promoting emotional balance, and normalizing female reproductive functions.

Chaste tree is a slow-acting tonic and requires long-term commitment. Results become evident after two to three months.

Dandelion (Taraxacum officinale)

Dandelion is one of the most overlooked herbs in North America. Viewed as a weed, it is a vital tonic for the liver, which is considered the control center for hot flashes. Improved liver health means fewer hot flashes. Dandelion also aids digestion and is a good source of potassium. The young leaves can be picked and added to salads, and the roots can be made into a tincture or tea.

Licorice Root (Glycyrrhiza glabra)

Licorice root contains Glycyrrhizin, a phyto-estrogen with estrogen-regulating properties. Besides acting on the two pituitary hormones, FSH and LH, licorice root has a calming effect and is used to treat insomnia, digestive disorders, and infection.

While suitable for occasional use, long-term use can cause high blood pressure, edema (water retention), and sodium retention. Women with high blood pressure, heart problems, diabetes, or kidney or liver disease should not use licorice root. As with other herbs containing phyto-estrogens, never take licorice root while taking chemical or synthetic estrogen-replacement therapy.

Motherwort (Leonurus cardiaca)

Menopausal women swear by it because it reduces the severity, frequency, and duration of hot flashes. Motherwort also increases vaginal lubrication, calms the nerves, and relieves anxiety and insomnia. Most commonly consumed as a tincture made from fresh flowers, a few drops can provide a sense of comfort and ease, calm fears, and relieve heart palpitations.

The best results come after frequent long-term use. Use the tincture up to six times per day for three months. Many women keep the tincture on the bedstand for use at night to combat night sweats.

Nettle (Urtica dioica)

Nettle strengthens and heals the adrenals. If you have consumed a lot of caffeine throughout your life, your adrenals are weak and need the support of nettle. Nettle is also high in calcium, which helps protect bones and maintain bone mass. Many women swear that taking nettle prevents night sweats and increases their daily energy. Fresh nettle can be steamed lightly and eaten as a green, or made into a satisfying tea or tasty vinegar.

Oatstraw or Oats (Avena sativa)

These act on the central nervous system, calming and strengthening the nerves. Oatstraw helps ease emotions, promotes a restful sleep, and strengthens the body's vital energy, renewing sexual energy and life force. Because it has natural calcium, oatstraw helps keep hair, nails, and bones strong. Oats have the same essential properties. You can consume this herb regularly by eating whole grain oats for breakfast in the morning.

Menopause Magic Tea

To allieviate menopausal symptoms, simply mix two teaspoons chaste tree berry, two teaspoons wild yam, and one teaspoon each of black cohosh, goldenseal, life root, oats, and motherwort.

Grind the mixture to an even consistency in a mortar and pestle, or use a clean coffee grinder. Place mixture into its own container. Use a heaping teaspoon of the mix in a cup of boiling water to make a tea. Steep for a few minutes, and then drink.

Ideally you can drink a cup three times a day. This tea will ease many symptoms by regulating hormones, nourishing the liver, and helping the body come back into balance.

Traditional Chinese Medicine

While much of our herbal lore in North America comes from the research and knowledge of indigenous cultures and early North American settlers, there are herbs from other cultures and continents that share a long-standing history of use and effectiveness treating hot flashes and menopausal symptoms.

Traditional Chinese medicine is based on balancing life-force energy. A traditional Chinese medical practitioner evaluates a patient's entire system, then treats the energy imbalance detected rather than the malady presented. Diseases are seen as symptoms of energy imbalance caused by stress, poor diet, lack of exercise, or poor coping skills. These factors inhibit the flow of energy through the meridians of the body, causing stagnation and imbalance. It is the imbalance that causes the ailment.

A qualified traditional Chinese medical practitioner performs an extensive examination, including questions about diet and lifestyle, an analysis of the many pulses, and a tongue examination. Treatment is prescribed based on the overall results. A combination of herbal therapy, acupuncture, moxibustion (the use of burning herbs), dietary and lifestyle changes, and Qi Gong (exercises that move energy) is commonly recommended.

Chinese herbs and acupuncture are now commonly used by North American women to ease hot flashes and night sweats.

Energy Imbalances

A young woman in her prime fertile years is said to have more yin energy, which is characterized as moist, receptive, and passive. As a woman approaches the perimenopausal years, there is an increase in the yang energy—dry, initiating, and active. As menopause arrives women are said to be more passionate about ideas, quicker to anger, and quicker to defend themselves. Traditional practitioners believe that hot flashes and menopausal symptoms are caused by these changes in energy, and the system's efforts to become accustomed to the new energy. Eventually the meridians become accustomed to the yang energy and the flow stabilizes.

Herbal formulas designed to relieve the particular symptoms of menopause treat the energy imbalances in the meridians.

In traditional Chinese medicine, hot flashes and anxiety are considered to be symptoms of a weakness of the heart meridian. Emotional irritability and irregular menstrual flow are symptoms of a weak liver meridian, and heavy menstrual bleeding and food cravings are symptoms of a weakness of the spleen.

Traditional Chinese Herbs for Hot Flashes

Most traditional Chinese medical doctors prescribe and mix their own herbs, and prescribe common herbal formulas, which are available in pill form. Made from recipes developed over generations of use, there are several herbal formulas commonly used for relieving menopausal symptoms.

Hot flashes and night sweats are generally due to a kidney deficiency, and are treated with the formulas Meno Peace (*Mai Wei Di Huang Wan*) or Kidney Yin Tonic (*Liu Wei Di Huang Wan*), which act directly on the kidney energy. Because the spleen is connected to fatigue experienced during menopause, a tonic for spleen chi deficiency and the immunenergy (*Shi Quan Da Bu Wan*) formulas are used to nourish the spleen and its meridian.

Two ingredients common to these formulas have become well known in North America: Dong quai (*Radix angelica sinensis*) and ginseng (*Panax ginseng*).

Dong Quai (Radix angelica sinensis)

An emmenagogue, dong quai can regulate the energy imbalances that cause hot flashes, insomnia, and night sweats. It is also balances the energies that control mental and emotional turmoil.

Dong quai is known to supplement the blood and aid in circulation. It also contains phyto-estrogens.

Ginseng (Panax ginseng)

While ginseng is known as a male tonic, it is highly useful to women during menopause because it contains steroidal glycosides, which help to regulate estrogen and progesterone levels. Ginseng is also an adaptogen and improves our natural response to stress, enhances immunities, and improves mental functioning. It also helps increase vitality, and uplift women experiencing depression and fatigue.

Other traditional Chinese herbs used to treat menopausal symptoms include: **Bao shao yao** and **Sang shen zi** for thinning hair; **Nuo dao gen** for night sweats; **Qing huo** for hot flashes; **Rehmannia** (*shu di huang*) for night sweats, irregular menses, dizziness, and premature graying of the hair; **She chaung zi** and **Tu fu ling** for vaginal dryness and lack of lubricating mucous; and **Fo ti**—an endocrine system tonic that rejuvenates, strengthens, and energizes—for premature aging, weakness, vaginal discharges, numerous infectious diseases, angina pectoris, and impotence.

The Best Remedy

As we age, we hope we become wiser, not just older. I have learned that hot flashes are no laughing matter, and through my research have come to understand that their treatment is not to be taken lightly either. Whether you choose to use traditional North American herbs, traditional Chinese medicine, or lifestyle changes to try to reduce your hot flashes and other menopausal symptoms, the best remedy is to make a wise decision.

Always Ask a Qualified Health Practitioner

While many North American herbs and traditional Chinese herbal remedies are available to the public, do not self prescribe. Herbs are powerful medicine and can easily harm when not used properly. Herbs should only be used under the direction of a qualified herbal practitioner. Locate a professional with many years of education and experience to use as your ally to help balance your body and make hot flashes a thing of the past.

Then, when the symptoms have passed, you can start to tell jokes about hot flashes, and really have the last laugh.

The Four-Step Herbal Cleanse

⇜ by AarTiana ⇝

Hunger is a natural signal that our bodies need nourishment. We get hungry. We eat. Problem solved. At least temporarily. The fact is, we need to eat a variety of foods to get the array of nutrients our bodies need to function. We all know that fast food, chips, and sodas aren't good for us, but did you know that certain foods can actually prevent us from absorbing the necessary nutrients?

So it's not enough to consume the right foods—our bodies need to be able to process them. That's where Dr. John Christopher's "Extended Herbal Cleanse" comes into play. The program, which originated at the School of Natural Healing, relies on implementing a mucusless diet: organic raw fruits and vegetables, whole grains, nuts, seeds, and legumes, with no meat, dairy, or breads, and no sugary,

refined, or processed foods. A juicer is an excellent investment, as it can be difficult receiving food's many nutrients (known and unknown) without one. Drink distilled water to eliminate toxins and stored minerals that cannot be assimilated. However, the distilled water will not wash away the desired minerals and assimilated nutrition from plants. If you wish to start this diet, eliminate all dairy and egg products first, as these cause most of the mucus build-up in the body that blocks nutritional absorption. Then eliminate sugary, processed foods, including bread; then meat. Replace with more raw fruits and vegetables—your nutritional absorption will improve, so these foods are enough. Rather than supplements, for extra nutritional support, drink three cups of tea per day made of alfalfa, red raspberry leaf, nettle, oatstraw, and/or horsetail. Add one heaping teaspoon of these herb(s) to eight ounces heated distilled water, and sweeten with raw unprocessed honey. Ground flaxseeds provide needed omega-3 fats.

If you decide to only do one cleanse, the colon is recommended. The other systems may rebalance themselves if toxins and old mucus have a way to leave the body. Also, take all of your medicinal herbs for six days—and rest on the seventh day. All of these cleansing steps are safe for as long as you need or want, and nonaddictive. If you wish to do them simultaneously, you can do the first three, then add the fourth step at least two weeks later. As herbs are basically food, there is no danger of overdosing—take enough to create the desired action. These recipes are provided for non-commercial use only. Mix the following powdered, dry herbs and place into size "00" capsules.

Note: While the "Extended Herbal Cleanse" has been historically used to cleanse, nourish, and even treat a wide variety of chronic ailments, you should review this program with a knowledgeable herbal practitioner before beginning any new regimen. If you are taking prescription medication or under other medical supervision, those practitioners should be consulted as well.

Step 1: Colon ("Fen LB")

2 ounces cascara sagrada (*Rhamnus purshiana*)
1 ounce barberry bark (*Berberis vulgaris*)
1 ounce cayenne (*Capsicum frutescens; C. minimum*)
1 ounce fennel (*Foeniculum vulgaris*)
1 ounce ginger (*Zingiber officinalis*)
1 ounce goldenseal (*Hydrastis Canadensis*)
1 ounce lobelia (*Lobelia inflata*)
1 ounce red raspberry leaves (*Rubus idaeus*)
1 ounce turkey rhubarb root (*Rheum palmatum*)

This makes about a three-to-six-month supply, depending on usage. Take 2 capsules an hour before meals three times a day, and monitor accordingly. If you become constipated, drink more water and take more capsules—up to 40 pills per day until it clears. It is ideal to stay on this cleanse for six to ten months and use it with distilled water and a mucusless diet.

As an additional, productive part of this cleanse, combine with a three-day juice cleanse. The best time for this is during a waning Moon. You will need 2 quarts of organic prune juice, 9 ounces of olive oil, 3 gallons of distilled water, and 3 gallons of organic, fresh-squeezed juice (apple, grape, citrus, carrot, tomato, etc.—stick to one fruit or vegetable during these three days).

Upon rising, drink 16 ounces of prune juice. Also, take 1 or 2 tablespoons of olive oil three times per day. Then, alternate 8 ounces of juice and water every 30 minutes. For instance, if you rise with prune juice at 7 am, at 7:30 am drink 8 ounces of juice, then at 8 am drink 8 ounces distilled water, and continue throughout the day until you have consumed 1 gallon of each. Since detoxifying is hard work for your body, allow yourself plenty of time to rest. Repeat the three-day juice cleanse once a month, with or without herbs, for best results.

Step 2: Liver/Gall Bladder ("Barberry LG")

3 ounces barberry bark (*Berberis vulgaris*)
1 ounce catnip (*Nepeta cataria*)

1 ounce cramp bark (*Viburnum trilobum; V. opulus*)
1 ounce fennel (*Foeniculum vulgaris*)
1 ounce ginger (*Zingiber officinalis*)
1 ounce peppermint (*Mentha piperita*)
1 ounce wild yam (*Dioscorea villosa*)

About a four-month supply—take 2 capsules 15 to 20 minutes before meals until you notice long-term improvement.

Step 3: Kidney/Bladder ("JuniPars")

1 ounce juniper berries (*Juniperus communis*)
1 ounce parsley (*Petroselinum crispum*)
1 ounce uva ursi (*Arctostaphylos uva-ursi*)
1 ounce marshmallow root (*Althaea officinalis*)
1 ounce lobelia (*Lobelia inflata*)
1 ounce ginger (*Zingiber officinalis*)
1 ounce goldenseal (*Hydrastis Canadensis*)

Approximately a six-month supply—take 2 capsules twice a day (morning and evening) with parsley tea for best results.

Step 4: Blood ("Red Clover Combination")

2 ounces red clover blossoms (*Trifolium pretense*)
1 ounce Chaparral (*Larrea tridentate*)
1 ounce licorice root (*Glycyrrhiza glabra*)
1 ounce poke root (*Phytolacca americana*)
1 ounce peach bark (*Prunus Persica vulgaris*)
1 ounce Oregon grape root (*Mahonia aquifolium*)
1 ounce stillingia (*Stillingia sylvatica*)
1 ounce cascara Sagrada (*Rhamnus purshiana*)
1 ounce sarsaparilla (*Smilax officinalis*)
1 ounce prickly ash bark (*Zanthoxylum americanum*)
1 ounce burdock root (*Arctium lappa*)
1 ounce buckthorn bark (*Rhamnus Frangula*)

About a six-month supply—take 2 capsules 1 hour after meals until you feel the bloodstream flowing and have more energy.

Tips and Treats
for Weary Feet

❧ By Krystal Bowden ❧

O ur feet faithfully support our weight and get us where we need to go as we go about our lives. Rarely do we think of them—except when they are hurting. We are more likely to complain that the toes are a funny shape or our heels are too callused, rather than think about how much they do for us every single day.

Our feet have a huge influence on our everyday health and feelings of well-being. Foot pain and other problems can lead to lower- and upper-back pain, neck pain, and headaches, or even poor posture. Feet, with twenty-six bones and more than 70,000 nerve endings, are also a very sensitive part of the body. No wonder a foot massage feels so nice.

The most simple foot-pain preventive measure can be done anytime and

anywhere. Just take a little time to notice how you stand. Do you typically place most of your weight on your heels? On the outsides or insides of your feet? Taking a look at the way your shoes are wearing can provide valuable insight. Any time you are just standing around (doing the dishes, talking to friends, or waiting in line for something), try to place your weight evenly across the foot: behind the little toe, behind the big toe, and across the bottom of the heel. This yogic practice helps alleviate foot and back pain and has the added benefit of improving overall posture.

Your nearest and dearest foot helper may just be Mother Earth herself. Every day, we are building up a static charge that at times we have felt as the shock we get after walking on carpet and touching something metal. Walking on the grass in your bare feet can ground this charge as surely as any other electrical charge. This is one reason that walking barefoot after a stressful day can be enormously helpful to our feeling of well-being.

If we harbor feelings of embarrassment about our feet, it is probably because of a problem that many people have after wearing closed-in shoes all day: smelly feet. But instead of being afraid of taking your shoes off, try making your own deodorizing spray to combat the problem. You'll need:

    1   cup distilled water
    ¼   cup cider vinegar (or witch hazel)
    7   drops tea tree oil
    3   drops lime, sage, or geranium essential oil

Take the cup of distilled water and add ¼ cup of either cider vinegar or witch hazel. Then add the 7 drops of tea tree oil and the 3 drops of the essential oil of your choice—lime, sage, or geranium. Add to a clean spray bottle and you are ready to go! Spray it on both before you put your shoes on and after you take them off. You can also add a little baking soda to your shoes at night and fill them with crumpled-up newspaper. The paper will absorb the moisture and the baking soda will help with the odors. Be sure to brush out the baking soda in the morning.

Athlete's foot is another all-too-common problem. To combat this malady, try this. You'll need:

10 drops tea tree oil

5 drops myrrh oil

1 cup liquid aloe vera

Simply add the tea tree oil and myrrh oil to a cup of liquid aloe vera. Apply this mixture twice a day (spraying works best), making sure to get in between the toes as well as the bottoms of your feet. If you have a problem with warts, apply one drop of neat lemon essential oil to each wart twice a day. If you are sensitive to citrus, try lavender instead.

Treat Your Feet

Pampering our feet is a wonderful way of thanking them for all the work that they do for us. Take an evening or a nice Saturday morning and set aside some time for a luxurious personal foot-pampering party. Try inviting some friends over to share in the fun! For the ultimate in foot fantasies, use the three-step process described below. But before you get started, find a comfortable seat that lets your feet rest flat on the floor and have all your materials gathered and prepared beforehand.

Step 1: Soak and Cleanse

1 cup oats

¼ cup lavender flowers

A variety of essential oils

Place cup of oats and the ¼ cup lavender flowers in cheesecloth or a clean cotton sock, and let it steep in a tub of very warm water large enough to hold both feet comfortably up to about ankle deep. If your feet are hot and swollen, allow the oats and lavender to steep for about 10 minutes, then add some ice to cool the water down. Then add essential oils depending on your mood. For an invigorating soak, add 2 to 4 drops of peppermint or tea tree for a pleasant tingle. Rosemary is also a nice choice, but won't add a tingling sensation. For a relaxing foot bath, add 1 to 2 drops of chamomile or 2 to 4 drops of lavender essential oil.

For a completely decadent foot bath, add a drop each of rose absolute and myrrh. Let your feet soak for at least 15 minutes, and then take a pumice stone and gently scrub the soles of your feet. It is unwise to try to take all the dry skin and calluses off in one sitting; this can be painful later. Just scrub very gently to take what will easily come off, and scrub a little more off next time you soak your feet. (It will give you an excuse to do this again soon!) Then, with a washcloth or a soft-bristled brush and a natural soap, thoroughly clean the feet, paying special attention to between the toes, the arch, and the sides of the heel. Swish your feet in the soak water to rinse them, and then place your feet on a nice, thick, soft towel and pat them dry. This is also a good time to trim your toenails because they will be much softer than usual.

Step 2: Massage

This is a particularly lovely part of pampering your feet. To prepare a massage oil, you'll need:

½ ounce grape-seed oil

¼ teaspoon jojoba oil

2 drops elemi essential oil

2 drops lavender essential oil

After blending the oils, pour the mixture out on your hand first to warm it to body temperature and then, starting at the heels and working up to the toes and back again, give a gentle massage. This is a good time to get the help of a friend or partner, so that you can totally relax. Using even pressure with the thumbs, and small circular motions on the heels and toes and longer strokes on the arches and ankles, work your way from heel to toe and toe to heel at least once. Use long strokes on the top of the foot as well. It is possible to do this on yourself; either rest your heel on a surface the same height as your seat or put your ankle on your knee. Be sure to avoid putting your foot in a position that is uncomfortable or painful; if you do, you will not get the beneficial effects of the massage. A very easy way to give yourself a foot massage is to add smooth river stones or marbles to your soaking water. As your feet are soaking, rub them back and forth over the stones or marbles for as long as you like.

Step 3: Moisturize and Protect

To help prevent dry, cracked, and callused feet, smooth a rich moisturizer over your whole foot and ankle, paying special attention to the bottom of your foot. To make your own moisturizer, you'll need:

½ ounce cocoa butter

½ ounce coconut oil

1 tablespoon beeswax

1 teaspoon jojoba oil

2 drops lavender, tea tree, rosemary essential oil

2 drops tea tree essential oil

2 drops rosemary essential oil

Melt the cocoa butter and coconut oil with the beeswax in a double broiler. When melted, add 1 teaspoon jojoba oil and stir until mostly cool. Then add 2 drops each lavender, tea tree, and rosemary essential oil. (If you add the essential oils too soon, they will evaporate instead of remaining in the moisturizer.) Cover your feet with clean cotton socks overnight or until the lotion is completely absorbed.

If you are a pedicure type of person, after you soak and cleanse your feet and trim your nails, take the time to push the cuticles toward the nail bed. You can soften them with a moisturizer, if necessary. Then, instead of painting them with potentially toxic nail polish, take a nail buffer and buff your toenails to a healthy shine. This generally lasts longer than a coat of polish and has the added benefit of increasing blood circulation underneath the nails.

If you are in a hurry but still need a little pampering, try using a salt scrub before taking a shower or bath. You can make a salt scrub by adding ½ cup of grapeseed oil to ½ cup of finely ground salt (such as canning salt), and adding 3 drops each of lavender and rosemary essential oil and 1 drop of tea tree essential oil. Place a large pan in the tub and massage the salt scrub all over your feet. Rinse well and empty the pan into the sink to help prevent your shower from getting slippery. A salt scrub also works well on the hands, elbows, and knees.

However you decide to treat your feet, be sure to take just a little time every so often to appreciate the part of the body that supports us, carries us, and keeps us in constant contact with Mother Earth.

Herbs
for
Beauty

Incredible and Edible Facials

❧ by Laurel Reufner ❧

True beauty—the glow of healthy skin—is desirable for a reason. Let's face it, when you know you look good, you feel good. And feeling good about yourself is the best beauty treatment/charm/aphrodisiac out there. We spend millions of dollars a year on skin and beauty products as though searching for the Holy Grail or philosophers' stone. The good news is that these magic elixirs needn't cost more than a few dollars and can be made from consumables already in your kitchen. Having looked through literally hundreds of beauty tips online (many posted by men), it is safe to say that this article is as much for the men as for the women. Men just usually don't want their friends to know that they enjoy a good facial as much as their wives or girlfriends do.

What follows are descriptions of items usually found in the kitchen that will help you have healthy, glowing skin with a minimum of cost or fuss. Look over the list and decide which ones you want to keep on hand for your regular beauty routine.

Almond meal gently exfoliates the skin. Almond oil is a useful substitute for olive oil and is a lovely emollient. As oils go, it can penetrate the skin more deeply, helping carry other healthy ingredients deeper as well. Almonds also can have a slightly bleaching effect on the skin.

Aloe vera is very soothing for sunburn and other forms of skin irritation. Some also use it as a moisturizer for its anti-inflammatory properties.

Apple cider vinegar is naturally astringent without being harsh and can help restore natural skin pH. It also contains alpha hydroxy acids, which help remove layers of dead skin cells, relieving itchy skin and leaving the rest looking refreshed and renewed. The vinegar helps ease burns, including sunburn. Finally, apple cider vinegar will help lighten age spots and remove blemishes. Apples can also be mashed and used in facials.

Avocados show up often in beauty formularies. Rich in vitamins A and E, they are wonderful for dry skin.

Bananas are wonderfully nourishing for dry skin, but also work on more normal skin when used with other ingredients. They are rich in potassium and other vitamins.

Carrots are high in vitamin A and also function as an antiseptic. If you need a cleanser for oily skin, try lightly steaming and mashing a carrot and mix in a little lemon juice.

Cucumbers are amazing on the face. They cool tired skin, soothe, and help heal. They can help fade unwanted freckles and make wrinkles less noticeable. Cucumbers also help ease the discomfort of tired eyes, sunburn, and windburn. Use cucumbers to help control oily skin.

Eggs are a staple in natural beauty care. Sometimes you use the yolk for all of the wonderful nutrients it contains and sometimes you use the albumen for its skin tightening/refining properties. Sometimes you use the whole egg. Egg yolks are moisturizing and full of antioxidants.

Honey, with its many uses, is one of nature's miracles. Used with the other ingredients listed, honey can help clear up acne-prone skin. As a humectant, honey draws moisture from the air into your skin, making it glow and look younger. It helps improve skin tone and smells yummy.

Lemons are another wonder food, good for so much more than lemonade. Lemon juice can be used to help bleach your skin (or hair), relieve sunburn, exfoliate dead cells, and help tighten and refine pores. The antiseptic, astringent properties of lemons make them useful in fighting acne or controlling oily skin. Mix some lemon juice with water and drink to help detoxify your body. To lighten skin, freckles, or age spots, try mixing milk and lemon juice in a 1:1 ratio. Leave it on your face until it dries and then rinse with cool water.

Milk does a body good, on the outside as well as the inside. The lactic acid in milk acts as an alpha hydroxy acid to help remove layers of dead skin cells and gives you a deep cleansing. Whole milk or cream helps feed tired, dry skin. Yogurt has many of milk's properties, helping clear the complexion, fight pimples, and balance your skin's pH.

Oats are wonderfully cleansing and soothing for sunburned, windburned, or otherwise irritated skin. An emollient and exfoliant, oatmeal helps clean and refine pores, heal dry skin, and clear up pimples. To make a simple oatmeal mask, grind some up finely and mix them with a little milk or yogurt to make a paste.

Olive oil is a wonderful all-purpose ingredient for use in home-beauty recipes. It's very healing for dry skin.

Rose water just feels great on your skin. It has rehydrating properties, makes a great mildly astringent tonic, and is good for your complexion.

Strawberries are yummy for oily skin, helping improve the skin's texture, minimize the oiliness, and give you a radiant, healthy complexion. The mildly astringent fruit also contains some alpha hydroxy acids.

Vitamin E is a wonderful emollient often used directly on the fine lines and wrinkles of the face, especially around the eye and mouth. Vitamin E is also useful in beauty recipes because, as an antioxidant, it helps increase the shelf life of beauty products containing oils. That antioxidant property is pretty nice for your skin as well.

Witch hazel is quite cleansing and most useful for oily complexions, but may be used on all skin types. Its styptic properties make it useful as an after-shave toner or lotion. Witch hazel also reduces redness caused by capillaries on the face, especially around the nose area. Add a few drops of a favorite essential oil to make your own toner.

Facial Basics

Let's touch on the basic steps to a good facial and then find out what can be done with these basic ingredients. At its most basic level, a facial is a four-step process. 1. Cleanse your skin, since it is fairly pointless to apply a mask to dirty skin. 2. Apply your mask and let sit while you relax. This usually takes between 15 and 30 minutes. 3. Completely remove the mask from your face and neck. 4. Moisturize, even if you have oily skin.

Our skin craves moisture, especially the delicate neck area where skin is thin and oil glands few. Furthermore, if oily skin is cleansed too harshly and left to become dry, your body might compensate by overproducing oil, compounding your oily skin problem. If you feel a moisturizer is too much for your skin, at least make a good toner to apply that will help even out your skin's pH, leaving it healthy and happy. Finally, if you can steam your face after cleansing it you'll get even more out of the facial, as the pores will have opened more and allow the mask ingredients to penetrate deeper and cleanse your skin better.

How often you make use of a facial is entirely up to you. Once a month can be an enjoyable, relaxing experience; however, a lot of research suggests that once, or even twice, a week gives you maximum benefits, not only helping you maintain healthy skin, but also by making time for you to relax and de-stress.

One final bit of advice on performing a facial: pay attention to *how* you apply anything to your face. This will help prevent unnecessarily stretching your skin, and prevent wrinkles later on in life. Always massage upwards and, usually, outwards. You need to massage the eye area inwards to prevent skin stretching in that area, and products applied to the nose are often done so in a downward motion.

How do you make the best use of the beauty ingredients in your kitchen? Well, the easiest way is to pick an ingredient that meets your skin-care needs and apply it to a clean face. Here are some simple recipes and suggestions for further use. Some of these recipes assume you have some additional items on hand, such as flour, sugar, salt (or sea salt), and baking soda.

If your skin is dry, a trip to the land of milk and honey is in order. Heat some honey mixed with milk in the microwave or a double-boiler. Let it cool enough so you don't burn your face. Apply to your face using a massaging motion and leave it on about 15 minutes. To make the facial a useful wrinkle fighter, use thick cream instead of milk. Rinse with warm water and pat dry.

Having oily skin, I like anything that helps tighten and reduce the pores around my nose. To help get that effect, mix 1 teaspoon unflavored gelatin and 1½ teaspoons milk and then microwave for about 15 seconds or until the gelatin is fully dissolved. Add a drop of essential oil, such as lavender, and then apply to your nose and chin for 10 to 15 minutes. When you peel off the dried mask, it should lift the impurities up and away. Rinse your face well with cool water and use a skin-balancing toner afterwards.

To cleanse your skin of nasty environmental toxins, mix 2 tablespoons crushed fenugreek seeds with 2 tablespoons yogurt. Soak the seeds in the yogurt for a couple hours and blend them into a smooth paste. Massage gently onto your skin and allow it to sit there for about 20 minutes. Rinse well with warm water.

Mmmm–Mmmm Good for Your Skin

(Delicious Face Masks)

This next facial is not only good enough to eat, but it sounds tasty. You might want to make extra and have it for breakfast! Take 2½ tablespoons yogurt and mix in 3 tablespoons mashed banana, 2 tablespoons mashed strawberries, and ½ teaspoon lemon juice. Leave it on your face for at least 15 minutes before gently wiping it off. Then rinse and use a toner/moisturizer.

Here's another facial that could do double duty for breakfast. Chop the ingredients that can be chopped and then toss it all into a blender: ½ banana, ¼ cucumber, 2 tablespoons honey, 1 strawberry, and 1 teaspoon yogurt. Blend it together, apply to face, and allow it to dry on your face before gently washing it off.

This facial mask formula is good for all skin types, helping exfoliate and revitalize your face while balancing its pH. Mash 1 small banana and mix it with 1 tablespoon each honey and lemon juice. Massage onto your face and wear it for 15 to 20 minutes. Rinse with warm water and finish with a toner and moisturizer.

This yogurt-lemon facial is also good for all skin types, particularly for dry or blemished skin. Mix together 4 tablespoons yogurt, 4 tablespoons flour, and a splash of lemon juice. Apply the resulting paste to your face and allow it to harden. Rinse it off with warm water and pat dry with a clean towel.

Cucumbers, grated or puréed in a food processor, make for a great facial mask all by themselves, acting as a mini-facelift. You will need to strain out the solids from the liquids or it will just slide off your face. If you want to help balance your skin's pH, mix the cucumbers with some thick yogurt. Remember to rinse your face well and use a moisturizer or balancing toner afterwards.

For a pH-balancing toner, mix ¼ cup apple cider vinegar with ¼ cup water. Gently heat it on low to fully combine the vinegar and water, then allow it to cool completely. The resulting toner can be left on your face without rinsing, or follow its use with a splash of cool water. Keeping toners and rinses in the refrigerator can provide an extra stimulating boost. For a gentler toner, try mixing 1 part cider vinegar to 9 parts spring water.

Here is a formula for another toner, using lemon juice and cucumber, that is good for those with acne problems or oily skin. Mix 8 ounces water with the juice of ½ lemon and 3 slices of cucumber. Let it all sit for 30 to 60 minutes and then remove the cucumber. Apply to face with a cotton ball or pad. This is another toner that feels great used straight from the fridge.

Mix equal parts of honey, glycerin, and lemon juice. Massage into your face and let it sit for about 15 minutes. Rinse it off and then follow with a toner or moisturizer. This recipe is good for moisturizing and controlling oily skin.

For a sweet facial mask, mix 1 tablespoon honey, 2 tablespoons sugar, 1 teaspoon olive oil, and 2 teaspoons lemon juice. Apply lightly to your face using your fingertips and leave it there for 5 to 15 minutes. Rinse off and use toner or moisturizer. This is a good formula—even for sensitive skin.

Women in India use this recipe to clean and moisturize skin. Mix together 1 tablespoon lemon juice, 1 teaspoon rose water, and ½ teaspoon honey. Apply to a clean, damp face, let it sit a few minutes, and then rinse well. This formula will keep in your refrigerator for up to three weeks.

To refine your pores, soften skin, and exfoliate at the same time, try mixing 1 tablespoon each of honey, baking soda, and lemon juice. Leave it on your face for 15 minutes before rinsing off. This will help control excess oil and acne.

Getting egg on your face every so often can be a good idea. This recipe uses 1 beaten egg, 1 tablespoon flour, 1 tablespoon milk, ½ teaspoon olive oil, and ¼ teaspoon salt. Mix all ingredients and let them age on your face for 20 minutes. Then rinse and moisturize.

Egg white mixed with a little milk works well as a pore refiner and skin tightener. If you want to give yourself an eye-lift without surgery, peel out the membrane found inside the egg shell and apply them to the corners of your eyes. Allow them to dry before removing them. Rinse well with cool water and moisturize.

An easy, moisturizing, and exfoliating facial uses ¼ cup oatmeal, 1 teaspoon honey, 1 tablespoon sugar, and some mashed, ripe banana. Rub this onto your face and let it sink in a few minutes. Follow by rinsing with cool water and adding a toner to balance the pH.

To make an avocado facial, mash up an avocado and mix it with a little milk and some oatmeal (ground is okay). Leave this on your face for approximately 30 minutes and then rinse off with warm water. For a richer mask, substitute yogurt for the milk.

Natural Means Edible

Remember the prime rule of natural beauty: you should be able to eat whatever you put on your face. When possible, buy from your local farmers' market and try to buy organic. Besides supporting local growers, the produce is usually fresher. Using organic produce helps you decrease the chemicals you put on your face.

If you grow your own food or you get a good deal at the local market, many of the fruits and veggies mentioned in this article can be done up in small batches and frozen for later use.

While I hope this article will help get you started, we have only begun to explore the benefits of kitchen facials, and encourage further learning. The skin is the largest organ of the human body—not only helping hold us together, but also helping filter out toxins and irritants while protecting us from the environment. Treat your skin right, and it will treat you right.

Skin-Care Products Crop Up Naturally

✎ by Karen Creel ✎

Every day we are bombarded with commercials on television and in magazines enticing us to buy the latest skin-care products. Hollywood stars and soap opera queens suggest we can share their beauty secrets, if we just buy their products. Infomercials, 1-800 numbers, and the Internet allow us to make our purchases at two in the morning. Many of these products cost too much for some of us—or maybe we're just not willing to pay a price that reflects the marketing, packaging, and endorsement fees that go into these products. Then, there are a number of products marketed as natural that aren't natural at all. A review of the ingredients makes you wish you had paid a little more attention in chemistry class. Some even include ingredients that can dry the skin or clog the skin's pores.

Fortunately, there are more reliable ways to take care of your skin. Making your own skin-care products is easy, inexpensive, and can be tailored to you and your family's personal needs. While the ingredients can be found at the grocery store, many can come straight from your backyard herb garden. Making small amounts of your own skin-care products doesn't require a huge garden. In fact, some herbs can be grown in containers—putting your own bath and body store at your back door.

Using herbs for skin care is a centuries-old practice. Recipes have been handed down from generation to generation, and the following herbs have retained their history as herbs for healthy skin. When planting a skin-care garden, keep the following basics in mind.

- Most herbs require well-drained soil, and a sunny location (at least six hours per day).

- Many herbs are drought tolerant and do not require any additional water in the summer months.

- Harvest herbs in the morning after the dew has dried, but before the hot sun diminishes their essential oils.

- Harvest herbs for drying and storing on a dry day, or the plants may mold.

- Take into account the size the plant will be when mature, and space according to directions. Place plants according to height, and according to sun requirements. Some herbs, such as the mints, can tolerate some shade and need more moisture.

- Plants in containers may need more frequent watering.

Skin Care Garden Herbs

Calendula (*Calendula officinalis*) is nature's greatest healer. Grow plenty of these pretty golden-petal plants to be used both dried and fresh in infusions of oil. Calendula plants may be purchased, but are easily grown from seeds after all danger of frost is over. Calendula grows in zones 3 to 10, but is treated as an annual in zones 8 to 10. Calendula also reseeds itself. Pick newly opened blooms in the afternoon and dry them. Remove the petals and store them for later use. Calendula is great for using in products for dry skin. This soothing antiseptic possesses wound-healing qualities and is a good choice for an overall skin conditioner. Salves made from calendula can also be used to treat minor cuts and abrasions, insects bites, and rashes. **Caution**: If you are allergic to ragweed, do not use calendula.

Chamomile-German (*Matricaria recutita*) has been used successfully in creams, lotions, and salves for eczema. A good choice for oily skin, chamomile also soothes sore muscles and serves as an anti-inflammatory. Chamomile self-seeds, and can be grown in zones 4 to 10. Gather the newly opened flowers daily and dry them thoroughly to prevent mold. Grow lots of chamomile plants to get a good crop of flowers. **Caution:** Chamomile is related to ragweed and the aster family. If allergic to any of these, do not use it.

Lavender (*Lavandula spp.*) comes in many varieties, so check with your garden center to see which lavender grows best locally. It is hardy in zones 4 to 10. When harvesting lavender buds, do so just before they open. Strip the stems of their leaves, tie them into bundles, and hang them upside-down in a dry, dark area until dry. Strip the buds off the stems to store. Lavender is rejuvenating, relaxing, fragrant, and has antiseptic qualities. It is a good choice for lotions or salves to relieve the discomfort of sunburn.

Mint (*Mentha spp.*) grows in zones 4 to 10. Mint is one herb that prefers moist rich soil and will tolerate partial shade. Its clean fresh scent cools and refreshes the skin. Because mint can be invasive, it should be planted in pots. You can place the pot in the ground, or above. Peppermint is a good choice for your skin-care garden.

Rosemary (*Rosmarinus officinalis*) is a perennial in zones 8 to 10. In other zones, rosemary should be considered an annual. It can be brought inside over winter. Rosemary softens the skin and is good for dry and/or damaged skin. It is antibacterial

Thyme (*Thymus vulgaris*) grows in zones 4 to 7. It should be treated as an annual in zones 3, 8, 9, and 10. The peak time to harvest thyme is just as the plant is beginning to come into bloom. Harvest the leaves by cutting the stems halfway down. After drying, strip the leaves and flowers and store them. Thyme is a muscle relaxant, an antiseptic, and an antimicrobial.

Included are a few recipes to get you started. I encourage you to explore further the many books available on natural bath and body products, and to plant your own beauty garden.

Calendula-Infused Oil

In a clean, 8-ounce jar, combine 1 cup fresh calendula petals and and 1 cup olive oil. Set the jar in a sunny window and allow the calendula petals to steep in the oil for a week. Strain the flowers through a piece of cheesecloth. Press the calendula petals through the cloth with the back of your spoon, getting as much oil out as possible. Pour the oil back into the jar. Refrigerate the infused oil if you are not going to use it immediately. It will solidify and need to be reheated. You can also use the oil as is to rub onto the affected area two to three times a day.

Calendula Salve

½   cup shea butter (I use unrefined)

1   cup calendula-infused oil

2   ounces beeswax (beeswax beads are easier to melt)

2   400 IU vitamin E capsules

Place the shea butter in a glass measuring cup and microwave for 30-second intervals until melted. Add the melted shea butter to the infused oil, and stir to blend. Add the beeswax and microwave at 30-second intervals until melted. Pour the mixture into three 4-ounce sterilized containers. Cover with lids. Allow the salve to solidify overnight before using it. This is great for minor scrapes, cuts, abrasions, and rashes. Use as a cream for dry skin.

Herbal Facial Steams

First, prepare yourself for this interactive treatment by pulling your hair back and removing all make-up.

Boil a quart of water. Lower the heat and add ½ cup dried or 1 cup fresh herbs to the pot. You may want to place them in a muslin bag or tie them in a square of cheesecloth. Remove the pot and allow the herbs to steep uncovered for about 5 minutes. Take off the lid and lean over to check the temperature. If it feels comfortable, place a terrycloth towel over your head and the bowl to trap the steam. Steam for about 10 minutes, then splash your face with cool water.

Herbs to use vary depending on the desired effect. Common steams include:

> Calendula for dry skin
>
> Chamomile for oily skin
>
> Rosemary to stimulate circulation

The water can also be used as a face soak. Strain the water and soak a face cloth in the water. Place the warm cloth on your face and leave for 5 minutes.

Herbal Salt Scrub

2   cups sea salt

1   cup sunflower or almond oil

1   400 IU vitamin E capsule

1   tablespoon dried herbs (combination
      of lavender, rosemary, mint)

Mix the ingredients and stir well. Spoon it into a clean container with a tight-fitting lid. While in the shower, gently massage a handful of the mixture into your skin, all over your body (avoid your face). Rinse with warm water and pat your skin dry. Do not use any additional soap as a cleaner or you will remove the beneficial qualities of the scrub.

A moisturizer and exfoliant, this scrub has a shelf life of several weeks if properly maintained. Do not allow water from the shower to get into the container.

Herbal Facial Toner

   2   cups spring water
   ½   cup dried chamomile
   ¼   cup apple cider vinegar

Place the water in a canning jar and heat for 1½ minutes. Add the herbs and screw on the lid. Shake. Cool the mixture before adding the apple cider vinegar. Place it in a warm, dark place. Shake the mixture daily and strain out the herbs after one week. Discard the chamomile. Store the liquid, and use it within six months.

Teen Girl's Garden

❧ By Kaaren Christ ❧

When a young girl reaches adolescence, her mind and spirit open to the wonder of nature in a new way. However, parents may feel the opposite is true as their daughter asserts her independence and begins developing new interests. Parents describe how their previously playful, gregarious girl has become sullen and moody—reluctant to participate in family rituals she used to enjoy. They talk about the daughter who used to delight in digging beside them in the garden, but now complains about getting her hands dirty. They bemoan the loss of the girl who used to help choose flower seeds from catalogues in winter months as they watch their teenager turn her attention to shopping for clothes and reading music magazines. This can be very distressing for a parent!

It's true. Your daughter undergoes tremendous changes during the teen years, teetering between the carefree days of childhood and the more complex, emotionally rich world of adulthood. She is becoming a woman, and, as beautiful as this transformation is, she will need your support and encouragement to find balance during this time. Previously influenced primarily by you, she is suddenly open and exposed to a wide variety of health and beauty products marketed specifically to her as a young woman. The choices and messages can be overwhelming. You can help her find her way by offering patience, nurturing, and teaching her the art of growing and using herbs that have properties particularly beneficial to women.

The Garden

Parents ask, "How can I teach my daughter about herb gardening for women if I can't even get her into the garden anymore?" The answer is modeling.

Adolescence is an interesting time. Certainly, young girls begin to pull away from parents and want more time with their friends. But ask any parents who have watched a child pass through the teen years and they will tell you that although it "seems" their daughter is ignoring them, she is actually watching her parents more closely than ever! This is a wonderful opportunity.

During your daughter's early teen years, you are likely sharing new information with her about her maturing body, romantic relationships, and her changing emotional needs. The world often presents a very commercialized and narrow view of these natural processes, but there are many opportunities for you to offer a gentler, more nature-based perspective. These opportunities can be found in your own garden.

To make use of this opportunity, you needn't insist your daughter join you in planting and harvesting herbs. This is likely to result in a terrible power struggle. Instead, you can plant a special area in the garden just for her, and quietly let her know that this is a way of celebrating her adolescence. Find a unique way to set her special area apart, but don't be too insistent that she join in your enthusiasm. Instead, quietly move her favorite garden ornament into the area, or casually pop into a garden center on the way home from shopping with her, and invite her to choose one of her own liking. Most girls will enjoy this adventure, and garden centers are overflowing with garden accents that range from the whimsical to the traditional. Whatever you do—don't criticize her choice! If she wants a porcelain frog holding a yellow umbrella but you prefer more "natural" ornament, now is not the time to impose your artistic or aesthetic views!

Remember, your goal is to celebrate both her childhood and her emerging adulthood. You are honoring her new place in the world. Whatever she chooses, smile and tell her it is perfect. Encourage her to place the ornament wherever she wants in the garden, and resist any inclination to reposition it. If your daughter enjoys crafts, you might suggest she make a sign for her garden using outdoor paints or markers. Take this decorating opportunity to show her what plants are growing in her special area, and talk to her about how they can be used once they mature.

Be sensitive to the moments when she is receptive to information about her garden. I would caution against sharing your enthusiasm in front of her friends or when there is a lot of activity going on. And don't expect a lot of excitement about your efforts. Remember, your daughter has a lot going on during this time. Just offer what you are doing on a regular basis, sharing your joy about how you are celebrating her growing up. In this quiet way, you are letting her know that she is entering a new world, and that you are there to support her.

Books

Everyone loves a gift. You might consider offering your daughter a book about women's health that includes a good section on herbal remedies on her tenth, eleventh, or twelfth birthday. Alternatively, you could pick up such books at the library and leave them on the coffee table where they can flipped through and discussed during quiet moments together. Books have a way of underlining what we think is important, and introducing the value of natural remedies early in a child's life can make it easier for them to accept this wisdom later.

Bringing Her Garden In

Eating habits change when children hit the teen years. Many parents find they spend less time preparing food for their daughters during adolescence because their girls begin to prepare simple meals independently according to their own schedules or prefer light snacks throughout the day. Adolescents also spend more time eating outside of the home, often grabbing whatever is available on the run rather than sitting down for a homemade meal. Although these things are true, your adolescent daughter also craves additional nurturing at this time, and food remains a wonderful opportunity to offer it.

As your daughter's special garden grows, take the opportunity to start bringing these plants and herbs into the kitchen to make herbal teas and other concoctions that will both nurture her and offer new opportunities to connect.

Teen Tea-Time Rituals

Drinking tea is a soothing, meaningful ritual that makes many young girls feel grown up and connected to adults. You might want to add a tea-drinking ritual to your daughter's day as well as your own, as a way of sharing a few moments of quiet time together each day. This is particularly meaningful during a time when life is generally busy and you are beginning to spend less time together.

Include your daughter in the creation of special teas made from the plants in her own garden, explaining how different combinations will treat some of the new feelings and situations she is encountering as her body and mind mature. Your daughter will feel nurtured by this, and you will have the pleasure of knowing you are helping her to balance her body naturally. The following are suggestions for teas that help with particular stressors during the teen years and are easily grown in most gardens.

Emotional Ups and Downs

Peppermint tea is enjoyed by most young girls, who find its pleasant flavor easy to drink. Combined with lemon balm and a bit of honey, the warm tea helps to stabilize mood swings and nourish her nervous system. Your daughter may prefer one variety of peppermint to another, so try planting two or three varieties and allowing her to experiment with them.

Menstrual Discomfort

If you have grown chamomile in the past and occasionally steeped a cup of tea for your daughter to encourage her sleep, you can continue this pleasant ritual even when she is sleeping more than ever before! Chamomile is also used to relieve the muscle aches that sometimes accompany menstruation. The addition of motherwort to chamomile tea will treat the occasional headache associated with fluxes in hormones, and you can also add a bit of fennel if your daughter experiences bloating during her menses.

Skin Blemishes

Blemishes during adolescence occur because of an increase in hormones that cause additional sweating. This results in an increase of oils in the skin's pores, which become trapped there. Pimples can also be caused by fluctuations in hormones or food allergies. An infusion of dandelion leaves, burdock root, and red clover can be used on a regular basis to cleanse the liver and purify the blood, allowing the skin to maintain its balance as toxins pass through in perspiration.

Beauty Rituals

During the early teen years, many girls express a desire to experiment with cosmetics. This is a great time to rearrange your own beauty cabinet (the one you previously banished her from!) and make room for your daughter to develop her own collection of favorite products. Young girls enjoy this newfound "permission" and will generally treat this new permission to be in your space with respect. Children love ritual and are very suggestive to symbolism, and this is one way a parent can show acceptance of their new interests and needs in a tangible way.

If you enjoy making herbal skin lotions, take the time to show your daughter how, and allow her to personalize her own products using herbs and essential oils that reflect her own tastes. If you haven't done this in the past, this is a wonderful time to take on a creative task together with your daughter, who has a strong need to express her individuality during this time.

Show, Don't Tell

Because young girls go through so many changes during their teen years, not only is it a challenging time for them but for parents as well. Particularly troubling for parents who value herbal remedies and natural health care approaches is seeing their daughter struggle to make sense of the new pressures to conform through use of commercial products. Taking the time to grow a special garden for your daughter and quietly sharing in the rituals associated with herb use will have much more power than lectures.

Henna for Hair

≈ by AarTiana ≈

E nhancing and coloring your hair naturally with henna can be a fabulous addition to your hair-care regimen. Unlike many chemical-based commercial products, henna does not damage hair. In fact, henna makes hair healthy. Henna binds with hair cuticles and seals them, which creates a thicker, shinier strand of hair that is easy to comb and manage. It helps turn frizz to curl or wave, and promotes resistance to damage like split ends. It is also a terrific tonic for scalp conditions (dandruff, hair loss), and, over time, works well to cover gray.

However, there is a catch: henna and chemicals don't mix (usually).

Before deciding if henna (*Lawsonia inermis*) is right for you, determine your long-term hair-coloring goals and lifestyle choices. Henna can react badly with the chemicals in most modern hair-care products (even some that say "natural"). If you wish to lighten your hair and are looking for alternatives to bleach or peroxide, henna is not for you—try researching lemon juice, chamomile oil, mullein flowers, and even potatoes, all of which are said to have a lightening effect. However, no matter the method, lightening hair causes damage, so treat it gently and deep-condition often. Others who should not consider henna include those who like using modern chemical styling products and/or change their hair color often—or have to, for career purposes (e.g., models and actors), as even the best hairdressers in the industry all demand use of chemical products. Lucille Ball, an avid henna user of her day, is an exception—her signature red hair was not changed when she changed roles!

The key to finding the right hair treatment product for you is knowing what you're getting into. This means exercising caution and always reading labels carefully. There are infinite products on the market that claim they are henna, but their ingredients reveal they have little or no henna. Since henna and chemicals almost always do not mix, many have discovered this fact the hard way. This article provides some tips on how to get started safely and to maintain natural hair care afterward.

Henna (red henna) provides a semi-sheer "stain" to the hair that your original color will show through. This stain ranges from a light pumpkin color all the way to brick red with rust or brownish tones. The so-called neutral or 'blonde henna' is not henna, but in fact **senna** (*Cassia obovata*) and is not blond, but clear, and does not lighten. It is used as a conditioning treatment, although henna actually does a better job. The so-called 'black henna' is actually **indigo** (*Indigofera tinctoria*), and is used to modify henna color. Please know your sources and make sure you are purchasing the pure powdered plant material.

Even then, you should try it out on small test-batches of hair from your hairbrush first to see how the color comes out. (Have an original "before" batch to compare them to when finished.) Once you have the intended color, look for reactions. Henna rarely causes allergies, but some other ingredients may cause sensitivity. Do skin tests first to make sure.

Ingredients for Basic Mix

Start with 100 to 400 grams of pure henna powder (short fine hair requires less, long thick hair needs more). If you are unsure, make a larger batch and freeze any left over in airtight, doubled ziplock bags for next time (use within two years).

Next, you'll need enough of an acidic liquid to make a yogurt consistency. Try lemon juice, vinegar, or wine, which will release the henna from the powder. You can also try very strongly brewed coffee (not instant), which enhances brown and tones down red.

Optional: Any combination of essential oils (3 to 4 drops per gram of henna) will enhance henna's coloring time: tea tree, cajeput, ravensara, and frankincense are best. Lavender, geranium, cardamon, cypress, and eucalyptus globules work too. These essential oils help disguise henna's earthy, haylike smell. Other conditioning oils include neroli, pine, juniper, and rosemary.

If the hair is dry, add 1 tablespoon olive, wheat germ, or other vegetable oil; any more and it may inhibit the coloring process. To lessen a flaky scalp, add 1 tablespoon powdered burdock root made into paste with boiling water.

To Modify Color (Optional)

The basic henna mix produces auburn tones, which you can tinker with for a lighter or darker look by making additional pastes separately (listed below) and blending them with the basic formula. As everyone's hair is different, getting the right color is a process of trial and error. If you're unsure, a good rule of thumb is to add the darker ingredients a little at a time. For instance, with burgundy/black, you can always add more indigo later. However, if you start off with too dark a shade, you'll have to wait for it to wash out. For the lighter colors like strawberry blond, the basic henna mix is the darkest ingredient, so go easy here, then add more henna later.

For more **gold** or **strawberry blond** tones, you need to have fairly light hair to start with, even if it is ashy. Use lemon juice as the acidic liquid, and/or add chamomile oil to the basic mix. Then, separately, using chamomile or mullein flowers, rhubarb root, and/or marigold (calendula) flowers, make a paste or very strong tea with boiling water and let it sit for 20 minutes. Add this to the basic mix.

For more **red**, yet to tone down orange tones, use red wine as the acidic liquid in the basic mix. Then, separately, make a paste or strong tea using beetroot powder, alkanet, pomegranate juice, hibiscus tea, and/or raspberry zinger tea with boiling water, and let it sit for 20 minutes. Add this to the basic mix.

For **auburn** tones, either use the basic mix as is, or use the suggestions below for brown, but not as much. You can also use nutmeg in the paste.

For **brown** tones and to lessen the red/orange tones, use at least some strong coffee as all or part of the acidic liquid in the basic mix, and lean toward rosemary and lavender essential oils. Separately, make a paste or strong infusion of dark hair herbs (sage, rosemary, thyme, nettle, lavender), walnut hull powder (allergy alert!), cloves, amla (darkens, creates a nice gloss, helps curl), and finely ground coffee and/or black tea with boiling water, and let it sit for 20 minutes. Add to the basic mix.

For **mahogany**, **burgundy**, or **black** tones, make the basic mix. Separately, make a paste with indigo (and optionally amla) by adding boiling water and letting it sit for 20 minutes. Use less indigo for mahogany, more for black—up to the same amount as henna. For mahogany, use some of the suggestions for brown with a little indigo. Mix them together. For black, make the basic mix of henna, rinse, then apply the indigo/amla paste separately.

Application

Mix the henna, acidic liquid, and essential oils in a ceramic bowl and leave overnight if possible. You can also add gentle heat (i.e., on the stovetop away from a burner when you are baking) for at least two hours. If you are modifying color, prepare those herbal pastes and then mix them into the henna mixture before applying it to hair (unless you are doing black, a two-step process).

Then put on your plastic gloves (the yellow kitchen-type ones are fine). Go to a place where you can be really messy (I like the bathtub with the shower curtain closed) and work it very generously into all of the hair, from roots to ends, taking care not to forget sections. It can feel heavy, so you may wish to rest while this procedure is happening. Wrap your hair very tightly in plastic wrap. Using a mirror, remove excess mixture from the skin, being careful around the ears (the shower helps here too). Wear something you don't have to pull over your head. You can then use a body heat cap (from Sally Beauty Supply) and sleep overnight. If you only have a couple hours, go in the sun or use heat from a blow dryer for at least the first hour, longer if you can.

To rinse, use a bucket large enough for your head to fit inside. Fill it with warm water, and invert your head into it, gently swishing out as much as you can. Flush the water down the toilet or dispose of it outside and repeat if needed. Then, in the shower, rinse most of the henna out—do not wash. Before it is all gone, add some thick conditioner all over, then rinse. This helps keep more color. You're done!

Maintenance

Ideally, you can use henna once a month, but it still works well when you can apply henna every two months. Schedule henna on the waxing-to-Full Moon, when hair hasn't been washed for two or more days, for best results. Remember that henna doesn't damage, so apply it generously from roots to ends, and concentrate on the roots of new growth.

You will discover you will not need to wash your hair as often, nor will you have to trim it as often if you are growing your hair long. Although a few people have no trouble with dry hair when using shampoos with sodium lauryl (laureth) sulfates, many do experience dryness. Some discovered that they can use conditioner instead of shampoo, called "conditioner only" (CO). The cheaper the conditioner, the more cleansing it probably is, without the harshness of shampoo. Others use CO sometimes and alternate it with natural shampoos (like Aubrey Organics) and deeper conditioners when needed.

I have fine dark hair with gray, and like coating the dry areas very lightly with olive oil containing essential oils. I make "shampoo" with 1 tablespoon soapwort and some sage, rosemary, lavender, nettle, and yarrow in a cloth tea bag. I add 2 cups boiling water. When it is warm, I pour this into my hair and let it sit to do its work (you can do other shower duties). Lastly, I use a vinegar rinse with essential oils. Make the vinegar mix ahead (2 cups vinegar, plus ½ teaspoon essential oils) and keep it in the bathroom. Use 1 teaspoon vinegar mix, add 2 cups warm water, pour this over your hair, then do a final cold rinse to seal. Henna is seductive, and you may find yourself experimenting—enjoy!

Internet Resources

Cartwright-Jones, Catherine. *Henna for Hair*. www.hennaforhair. com

Kolander, Cheryl. "Karma-Free Silk Protein Deep Conditioner." www.aurorasilk.com/shop/silk_shampoo.shtml

Long Hair Community. www.longhaircommunity.com (Look in Forum Archives for more natural henna and hair care recipes.)

Banish Blemishes
the Wise Woman Way

⊰ by Susun S. Weed ⊱

When you look at your face in the mirror, do you see spots? From harmless freckles to nasty acne, spots on our face usually make us frown, and that makes ugly wrinkles. Smile instead. You can banish blemishes of all kinds—without making a dent in your budget—by using common plants from your kitchen, your yard, or your health food store, the Wise Woman Way.

Wise women use herbs simply—one at a time. And wise women use local, common herbs instead of hard-to-find exotic herbs. Wise women know that herbal medicine is people's medicine, the medicine of the earth. The Wise Woman wisdom here can help you face the world with a clearer complexion and be more in charge of your health; but do seek further advice if blemishes linger or rapidly worsen.

Freckles: St. Joan's Wort Oil

A few freckles certainly aren't a problem that needs a remedy; neither are a lot, though skin so fair it freckles is more prone to sun damage. Instead of bleaching away freckles with lemon juice or plant acids, wise women prefer to prevent them.

To prevent freckles, and sunburn too, I use the red oil of St. John's/Joan's wort instead of sunscreen on all exposed skin. St. Joan's wort (*Hypericum perforatum*) nourishes the skin, helps prevent damage from the ultraviolet rays of sunlight, promotes an even tan, softens and prevents wrinkles, and cuts down on freckles, too. If I'm careless and get sunburned, lavishing applications of St. Joan's wort oil as frequently as needed to quiet pain helps heal my skin and ease any worry about long-term damage.

Hypericum oil is an old favorite. Its use goes back hundreds of years in the European tradition and it was, and still is, used by many North American Indians. The small green leaves and sunny yellow flowers contain highly pigmented active ingredients, such as hypericin, that seep quickly into fat or alcohol, staining them bright red and providing powerful, but safe, home remedies.

To make your own St. Joan's wort oil, harvest the flowers or flowering tops on a hot, sunny day. Immediately put them into a jar and pour pure olive oil to the very top of the jar. Close tightly with a lid, label, and put the jar onto a dish to catch any overflow. Steeping the oil in a cool, dark room away from the sun will help keep it from going rancid. If you wish to make a tincture, substitute 100-proof vodka for the olive oil. Either way, wait six weeks before using your remedy.

St. Joan's wort oil penetrates the skin and heals it from deep within. It carries an antiviral principal that is especially effective in relieving herpes outbreaks, and even better at preventing them, if used at the first suspicion. As a relieving application for those with shingles, nothing, herbal or pharmaceutical, is more effective, or quicker to act. I've even known it to permanently relieve pain that lingered for decades after an episode of shingles. Hypericum is an excellent anti-inflammatory, with a good track record of helping ease the muscle/nerve pain experienced by women with fibromyalgia, and of quickly quelling the inflammation of acne and rosacea.

Russian healers think so highly of Hypericum that they say: "It is as impossible to make bread without flour as it is to heal people without St. John's wort." All wounds, sores, burns, rashes (especially those that originate in the nervous system), blemishes, and discolorations such as freckles, are, they say, healed by St. Joan's wort oil.

Red Blotches: Honey and Roses

Red blotches and other skin discolorations have a range of causes, including overindulgence in alcohol, pregnancy, use of birth control pills, menopausal hormone treatments, and getting older. Removing them can be as simple as removing the causative substance. But if your blotches and blemishes are stubborn, then come along to my Wise Woman garden where bees buzz in rosebushes and sweet scents waft on the air, where honey and roses create clear, beautiful skin.

Honey has long been favored as a reliable healer and nourisher of the skin. It is so hydroscopic (water-loving and water-attracting) that it can hydrate even the driest skin. Its antifungal and antibacterial effects are powerful enough to kill any pathogens on the skin. Raw honey—which contains protein-rich pollen and antimicrobial propolis—is considered more regenerative than regular pasteurized honey, but any honey heals. Impressive scientific evidence has accumulated showing honey's ability to speed wound healing, prevent scarring, heal skin ulcers, and counter blemishes and pimples.

A honey mask is a wonderful way to even out skin tone, loosen and eliminate blackheads, and bring a rosy glow to the cheeks. Begin a honey facial by washing your face with witch hazel extract on a washcloth. Then, apply rose water in the same way. Finally, starting from the forehead and working down, pat honey over your entire face. You can even cover your eyelids, but do it last, or have someone else do it for you. Then lay down with your eyes shut for at least ten, but no more than thirty, minutes. Finish by rinsing the honey off with splashes of tepid water, then blot dry and apply a mist of rose water or calendula tincture.

Roses calm the skin and are sought after by those with blotchy, reddened skin. Attar of rose, or rose oil, has been scientifically shown to relieve radiation burns and has proven itself effective in hundreds of cases of skin ulcers that antibiotics failed to cure. But it can be too expensive, and too strong, for regular use. Rose water or rose hydrosol are better choices: easy to buy and fairly easy to make.

For a simple rose water, place a cup of rose petals (chemical free, please) in a jar with a cup of cold water and a tablespoon of vodka; cap tightly and let sit (out of direct sunlight) for two or more weeks before using. Acid components in rose water make the skin softer, moister, and much less prone to inflammation.

Rose water is a special ally for the skin of women of all ages: newborns, menopausal women, and very old crones.

Blackheads: Witch hazel

Blackheads are pores that are clogged with natural oily skin secretions, make-up, and air pollutants. When these accumulate and oxidize in an open pore, they appear black. When the pore is closed, they appear white and are called whiteheads. Both blackheads and whiteheads are known as comedos.

A facial steam loosens existing comedos, allowing them to be scrubbed off with applications of ground oatmeal or ground almonds. To make a facial steam, throw a large towel over your head and hold your face over a pan of steaming hot water, which could contain nice-smelling herbs such fennel, chamomile, or rosemary. Five minutes is about the right amount of time to steam your face. Be sure to remove the pan from the stove before steaming to prevent fiery accidents.

The best medicine is always prevention, however, and that means keeping the pores toned and the skin well washed so blackheads can't get a foothold. But washing with soap and water can dry and irritate even the oiliest of skins; instead, Wise Women use witch hazel (*Hamamelis virginiana*) extract, an herbal remedy that's still for sale in drugstores.

Plain witch hazel extract works just fine, but if you want to be fancy, you can get witch hazel extract with rose, lemon, or aloe vera. I use a teaspoonful on a dry washcloth, morning and night, to remove city grime, road dust, pollen, and excess skin oils from my face.

Whether plain or fancy, witch hazel normalizes all skin types. Applied topically, once or twice a day, it soothes and heals dry skin areas, calms oily areas, tightens pores, and creates a firmer, finer complexion with far fewer blackheads and blemishes.

Witch hazel is a favorite herbal astringent, and its soothing, cooling properties are renowned for relieving the sting of insect bites, the itch of poison ivy, and the ache of facial outbreaks. Don't restrict its use to your face; let witch hazel ease spots anywhere on your body.

And when pimples threaten, a mixture of half witch hazel and half vinegar, applied hourly, can head them off at the pass.

Pimples: Yarrow

Pimples are localized bacterial infections, like big, tender whiteheads, but more difficult to treat because the bacteria that inflame the pores are deep under the skin and hard to reach. Pimples most commonly occur on the forehead, nose, chin, back, and shoulders, and can cause scarring if not treated properly and promptly. Pimples are fed by hormonal changes and so are most bothersome during puberty and menopause, but some women get pimply outbreaks every menstrual cycle. Pimples can be brought on by irritation from rubbing or washing the skin, some cosmetics, and drugs such as lithium carbonate, asthma medications, and steroids.

Remedies against pimples need to 1. kill infective bacteria on the skin while maintaining healthy skin bacteria, 2. ease pain and aching, 3. counter redness and inflammation, and 4. help prevent the formation of scar tissue. Common yarrow does it all and more, especially when used as a mist.

Yarrow (*Achillea millefolium*) is clear skin's best friend, and a pimple's worst enemy. Yarrow's beautiful white flowers and spicy-smelling finely cut leaves make it easy to find; "wound wort" or "milfoil" is found in meadows throughout the temperate regions of the world. The tincture is easy to make and readily available at stores.

To make yarrow tincture, harvest the leaves, stems, and flowers of white yarrow in full bloom, usually in midsummer. Cut these into one-inch pieces, and put them into a bottle, filling it to the top. Then add 100-proof vodka, right to the top. After capping and labeling your tincture, let it sit for at least six weeks.

A small spray bottle filled with yarrow tincture is the best way to apply a mist on the face or to any other area that is in need of infection-proofing. Twice daily use—first thing in the morning and last thing at night—cuts down on, or eliminates, pimples, acne, and sometimes even rosacea, usually within a month.

The antibacterial properties of yarrow are legendary, and supported by hard scientific evidence. Yarrow successfully kills all disease-causing bacteria it encounters, including strep and staph, while allowing beneficial bacteria to remain. Antibacterial soaps, on the other hand, kill both the bacteria that cause disease and those that prevent disease. The skin of members of households using antibacterial soaps have been found to be teeming with antibiotic-resistant bacteria. Instead of dangerous chemicals, Wise Women use yarrow tincture.

A mist of yarrow tincture on the face and back not only kills bacteria, sending pimples running for the hills, but also acts as a local pain killer, an anti-inflammatory, and a pore-tightening astringent. It can be used instead of witch hazel, or in conjunction with it. This yarrow tincture is especially effective when used after a facial steam.

Acne: Poke Root and Calendula

Acne is a skin condition that includes the presence of black-heads, superficial pustules, tender nodules, cystic nodules, and deep pustules (which lead to scars). The most common of all skin problems, acne occurs mostly in adolescent boys, although people of all sexes and ages may be afflicted. The severity of acne is determined by a complex interaction between hormones, keratin-producing cells, sebum, and bacteria.

Acne is so different in different people that it is best to develop an individualized approach to treatment, but, in general, you will want to 1. counter infection, 2. counter inflammation, 3. ease hormonal overloads, 4. prevent scarring, and 5. improve nutritional status.

Poke root (*Phytolacca americana*) is a one-stop shopping trip for those wishing to clear acne. One of the strongest anti-infectives available, poke root also dramatically reduces inflamation, eases hormonal disruptions by improving kidney and liver functions; and helps prevent scarring by countering destruction of skin cells.

This powerful herb is used only internally, and only in tincture form (capsules are poisonous). And, poke root is used in the tiniest of doses: 1 to 2 drops per day to start with, gradually increasing to a maximum of 4 drops taken twice a day. Poke root tincture is easy to make, but may be difficult to buy. (Online outlets may have it for sale. Try redmoonherbs.com.)

To make a poke root tincture, harvest poke roots in early December when frost has killed all the top growth, wash them, cut them into chunks, and fill a jar first with the root pieces and then with 100-proof vodka. After labeling and tightly capping the jar, I wait patiently for at least six weeks before I decant it into a dropper bottle for cautious use.

Those who have access to poke—it is a common weed on the east coast of North America—may also wish to experiment with the berries. The seeds of the berries are poisonous, but they are so hard that poisoning never occurs unless they are ground to a powder. The usual anti-inflammatory dose is one or two whole dried berries a day. I have taken this remedy myself on numerous occasions and can vouch for its safety.

Other infection-fighting herbs useful to those dealing with acne include **yarrow tincture** (*Achillea millefolium*), **echinacea tincture** (*Echinacea augustifolia*), and **goldenseal tincture** (*Hydrastis canadensis*). All can be misted onto affected skin to counter local bacteria. For best results, use at least two different ones alternately. Internally, however, it is best to choose one and use it consistently for at least three months. Internal doses are as follows: a dropperful of yarrow tincture taken two or three times a day, or 4 dropperfuls of echinacea tincture taken three to four times a day, or 10 drops of goldenseal tincture, taken no more than twice a day. I find combination products (such as goldenseal and echinacea together) much less effective than single herbal products. I do not consider any herb in a capsule safe.

I've saved the most famous herb for last: the **pot marigold** (*Calendula officinalis*), a skin-care favorite around the world. Used as an oil, a mist, or a facial, calendula soothes inflamed skin, hastens healing, counters infections, tightens pores, and improves skin tone.

Calendula flowers are like little suns, with sunny rays of yellow and orange surrounding their glorious golden centers. Sunshine's anti-acne benefits concentrate into calendula.

Both infused calendula blossom oil and calendula flower tincture are anti-inflammatory, antiseptic, antifungal, and astringent, yet gentle enough for the most sensitive skins. Calendula is scientifically validated in its ability to quickly heal even hard-to-heal wounds and ulcerations—and to prevent scarring—making it an ideal ally for those with acne. Use of the tincture externally has been shown to hasten the rebuilding of the collagen matrix of the skin and to vastly increase the rate at which wounds heal and new capillaries are formed. Calendula is currently used medically to help prevent severe infections including gangrene and tetanus, to prevent and heal rashes and irritations, and to wash abscesses and burns. Its ability to counter skin cancer is well established, though not in all cases, of course.

Calendula oil and calendula tincture are marvelously easy to make at home. Of course, you can buy them already made. Weleda sells exceptionally fine calendula products.

Remedies made from fresh calendula blossoms are best, and calendula is quite easy to grow, even in a pot on a windowsill. But the dried blossoms can be used to make a tincture if you can't find or grow fresh calendula. To make your own calendula oil, simply fill a jar totally full of fresh calendula flowers, then add pure olive oil. Or fill your jar only half full of dried blossoms, and then fill the jar to the top with 100-proof vodka to make a tincture. Label, cap well, and wait for six weeks before using either one.

In terms of nutritional advice for those with acne who frequently focus on eliminating "bad" foods, no scientific studies have found adverse connections between acne and the amounts of chocolate, meat, fat, or dairy products in the diet. In fact, numerous studies strongly indicate that daily consumption of 2 ounces or more of dark chocolate, ½ cup or more of organic yogurt, and small amounts of organic meat help prevent and even eliminate acne.

Nutrients known to be needed in large amounts by those dealing with acne include vitamins A, B6, and E, and the minerals selenium and zinc. As these vitamins in supplement form can have detrimental side effects, including increased risk of hip fracture in women, it is best, Wise Women say, to increase the amounts of these nutrients by dietary measures.

All orange, red, yellow, and green plants, such as tomatoes, sweet potatoes, and kale—when well-cooked (but not when raw or steamed)—provide the precursors to vitamin A. Baked potatoes, lentils, and fish are excellent sources of vitamin B6. Nut butters are superb sources of vitamin E. And seaweed and mushrooms (wild or cultivated) offer lots of zinc and selenium.

Anti-Blemish Masks

Smearing lovely things on your face and stretching out while your skin feasts (or gives up its excess oil) is a delicious way to counter and prevent blemishes. Here are a few masks you may try.

To Remove Oil

Clay mask: Wipe your face with witch hazel. Mix any type of powdered clay—best if it is white or gray, and kaolin is very nice—with water to make a slippery paste. Stroke the clay paste over your face and allow to dry. Brush the clay off and rinse your face with cool or tepid water. Mist with yarrow or other anti-infective tincture. Twice weekly clay masks are helpful for those with acne and many pimples. Others find that a clay mask once or twice a month is enough to keep skin vital and blemish free.

Egg white mask: Whip one egg white and fold in a table-spoonful of lemon juice. Wipe your face with rose water or witch hazel, then apply the mask evenly. Allow it to dry. Brush it off, then rinse well with cool or tepid water. Finish with a spritz of rose water. This astringent face mask frightens blemishes away.

To Moisturize, Heal, and Soothe

Olive oil mask: Spread a generous amount of extra virgin olive oil over your face and neck, and, if you wish, into your hair. (For extra effect, steep fresh rosemary in the olive oil overnight before using it; or use infused oil of calendula or Hypericum.) Wrap a hot, damp cotton towel around your entire face, leaving a nose hole for breathing. Replace it with a fresh towel at least once. When done, remove excess oil with witch hazel (and sham-poo your hair if needed). Follow with a mist of yarrow tincture or rose water.

Smile

With the aid of a few simple herbs, you, too, can put your best face forward. Why not get started today?

Herb
Crafts

Crafts for Kids Unfold Outdoors

⪢ by Sally Cragin ⪡

When my son had just turned two, we visited a good friend in the woods with a meadow nearby. His field was full of milkweed pods that had just popped, so we gathered up dozens. I wasn't sure what to do with the seedpods, until I found a beautiful bare branch that looked like a miniature tree all by itself. One evening, I put Christopher on my lap and spread out supplies.

We put the branch in a small vase and then I held a pod and asked him to pull out one of the "catkins" (the little fluffy seedpods) and pull off the brown oblong seed. Then I dipped the end of the fluff in white glue and together we stuck it on the branch. I was amazed at the concentration he showed for this craft, especially since he had previously been mildly distressed when first touching the milkweed fluff.

We covered six or seven smaller branches and slowly a Dr. Seuss-style tree emerged. I then asked him if we should paint some glue on, and then pour silver glitter on that. He smiled and said yes. And so now we have a very interesting milkweed tree growing year-round in our window.

I write this story to make a simple point: you don't have to have a "destination" in mind when working with nature or recyclable crafts. I teach craft classes at Fitchburg Art Museum (in Massachusetts) and am constantly reminding my students that no one needs a "kit" to make something lovely. All that's necessary are supplies along with desire, patience, and time to let a nature craft unfold.

Getting Started

These are general suggestions—some of these objects are probably in your house or near to hand. Growing herbs from seeds can be tricky, but starting with "six-packs" during growing season can give you a head start on always having fresh herbs around. And if you have a garden you can prep with your own compost, and plenty of sun, you and your child can enjoy gardening together. And yes, weeding is a craft also!

Herb Staples

Rosemary	Lavender
Pine needles	Basil
Parsley	Thyme
Oregano	

Art Staples

Poster paint	Brushes
Glue and glue sticks	Markers
Glitter	Tape
Construction paper	Card stock
Stick cardboard	

Recyclable Staples

Strawberry baskets
Corks
Styrofoam supermarket trays
Colorful bottle tops from detergent, soap,
    and shampoo bottles

Nature Staples

Pods	Pine cones
Leaves	Shells
Pebbles	Twigs
Milkweed pods	

Always Useful

Buttons	Beads
Wire	Pipe cleaners
Bottle caps	"Googly eyes"

A Few Words about Getting Organized

Even if you're crunched for space, do consider making a corner a permanent craft area so that you're not constantly bringing supplies out and putting them away, depending on your child's age. (However, keeping paints and glue on a high shelf makes sense for a number of years.) You can help teach your child about being organized by having your supplies in clear shoeboxes or in a plastic three-drawer bureau to logically separate materials.

Lessons children quickly pick up can include keeping lighter, more fragile supplies away from heavier objects, preventing paints and markers from inadvertently marring clean construction paper and card stock, and possibly even keeping chemicals away from natural items.

Carnival of Smells

Make a game of learning with a carnival of smells. Fresh herbs are the best, but even dried herbs from your pantry can make for an interesting game. Choose herbs with a distinctive aroma: oregano, basil, parsley, thyme, dill, rosemary. Have your children smell all five, and then close their eyes while you put a half teaspoon of each herb on a plate. See if they can remember each smell. (This will be easier if each child takes a pinch of the herb.) An older child might be able to describe the smell using the language of imagery (oregano smells like the pizza parlor, basil smells peppery, etc.).

Car Freshener

Ingredients: At least 2½ feet of yarn or ribbon, white pine branches, rosemary sprigs, lavender.

Depending on your child's fine motor abilities, this can be as simple or as elaborate as you like. Gather at least a half-dozen branches or sprigs of whatever herb you choose. Tie the stems together, and then wind the ribbon or yarn around your herbs so that they are bunched together. Once you've reached the tips of the herbs, bring the yarn back around so you're making a bundle. **Advanced tip:** Tie the ribbon or yarn in the middle, so that you're winding both ends at the same time. This method requires a grown-up to hold the bunch. Once you're done, make a label that says, "tuck on dashboard or on space behind back seats." Sunlight makes the herbal smell bloom. You can also do this craft with bracken fern (which has a spicy smell) and other grasses. However, remember that many people are allergic to goldenrod and its various little siblings, so you'll want to discourage your little herb harvester from choosing plants that are just "pretty"!

In the Kitchen

Simple Teas

Ingredients: Sprigs of mint (peppermint or spearmint).

A handful of fresh mint leaves (plucked from the stalk) added to a glass quart pitcher makes lovely "sun tea." Watching this tea darken in the sun can be very exciting for a small child. If you have a variety of mint in your garden, you could even make "glass at a time" mint tea and see if you can distinguish each taste. Mint tea is also a wonderful base for homemade lemonade.

Cardamom Iced Chocolate

Ingredients: Cardamom pods and seeds can be used, or just cardamom seeds.

Grind, with mortar and pestle (or in clean coffee grinder), a half-dozen pods and seeds. If using seeds, a half-teaspoon is plenty. Make hot chocolate the way you usually do, whether with a mix or by adding two tablespoons cocoa to one tablespoon sugar per cup of milk. When hot chocolate is ready, add a pinch of cardamom. It's very aromatic and a little goes a long way. Chill your hot chocolate and enjoy a spicy Indian-style beverage! Add a pinch of cinnamon and note the distinction in tastes.

Herbed Butter

Ingredients: Butter or spreadable butter, french or sourdough bread slices, garlic, basil and/or parsley leaves. Variants: oregano, thyme.

Everyone loves garlic bread, so why not add some herbs to the mix? Start with a half-stick of butter, or less, depending on the number of slices (a tablespoon of butter seems to do three slices of French bread at our house). Cut basil or parsley leaves into a fines herbes consistency. Figure at least a tablespoon of herbs per half-stick of butter, and at least a clove of garlic. Children love using a garlic press, even if they're not wild about the taste. With softened butter, even small hands can "mash" the herbs in (or very, VERY clean hands can squeeze the herbs in). Spread the mix on your bread, and put it under the broiler or in the toaster oven. And you know how to cut basil leaves, right? Children love helping on this step: stack three or four basil leaves and then start rolling them from the stem to the tip. When your little cylinder is complete, cut into shreds. (**Note:** This is the step for the big people to do.)

Herbal Bath Ball

Ingredients: Dried lavender buds, rosemary leaves, mint leaves, clean screw-top jar, new tea ball.

This can make a lovely gift for a grandmother or anyone in the family who's known to escape to the tub! And it's easy for a small child to do the measuring. Mix equal amounts of dried lavender buds, rosemary leaves, and mint leaves in a clean jar with a screw-top. Buy a new tea ball and write the following directions on a card that is tied with a ribbon around the jar: "Herbal bath ball—fill tea ball and hold under running water as you draw the bath." For extra-strong pungency, include a small bottle of lavender oil with this gift, and include this notation: "Add two drops of lavender oil to herbal mixture in tea ball."

Flowers and Petals and Leaves

Petal Collage

Ingredients: Flower petals, card stock, glue (white glue or glue stick).

Unless you want to go to the trouble of drying and pressing your petals and then making a collage, this is definitely a temporary delight. Have your child collect a variety of flower buds—you may want to go along so that prize blooms don't get topped! Sort them into colors and then, with fingertips or blunt scissors, pull off the petals. Glue them on the paper. You can make a variety of scenes—blue/purple petals make ocean waves, red/orange/yellow petals can be butterfly wings. Green petals can be trees or bushes. This is a very interesting way to have your child really look at shapes and distinguish heart shapes from banana shapes and circles from scalloped shapes. If you do these collages on card stock or a meat tray, they will be more durable.

Fern Trees

If you live in an area where ferns are abundant, you can have a very enjoyable interlude by using a magnifying glass to examine the fronds of a fern. What do the fronds look like? (Christmas trees? Dragon tails?) Can you make a collage with a frond, and then paste colored bobbles or stickers on for an Xmas-in-summer design? Some ferns are also very sweet-smelling, and if you gather them and tie loosely with a thread and then hang them up, you have an unusual drawer-sachet (putting dried ferns in muslin bags will keep the crumbs from scattering).

Lavender

What a blessing lavender is—the leaves have a wonderful smell, and the flower buds can be steeped for tea or even added as an ingredient in muffins.

Evergreen Crafts

Pine Needle Crafts

Virtually every state in the union has some variant of evergreen, and the pungent, tarry smell evokes memories of summer camp and long warm nights. Pine needles, branches, and cones can form the basis of a variety of crafts.

Pine Cone Folks

Ingredients: Pine cones, pipe cleaners, googly eyes, scraps of fabric.

Wind a pipe cleaner around the top and the bottom of a pine cone to make animals and people. A squat pine cone can be a little dog, while a long, thin pine cone can be a dachshund or a skinny person. These don't need much more for decoration—perhaps a green leaf for a hat or a scrap of fabric for an apron.

Pine Needle Hedgehogs

Ingredients: Pine needles, clay.

Whether you use air-drying clay or plasticine, your child can easily make a hedgehog by sticking pine needles into a ball. Don't forget to pinch one end for the little snout!

Miniature Spruce-Branch Yule Tree

Ingredients: Spruce branch, large-hole beads such as those used for corn-rowing, bottle top from detergent, shampoo or soap bottle, spool or Styrofoam square.

If you take the tip of a spruce branch and cut it off at three or four inches tall, you may notice it looks like a little Christmas tree. Have your child stick it in a bottle-top, spool, or Styrofoam square—whichever looks best to you. Next, "decorate" with large-hole colored beads, or single strands of tinsel. Make a tiny tree-topper out of two stick-on stars stuck together. You and your child can have all kinds of fun figuring out different decorating schemes. You can even glue some Cheerios on a flat button as a plate of cookies for Santa!

Pine Needle Brushes

Ingredients: Long pine needles, Styrofoam tray, poster paint, paper or card stock.

Whether you use a "brush" made of three pine needles (white pine) or thirty, kids enjoy seeing what interesting designs they can make using an unusual brush. Pour a dollop of poster paint in a clean Styrofoam tray (or other washable tray) and swish the needles. This kind of marker makes all kinds of interesting effects. Try red paint on green paper, or the reverse, for an interesting Christmas card, or orange paint on black paper for Halloween decorations. Or, cut out red paper hearts and use white or pink paint for swirling. See if your child can make ocean waves or clouds or "bubbles" by swishing the needles around.

Balsam Fir Pillows

Ingredients: Pine needles, screen, linen fabric, ribbon, twisty-ties, needle and thread.

Collect lots of pine needles and dry them on a screen. When the needles are less flexible, take a pair of utility scissors and cut them into small lengths over a paper plate or piece of paper.

You'll need a lot to fill even a small pillow, but the results are fragrant. I'd suggest a scrap of linen for your pillow. You can paint a pine cone design on the fabric ahead of time while you wait for the pine needles to stiffen up. And if you don't care to sew, cut a 5 × 5-inch square. Have twisty-ties ready and put several tablespoons of pine needles in the center. Squash together in a mound and then start rolling the fabric. Needles will try to escape out the edges, so twisty-tie one side, as if you're making a Christmas cracker. Pull the fabric tight and add more needles, and then twisty-tie the other side. Tie ribbon over twisty-ties for an instant no-sew pine needle "cracker."

Rocks and Pebbles

(Yes, we're getting even farther away from herbs—but what is more natural than a rock?) If you and your kids spend a lot of time in the car together, and you live in a hilly part of the country, try to interest your child in the roadcuts you're driving by. Unfortunately, stopping on the highway (unless at a rest stop) is the sort of behavior that immediately prompts some well-meaning passerby to pound 911 on the cell phone. But if your kid loves rocks, see about contacting an area rock/mineral club to get some information on what's actually under your feet. Since much of North America was once glaciated, there are lots of rocks and pebbles that aren't necessarily indigenous to your area. A simple primer on rocks would say this: white probably means quartz and feldspar, layers means sedimentary, and speckles means an igneous or metamorphic rock.

Twigs and Sticks

Twiggy Birdfeeder

Ingredients: Thin, branchless twigs, plastic strawberry basket.

How many twigs can you stick in a strawberry basket? When you have finished, your child will have a very interesting twig assemblage. Display it on a shelf, or tie strings to the four corners, gather them together, and hang it from a tree with a slab of suet in the center. (An aluminum pie tin with a hole in the center just over the top of this might discourage squirrels.)

Twig Assemblage Out of Doors

Make yard work fun for your little one. Encourage your child to pick up twigs and sticks. When you have a good-size pile, make a "temporary hut" by stacking. A good way to start is by taking three long twigs with Y-branches and making a "tipi." Then start stacking. This is a great place for small plastic or ceramic elf dolls to live.

Variant: Wrap pipe cleaners around twigs and assemble. Or stick twigs in lumps of air-hardening clay to make a miniature forest scene.

A Memorably Scentual Wedding

❧ by Kaaren Christ ❧

I have a garden of my own, Shining with
flowers of every hue; I love it dearly while
alone, But I shall love it more with you.
　　　　　　　　—Thomas Moore

A h, love. It blooms in every hue
imaginable and no two pair of
starstruck lovers are ever the
same. Because of this, wedding ceremonies are also one-of-a-kind occasions
that reflect the unique personalities,
families, histories, and dreams of the
couple being married.

For couples who share a love of
nature, the use of herbs on their wedding
day will add romance, meaning, symbolism, and extra beauty to an already special occasion. Herbs are sensual, specific
to geographical areas, and rich with
folklore. Many are wonderfully aromatic and can infuse your celebration
with scents that will have the power to

trigger vivid memories of your wedding for years to come. Herbs also lend memorable flavors and visual appeal to specially prepared foods your guests will enjoy. Herbs can be used to create stunning bouquets, tosses, centerpieces, crafts, and keepsakes your friends and family will always cherish.

Careful choosing of particular herbs will reflect the personal characteristics of the happy couple, add a deeper level of meaning to the rituals, and invite guests to experience love and commitment anew in their own lives.

Whether you are calming preceremony jitters, designing a menu, decorating, or creating mementos—herbs can be a delightful and meaningful addition to your wedding.

Soothing the Jitters

Few couples arrive at their special day without having experienced a few normal jitters beforehand. After all, not only is marriage one of the biggest life decisions we make, but a wedding is often the largest celebration we ever plan in our lifetime!

Thankfully, we can begin to enjoy the wonders of herbs even during the planning stage. Many herbs have healing or medicinal properties and can be used by the couple before, during, and after the festivities to invoke a sense of calm and peace.

In the form of aromatic waters, teas, and body oils, herbs offer many soothing remedies to ease anxious feelings related to the excitement and planning of your big day.

Herbal Baths

Herb-scented baths combine the soothing effects of hydrotherapy and aromatherapy to offer the anxious bride and groom (together or separately!) a well-deserved reprieve from guest lists and menu planning. Bathing has been a common prescription for bothersome physical aches and pains, as well as emotional troubles, for centuries. The warmth of a freshly drawn bath alone relaxes tense muscles, and a few drops of essential oil rising in the steam encourages deep breathing and improves circulation.

You can enjoy relaxing herb remedies in the bath in a number of ways. Dried or fresh herbs can be placed in a small cheesecloth bag or into a loose tea holder, and then placed under the running water. You can also make an herbal infusion by pouring boiling water over the herbs of your choice, and allowing the mixture to steep for thirty minutes. The resulting liquid is then poured into the bath. If you are getting married in the late spring, an infusion of blackberry leaves to the bath water will restore youthfulness and vibrancy to skin after a long winter.

Adding a few drops of essential oil to bath water is another way to enjoy the soothing effects of herbs. Lavender, orange, chamomile, and ylang ylang are some of the most common essential oils used for relaxation and can be blended to suit individual preferences. Other soothing herbs include lemon balm, rose flowers, and violets.

Recipe for Relaxation

2   drops lavender essential oil
1   drop orange essential oil
1   drop chamomile essential oil
1   drop ylang ylang essential oil

Add the above to a very warm bath, and stir gently to blend. Sink into the water and breathe deeply.

If you are bothered by dry skin, you can combine relaxation with skin protection by adding a small amount of vegetable or nut oil to the bath water. While some people like to add oil while the water is running, you could benefit more by soaking for a little while first, allowing your pores to open before adding the oil. Bath oils made with vegetable or nut oils float on the top of the water and coat the skin as you rise out of the bath. If you prefer a bath oil that mixes with water, you will need to use a castor oil instead.

You can achieve different effects from an herbal bath by altering the water temperature. Generally, water that is close to your body's internal temperature will be most relaxing, but warmer baths can help induce sleep. A cooler bath is perfect when you have a busy day of planning ahead and just need a quick lift. Generally, taking very hot baths should be avoided because they can cause exhaustion, lightheadedness, and dry skin.

Sharing the Pleasures

Couples who enjoy bathing together find the process of finding just the right "blend" of herbs for their baths a romantic, creative process that brings them closer and offers time to share thoughts and feelings about their life together. This is particularly important during the somewhat hectic wedding-planning stage.

Because scent is very evocative of memory, the simple act of sinking into their "personalized" herbal bath will bring them a wonderful sense of peace and togetherness, even when miles may separate them.

Hand and Foot Baths

Given that many couples plan wedding rituals involving the exchange of rings or a walk down the aisle, extra attention to the hands and feet prior to the wedding is in order. A hand or foot soak using essential oils or an herbal infusion can create the same effect as an herbal bath and is a quick and easy way to remind the body to relax and enjoy. It also prepares the hands and feet to look their best under the spotlight!

Hand baths can be enjoyed at the kitchen table or in a comfortable chair while listening to relaxing music. Choose your favorite combination of relaxing or invigorating herbs and make a strong infusion. When the herbal hand bath is just right for soaking, rest your hands in the water for about ten minutes. Plan to follow the soak with a luxurious hand massage using herbal lotion. You can easily apply the lotion to your own hands, but I recommend taking turns with your loved one, pampering each other in this way. Finish each other's hand treatment by rubbing a small drop of citrus oil into the cuticle and base of each nail. For best results, apply soft kisses to the finished product.

Feet can be similarly pampered using specific herbs. Wormwood, sage, burdock, and mustard seed are all recommended. A quick buffing of the heels and soles of the feet with a natural pumice after the soak will have you ready to dance down the aisle! These "mini baths" for hands and feet are perfect when you don't have time for a complete bath but still want the emotional benefits of inhaling aromatic water vapor.

Tea for Two

Don't forget the many benefits of herbal teas as you approach your wedding day. Taken as part of your daily routine, herbal teas can help you let go of worries and will encourage a restful sleep. The rhizome and root of *Valerian officinalis* have long been used to treat nervousness and anxiety. To make valerian tea, add one-fourth teaspoon of the root to a cup of water and drink the infusion three times throughout the day. If you plan to enjoy wine or spirits on your wedding day, valerian can safely be taken right up to the last moment because it will not interact with alcohol.

Sweet woodruff can also be used for relaxation. Taking two teaspoons of this dried herb infused with a cup of water will help to calm a nervous stomach.

Herbal Delights to Dine On

Weddings often include time-honored culinary rituals that use herbs and wildflowers in creative and memorable ways.

Edible flower petals sprinkled onto fresh greens make a delightful first course to a romantic meal, and fresh mint sprigs can be added to a colorful punch. Rosemary or other savory herbs can be baked into fresh loaves of bread, and there are endless combinations of herbs that can be added to traditional dishes to give them a more memorable flavor.

Many wedding celebrations involve a special cake that is symbolic of love, commitment, or the joining of families. This is a another wonderful opportunity to showcase herbs and other delights of the garden!

If personalizing your wedding cake with decorations is your goal, make use of edible flowers. Pick blossoms of common edible garden flowers on the morning of the feast, making sure you collect them from plants that have never been touched by harmful chemicals. A romantic sprinkling of violet, carnation, orange blossoms, or pansy petals over a traditional white wedding cake is stunning. Other popular edible flowers include calendula, lilac, squash blossoms, and mint flower. You might also consider using candied violets or rose petals at the base of your cake, which will sparkle in the sunshine or by candlelight and add another level of visual beauty to the cake. Rose petal jam is also beautiful layered between white sheets of fluffy cake.

A little placard set in front of the cake with information about the flowers used in the recipe and the meaning of your choices will add to your guests' enjoyment.

Herbal Rituals, Décor and Keepsakes

Decorating to honor special occasions is seemingly human nature, and weddings are certainly no exception. From confetti to bouquets, centerpieces to mementos, herbs can be incorporated in your décor every step of the way. The opportunities to personalize your celebration are endless!

Blessing Herbs

The common practice of wedding guests showering the new couple with rice or paper confetti after the exchange of vows and as they leave the ceremony has fallen out of favor in recent years, with groundskeepers and custodial employees at places of worship citing reasons of practicality and cleanup. Outdoor ceremonies are problematic as well, since cleaning up small bits of paper is not practical or ecological and rice may not be the best food for local birds. This is another perfect opportunity to bring herbs into your ceremony.

A beautiful mix of dried herbs blended with dried flower petals can be packaged into small paper cones and given to the guests so they can sprinkle the new couple with blessings after the ceremony. This creates a sweet-smelling shower and a brilliant display of color that works beautifully outdoors because it can be left on lawns or pathways to naturally decompose and does not require cleanup.

Depending on the season in which you marry and the color schemes you are using, you can blend blessing herbs to complement your theme. If blue is your chosen color, a blend of lavender, Johnny-jumps-ups, and white rose petals would work beautifully. If you are enjoying an autumn wedding, a blend of rosemary, heather, and daisy, with accents of ivy, will lend a splash of fall color to the ritual. A winter wedding blend might begin with rosemary and heather, but also include dried red berries and white rose petals as seasonal accents. If creating these blends yourself is beyond your ability or desire, there are many companies specializing in the creation of herbal products that can be found on the Internet or by visiting your local library.

Bouquets and Tussie Mussies

Tussie mussies are a kind of bouquet perfect for the herbal-inspired wedding because their beauty comes from their use of local herbs and wildflowers. Additionally, each bouquet becomes uniquely momentous depending on the meaning associated with each chosen flower. They have been used in Britain for centuries, and enjoyed increasing popularity during the Victorian era when entire conversations between courting couples were accomplished using only the flowers in the bouquet as words. This was during a time when dating was a much more "reserved" ritual, and contact between lovers was limited by social convention and a sense of propriety. "Specialists" in the language of tussie mussies claim that they not only can tell you the "message" of an herb bundle, but also where the individuals are from by identifying the local flowers and herbs used.

Couples today can have great fun designing their own tussie mussies, which can be used either as bouquets to hold or as corsages. They are often held together and accented with a piece of antique lace from a grandmother's dress or with some other material meaningful to the couple. It is great fun for guests to have printed information about the flowers and their meanings to enjoy. This information can easily be included in a wedding program, or can be added to thank-you cards.

Herbs for Tussie Mussies

Some of the traditional herbs and wildflowers used in tussie mussies, and the meanings attributed to them are listed below:

Chamomile: Wisdom and stick-to-itiveness
Dill: Survival and strength in the face of adversity
Scented geranium: Happiness
Bee balm: Virtue
Calendula: Hopefulness
Angelica: Inspiration
Parsley: Merriment
Yarrow: Health
Lavender: Devotion
Marjoram: Marital bliss

Decorations

You can adapt almost any modern-day wedding decoration to include herbs and wildflowers. Ordinary indoor and outdoor areas can easily be transformed into magnificent romantic spaces that capture the imagination and timelessness of love. The only limit is your imagination. If your imagination has been somewhat used up by planning, here are a few ideas to get you started.

Invitations

Invitations are an opportunity to give your guests a sneak peek into what to expect at your celebration. One way to surprise your guests is to scent the invitations. You can do this by dabbing a bit of cotton batting with a few drops of your favorite essential oil and placing it into a box or a bag with the bundle of invitations about a week before mailing them. The oil shouldn't touch the paper; it should just be enclosed with it. The guests will enjoy a gentle hint of the sensory pleasures they can expect to enjoy upon attending. You can also include a special poem or quotation that includes a specific herb or garden sentiment on the invitation, or choose stationery with images of your favorite flowers.

Swags and Wreaths

Herbal decorations bring a sense of simplicity and hominess to a wedding celebration. Although they can be purchased ready-made from craft stores, they can be made relatively inexpensively and easily if you have access to gardens, countryside, and a bit of local plant wisdom. And, as in the tussie mussie, local varieties can add a wonderful sense of local pride and community.

Wreaths can be hung at the end of church pews, or used as centerpieces on tables, with a chimney and candle placed in the middle. They can also be placed on entrance doors. Swags are particularly beautiful placed above or behind the couple during the exchange of vows.

Keepsakes and Mementos

Most couples spend a great deal of time trying to find the perfect way to thank the friends and family who have helped them celebrate their commitment and plan their wedding. Herbs make it easy to send your treasured guests on their way with a little reminder of the day—and of your appreciation.

Flavored vinegars are a beautiful and useful gift your guests will treasure for meals to come, and will always remind them of your celebration! Small bottles can be purchased inexpensively that will hold a few sprigs of your favorite herbs—possibly clipped from your own garden. You can use burlap string or ribbon to tie a homemade label around the neck, or use hand-scribed labels that affix right onto the bottle. You might include an herbal verse on the label, or put a thank you note right onto the bottle, with the date of the wedding added. You can also use the same vinegar you served on a salad to add to the strength of the memory. Here are five suggestions for enjoyable herb vinegar combinations:

1. Rose petals, violet petals, and rice vinegar
2. Coriander leaf, garlic, and rice vinegar
3. Borage, dill, shallots, and white wine vinegar
4. Sage, parsley, and red wine vinegar
5. Raspberries, mint, and white vinegar

Sachets and Dream Pillows

For the one who sews, sachets and dream pillows are easy-to-make keepsakes that are very sentimental and a pleasure to receive. Sachets are typically small pockets or tied bags of thin material filled with scented, crumbled herbs and placed in drawers or closets where they can gently scent clothes. A dream pillow is essentially the same idea, but is given with direction that the bag is meant to be placed beneath the pillow, where the scents coming from it will reach the sleeper and bring good dreams.

Any herbs can be blended, but it is especially memorable to use the same blend that has been used somewhere else in the celebration so that it strongly evokes the special memories of the day. Both can be given with an attached thank you for your guest.

For Years to Come

Couples who enjoy an herbal-inspired wedding often return to their herbal rituals as they celebrate the timelessness of their love on anniversaries. Personally chosen combinations of flowers and herbs are re-created and shared with loved ones, and special recipes from their wedding day are used to celebrate the couple's ongoing commitment to one another. With each passing year, these rituals become more meaningful and powerful and are enjoyed by all.

Home Crafts for an Herbal Atmosphere

❧ by Zaeda Yin ❧

Making herbal crafts at home is an enjobable activity for the whole family. Homespun items using herbs, flowers, buds, roots, leaves, and spices cost a mere fraction of any similar items purchased from herbal-themed shops or health stores. Herbal crafts appeal to the human senses of sight, smell, touch, and taste. Nothing is more satisfying than putting your own personal touches around the home, creating an "herb-filled Aladdin's Cave" or a "scentual household."

The motivation for this article stems from memories of a visit to an old friend's home on the island of Tasmania, where an entire room was dedicated to herb crafts.

It wasn't just a room full of herbal items—it was more like an herbal treasure trove! This was an eye-opener.

The burst of divine fragrances upon entering the room was enough to excite or inspire anyone without a blocked nose! There was a glass cabinet displaying an assortment of potpourris in antique and modern jars and bottles. Bookshelves were resplendent with collections of herb-filled dolls, teddy bears, and other soft toys. One shelf was beautifully arranged with herb sachets in ziplock plastic bags for preservation.

Pomanders were strategically hung around for capturing a little "romantic light," reminiscent of bygone "olde worlde" eras. An old oak cupboard was used for storing craft materials collected over the years. Bunches of dried roses, lavender, and other flowers with leaves intact hung from the ceiling on one side of the room. Sofa cushions had lovely cotton bags of potpourri inserted in between or zipped inside cushion covers.

The guest room where I stayed several nights had a giant lavender- and chamomile-scented cushion on the bed. Curtains and drapes were lined with herbs sewn into them. Needless to say, I had the best sleep in years. Credit for this goes to the herbal atmosphere created by the three generations of inhabitants in this particular home, who emphasized that herb crafts kept them "cool, calm, collected; healthy, wealthy, and wise." Not that they were at all inclined to sell any of their craft items. (Begging didn't work, I tried.) However, they generously shared their methods for some herb crafts, which are described below.

Dry Potpourri

Dry potpourri is easiest to make in large quantities. Gather dried herbs, flowers, spices, essential oils of choice, and fixative in a large glass bowl. Mix the contents and store in a sealed, airtight container. Allow the mixture to mature for at least six weeks. Stir the contents a few times each week. During this process, the essential oils will be absorbed by the fixative and both will fuse with the dried herbs to maintain longer-lasting fragrance. When using spices, they should be crushed, but leave some whole for adding texture to the finished product. Wash, sterilize, and thoroughly dry an assortment of clear or pastel-colored screw-top jars. After the maturing process, the potpourri can be transferred to these jars and sealed. Tie some ribbons around the screw-tops for an appealing effect. Label the jars and store in a cool cupboard. Leftover potpourri can be placed in ceramic or terra cotta bowls around the house.

Traditional Rose-Lavender Potpourri

This is a very common dried potpourri favored by herbal hobbyists. It is made by following the instructions above.

    1   cup lavender flowers
    1   cup rose petals
    1   cup rose-geranium leaves
    2   teaspoons ground cloves
    2   teaspoons crushed allspice
    1   teaspoon crushed cinnamon
    3   tablespoons orris root granules
   60   drops rose geranium essential oil
    8   drops lavender essential oil

Whole-Spice Necklaces

During ancient times, herb and spice necklaces were used for adornment and to ward off malevolent entities. They were also believed to prevent diseases, draw good luck, and help achieve harmony with Mother Nature's energies. Enticingly fragrant necklaces can be made by stringing whole pieces of spices with thick threads, or thin but sturdy cords. As most spices are naturally hard, they are durable and will not disintegrate easily. Select spices that are smooth so there is no friction against the skin.

Begin with small specimens for the back of the neck, then move down to medium-size spices and a large specimen as the pendant. Examples of spices for use in making a spice necklace include whole allspice, nutmeg (drill holes in them), cloves, cinnamon quills, and star anise.

For a dash of color, add bright wooden beads or those made from rosewood and white sandalwood to the strand. When not wearing your spice necklaces, hang them around the home as deodorizers. Alternatively, store them in natural fiber pouches to scent drawers or handbags.

Flower and Herb Cushions

Cushions filled with cotton wadding, dried flowers, and herbs and spices with a few dabs of essential oil are easily made in many shapes and sizes. Whether hexagonal, heart-shaped, rectangular, square, or kidney-shaped for fitting behind the neck during rest, herbal cushions are stimulating and make cozy additions to home décor. They can be any size, firm or floppy—whatever you deem to be the most eminently snuggable. (Polystyrene granules are optional.)

To create a basic—yet gorgeous—herbal cushion, sew a cushion "casing" with plain cotton cloth in the same shape as the cushion cover that you have in mind. The cushion cover itself should be of appealing materials such as silk, velvet, linen, lace, or satin. When the casing is sewn, insert the wadding. Generously spread dried flowers and herbs all over the wadding before sewing up the opening and putting it into an attractive cushion cover. Alternatively, instead of spreading dried flowers and herbs around the wadding, a few small pouches of favorite herbs and flowers can be sewn at intervals to the inside of the cushion covering.

Pomanders

Centuries ago, highly scented balls of pomanders used to pack a punch for deodorizing clothing and controlling foul smells. They were also alleged to cure insomnia and prevent fainting. Pomanders were also widely used for ridding pestilence and disease prevalent in those days. The balls were hung on the ends of chains from the neck or waist or stored in cloth sachets for pinning to the insides of clothing layers. There was a roaring trade in exquisite silver and carved wooden balls specially made for carrying pomanders or fixing them to walking sticks.

During the sixteenth century in Venice, the popular fashion of the day was for ladies to wear hairpins decorated with miniature pomander balls. Today, pomanders still retain an intrinsic charm and appeal. Early pomanders were made by melting beeswax, adding herbs and spices, and then rolling the cooled wax into balls. Modern pomanders generally are composed of an orange as a base, cloves, some small flowers, and petals. In recent times, oasis balls from craft stores or florist shops have become popular bases for making pomanders.

Rosebud and Petal Pomander

Gather dried rosebuds of different colors with stems intact. Obtain an oasis ball with a hole drilled through the middle from a craft store and cover it with a thick coat of craft glue. Press the stems of the dried rosebuds into the oasis ball until it is fully covered. Ensure that the craft glue is thoroughly dry before decorating the pomander with ribbons and silken threads. Insert a length of ribbon through the middle of the pomander ball for suspending. Rose essential oil can be randomly dabbed on the rosebuds for added fragrance.

Lavender Fan

Lavender fans are very handy. They can be hung on walls, dressers, and other places for a fragrant, decorative touch. In addition to perfuming drawers and cupboards, they are useful for fanning oneself to help clear the sinus or a blocked nose, making breathing easier. The materials required for making a lavender fan are as follows:

Dried lavender flowers

Durable craft glue

An oval straw base from craft store (any size you like)

Lavender material or cloth, cut to the same oval shape

Stiff cardboard of similar shape, but cut ½ inch smaller around the edges

A strip of lovely lace to go around the circumference of the fan

A small amount of polyester wadding (best if from a haberdasher's shop)

Glue a thin layer of wadding to the cardboard and trim to fit. Wait for the glue to dry completely. Cover the wadding with dried lavender flowers and fix the piece of material or cloth over them. Gently turn this lavender "bag" over without dropping any contents. Glue the overlapping cloth to the back of the cardboard. When this dries, glue the strip of lace around the cardboard. Those with strong fingers and sewing skills may want to hand stitch the lace instead. While gluing or sewing the lace strip, make sure that it is visible when turned over again. Glue the lavender "bag" to the straw base and attach several strips of attractive ribbons.

Herb Sachets

Herb sachets are easily made with dried flowers and spices. Popular ingredients are rose, lavender, chamomile, mint, jasmine, and orange blossom, but use only the ones that appeal to you. Cut a 4 × 3-inch piece of cotton or linen cloth (or a 6 × 5-inch cloth if a larger sachet is required). Hand stitch or sew with a machine on three sides to make a rectangular pouch or sachet. Turn it inside out. Fill the inside with flowers and herbs after mixing them with 2 drops of a favorite essential oil. Secure the opening at the top with cotton thread and tie a ribbon around it. Use the sachet for perfuming lingerie or linen or carry in your handbag to be taken out for a refreshing sniff—to relax, de-stress, or invigorate whenever required.

Wreaths

Wreaths are displayed during most festivities and in home decorations that uplift dull corridors or blank walls. As well as accentuating the home, they provide color, atmosphere, liveliness, and ambience year-round. An herbal wreath hung above a lit fireplace during cold winters embraces the living room with pleasant aromas. Always take into consideration the size you desire, as a completed wreath is always bigger than the base.

Bases for creating wreaths vary in size from small to large and are usually round or heart-shaped. They are commonly made from grapevines, raffia, straw, cane, or thick wire. Florists' oases used for securing floral arrangements into place are also necessary in modern wreath-making. They are dipped in water to help fresh flowers and herbs retain moisture.

Other materials for making wreaths include flowers, herbs, leaves or foliage, sphagnum moss, natural carpet thread, strong but thin wire, florists' staples, green florists' tape, and scissors and ribbons for making bows. For something unique, use rows of different colored flowers and herbs that are complementary.

Simple Wreath-Making for the Beginner

Cover the base, wire, and oasis with pliable sphagnum moss to prevent light from showing through the finished item. Secure the moss and other materials by winding fine wire firmly around them. Flowers and herbs must be bunched together in sprigs of three to six pieces. Place two or three bunches on the base with the stems facing diagonally upward to form a curving row. Wind the bunches with wire. Continue placing flower and herb bunches in layers, one above the other, securing them with string. Make sure that the stems from the first row are totally covered and curving in the same direction. Contours of the wreath can be softened with small sprigs of baby's breath flowers. Repeat this procedure until the entire wreath is covered.

Gently turn the wreath over to fix a strong wire loop for hanging the wreath. The loop should not be visible in the front. Turn the wreath back to the front. Make a bow with streamers for attaching to the wreath top or bottom with wire in the center. If it tickles your fancy, ribbons may also be wound around the wreath. Remember to use a spray bottle of water to regularly mist wreaths which contain fresh components. To achieve a further fragrant "oomph," try diluting essential oil in alcohol for misting.

Herb
History,
Myth, and
Lore

Mistletoe Mysteries

❧ by Patti Wigington ❧

Everyone is familiar with mistletoe. It's that cute little bundle of leaves and berries we hang in our doorway around Yule—and then we spend plenty of time trying to maneuver the object of our affections into position beneath it. We coyly glance up, and whisper, "Oh, look where we are! You know what that means!"

And then if our intended is a good sport, we pucker up.

Known far and wide as the holiday kissing plant, mistletoe also happens to have a somewhat more complex history. In fact, the North American variety of the plant is actually a botanical parasite. How unromantic is that?

Let's travel back in time a bit. The ancient Greek physician Dioscorides wrote his five-volume *Materia Medica* around 50 AD, which established him

as the guy to go to for whatever might ail you. As one of the most influential herbalists in history, Dioscorides discovered that his patients could be cured of external tumors with the use of mistletoe. He wrote that mistletoe "has the power to disperse, soften, drawing and assisting tumors of the parotid gland and other lesions . . ." He even found that adding a pinch of frankincense helped soften old ulcers and malignant lumps and bumps of the skin. A few decades later, Pliny the Elder wrote *Natural History*, and expounded on the use of mistletoe in the treatment of both "scrofulous sores" and epilepsy.

Pliny went on to describe mistletoe as not just a medical herb, but as a plant that could be used in ritual and magic as well. As the Romans moved into the island of Britain, the Druids became a focus of interest. The oak tree was sacred to the Druids, and so the leafy green parasitic plant that grew upon it was considered a gift from the Divine. According to Pliny, Druid elders performed a ritual in which mistletoe was harvested from the oak using golden sickles and caught in a white cloth. The mistletoe was gathered during the waxing Moon phase and then fed to animals to ensure fertility in the coming season. Two white bulls were sacrificed as part of the rite, and prayers were sent up to the gods to bestow prosperity upon the villages.

The Druids weren't the only ones celebrating with mistletoe. The Roman festival of Saturnalia is one of the most ancient documented traditions of the Winter Solstice. During this seven-day celebration, gifts were exchanged, much wine and food was consumed, and there was dancing and music. Work was suspended during Saturnalia, courts were closed, and general merrymaking and debauchery took place. Saturn was an agricultural god, and so to keep him happy, fertility rituals took place under the mistletoe during the party.

In Scandinavian countries, warring clans could negotiate a truce under the mistletoe, which was considered a plant of peace. In the Norse Eddas, if a pair of enemies accidentally ran into each other under a growth of mistletoe in the forest, they had to lay down their arms and cease fighting until the next day. The plant was so well known amongst the Scandinavians that it even figured into their folklore and legends.

According to Norse myth, the goddess Frigga honored her son, Baldur, by asking all of nature—plants and animals, iron and stone, wood and water—to promise not to harm him. Unfortunately, in her haste, Frigga overlooked the mistletoe plant, so Loki—the resident trickster—took advantage of the opportunity and fooled Baldur's blind twin, Hod, into killing him with a spear made of mistletoe. Baldur, a gentle and beautiful god, was greatly mourned by Odin and the others, so they later restored him to life. As thanks, Frigga declared that mistletoe must be regarded as a plant of love, rather than death, and so kissing beneath its leaves celebrated Baldur's resurrection.

In a tale similar to that of Frigga and her son, as punishment for its participation in the act, the plant was forbidden to grow in the earth, and was thereafter relegated to freeloading off more virtuous trees, such as the oak or ash. As Christianity spread throughout the world, a legend popped up in France that the cross upon which Jesus died was made of mistletoe, thus earning it the name herbe de la croix.

From medieval times onward, the use of mistletoe has been recorded in many folk remedies and superstitions, particularly in more rural areas. Sprigs could be cut and harvested, tied in bundles, and placed over a doorway to ward off demons. In some countries, mistletoe was placed in the stable to keep cows and livestock safe from any mischievous witchcraft. In both Italy and Sweden it was believed to be a fire repellent. To country folk, the plant was known as the best remedy for a barren woman—mistletoe was the cure-all for problems with conception, because the method of its propagation was a mystery to early cultures. In an interesting paradox, some Native American tribes, such as the Cherokee, used certain species of mistletoe to induce abortion.

Not too long ago, before we spent all our free hours watching television and playing on the Internet, people spent a good part of their leisure time visiting friends and family. Besides providing the company of others, socializing performed an important function—matchmaking. During the winter holidays, particularly in England, a homeowner would hang sprigs of mistletoe in his doorway. Loosely following the Scandinavian tradition of laying down one's arms, if a young lady was caught under the mistletoe by a young gentleman, it was perfectly acceptable for him to give her a chaste kiss. Many romances bloomed from this tradition, and in some areas, a girl who wasn't kissed under the mistletoe at Yuletide was doomed to spend the next year unmarried.

Although we know that mistletoe is a good way to sneak a smooch out of our significant other—or potential significant other—this little plant is a botanical oddity. There are two types of mistletoe. The common North American variety, *Phoradendron flavescens*, grows on trees as a hemiparasite, and the European type of the plant, *Viscum album*, is capable of either growing on other trees or rooting as a shrub in its own right. As immigration and settlement became more commonplace, the traditions associated with the European mistletoe were applied to the North American variety as well.

A true parasite, North American mistletoe doesn't have any roots of its own. Instead, it has little extensions known as holdfasts, which grip onto the bark of the host plant and suck the nutrients out of it. A mistletoe plant can be either female or male, yet only the female has berries, which are lovely, but toxic to humans.

One of the amazing things about the mistletoe berry is that while it can be deadly when ingested by humans, birds seem immune to its poisons. Good thing, because the propagation of the mistletoe plant itself is dependent on the birds that consume the berries but do not digest the seeds. The seeds are most likely to flourish and grow if a bird deposits them on the same species as the original host plant. In other words, a bird may eat mistletoe berries growing on an apple tree, and then fly several miles away to excrete the seeds on a completely different apple tree, ensuring the continuation of the mistletoe.

Because it's unusual for a flowering plant to be parasitic, mistletoe has been the subject of a lot of studies. Modern researchers are learning what the Druids knew so long ago—that this odd little green parasite has healing properties. Although herbal healing has often been dismissed as superstition by the medical community, the discovery of a mistletoe-based product may change the way physicians view herbs. This extract is made from different varieties of mistletoe, based upon which host plant they use, and clinical trials are being done to determine its effectiveness as a cancer treatment. While using mistletoe against cancer was mentioned as early as the 1920s, only recently have scientists found that mistletoe kills cancer cells in the laboratory, and can stimulate the immune system, which in turn fights off disease.

One of the best things about mistletoe is that as a parasite, it's actually pretty easy to grow on your own. You just have to be willing to sacrifice another plant as a host. Christmas mistletoe is harvested while still immature, so don't use those berries to start your plants. Instead, wait until March or April and then pick some fresh, mature berries. If they're plump and white, they're ready to be picked. Try to obtain one from a host plant similar to the one you wish to use as a host for the new growth.

Select a good hardy branch on a mature tree—at least fifteen years old—and make several small incisions in the bark. Higher up is better so that sufficient sunlight can reach the seedling. Remove the seed coats from the seeds, and place the seeds inside the bark. Remember that birds love these berries, so be sure to cover the seeds with some jute or other protective covering—otherwise your birds will feast, and you'll have no mistletoe at all.

Plant plenty of seeds, because both males and females are needed to propagate the new growth, and the germination success rate is fairly low—around 10 percent. Over the next three to five years, the host branch will begin to swell up, and eventually your mistletoe will reach berry-producing size.

Because of its long history as a healing herb, it's no wonder that modern Wiccans and Pagans have found ways to use mistletoe. Traditionally, a tea is brewed using the mistletoe leaves in hot water. Once the leaves have steeped, they are strained out and removed. Another option is to make a cold infusion from the leaves and sweeten it with honey or sugar before drinking.

When ingested in small amounts, as in teas or extracts, there are rarely side effects from mistletoe. However, consuming large quantities of mistletoe leaves or berries has the potential to be fatal—particularly in children, who have been known to nibble the pretty berries during the holiday season. The use of mistletoe is also not recommended for pregnant women or nursing mothers. If you believe someone is suffering from mistletoe poisoning, get them to an emergency room immediately.

If you're not comfortable taking mistletoe internally, never fear. It can be used in a variety of ways during ritual and spellwork. Consider all the properties of this leafy green plant, and think of all the wonderful applications. Here are a few:

- Use stalks of mistletoe in a healing ritual for an ailing friend, or place the leaves in a pouch for the ill person to carry with them.

- Place dried leaves in a sachet or pillow for a woman who is trying to conceive a child.

- If you're trying to draw love your way, why not hang mistletoe over your doorway or use it in a love spell?

- Use mistletoe in a ritual to end strife and discord in your life. After all, the Norsemen laid down their arms when they met beneath a growth of this plant.

- Adorn your house with mistletoe boughs year-round if you can, to protect your property and family from fire, bad fortune, and negative magic.

For thousands of years, this small parasitic plant has found its way into our homes and our hearts. Pick some up commercially, or better yet, grow your own, so you can take advantage of all the magic and mystery that mistletoe has to offer.

Paracelsus, Plants & the Doctrine of Signatures

＊ by Mark Stavish ＊

That which is Above, is like that which is Below; that which is Below, is like that which is Above, to accomplish the miracle of the One Thing.
—The Emerald Tablet of Hermes

AS ABOVE

SO BELOW

Plants have always been the touchstone of medicine, from the Stone Age to the Space Age, and even when newer and better ways of delivering their healing power is presented, in the end, plants are the basis for the majority of medicines past, present, and future.

While our understanding of plants has changed considerably over the last two hundred years, one thing remains certain: from the occult perspective, plants are living things that allow us to be connected to worlds and experiences beyond daily life.

Magic: Where the Past Is Present

Modern magical practices owe their existence to their predecessors, those magi of the Renaissance who resurrected the magical worldview and made it acceptable in the late fifteenth century. The Western esoteric traditions fundamentally consisted of several schools of thought that found their common ground in the occult practices of astrology, ritual magic, and alchemy. Together these three areas form the practical work of Hermeticism.

Despite minor differences in doctrine, all schools see the universe as existing in dual form—what we experience with our physical senses, and what exists invisibly that our physical senses cannot directly experience. These two polar ends of existence are connected by a series of interconnected worlds or planes, going from the most abstract to the most concrete (also known as our material world).

What unites them is that in their own ways, each world is a slightly distorted reflection of the other. Thus, while not perfect, knowledge of one world can give us knowledge of another. The analogy that may best describe these various worlds or planes of consciousness and matter is the musical keyboard, on which one plays the same notes, but at different octaves, to achieve different combinations of sounds.

Herein lies the key to Hermeticism and all magical operations—the Hermetic Axiom, or "That which is Above, is like that which is Below; and that which is Below, is like that which is Above; to accomplish the miracle of the One Thing." To know one set of notes and one or two octaves allows us to understand the same notes and their possible effects (or sounds) at other octaves higher or lower in the scale.

Note that it is described as the One Thing. Contrary to appearances, the universe is a single, united being. More importantly, in order to understand how its invisible and psychic laws work, and how the great mysteries of creation take place, all we need to do is to study and understand the material world in which we live.

Prior to the Age of Reason, when the universe and fields of learning began to be divided up into neat little boxes (a task completed during the Industrial Revolution), everything was seen as existing in an interconnected tapestry or harmonic scale of ideas, energy, and matter. To learn and master one subject well would lend itself to learning and mastering another subject well, and possibly even mastering all fields of knowledge. This ideal was found in the Renaissance man, a person of immense knowledge, skill, and wisdom. During the Renaissance the study of Hermeticism was seen as the capstone of personal intellectual, scientific, and spiritual learning, and within it—alchemy as the crown, or Royal Art, as it was called.

Paracelsus (1493–1541) is the most well-known of Western alchemists. His writings on the use of plants for healing physical and spiritual illnesses has been the basis for alchemical pursuits for almost five hundred years. Born in Einsieden, Switzerland, in 1493, Philippus Theophrastus Bombastus von Hohenheim studied medicine at Basel University, which at the time included the study of alchemy. He later studied minerals and mining-related diseases in the Tyrol region. His travels took him across Europe and to the Middle East, where in Constantinople he is said to have confected the philosophers' stone. Using the pseudonym of "Paracelsus" he returned to Basel in 1526, where Erasmus obtained a lectureship position for him at the University. Lecturing in German rather than the conventional Latin of the day, Paracelsus was forced to leave Basel in 1528. Eventually he moved to Salzburg, where he died thirteen years later.

The work and teachings of Paracelsus form the basis from which most modern alchemical practices are derived, as well as several schools of alternative medicine—principally homeopathy. In homeopathy, we hear the words of Paracelsus, "Where there is disease there can also be found the roots of health. For health must grow from the same root of disease, and where health goes, there also disease must follow." Other schools also clearly bear his mark, even if it is not recognized as such—including aromatherapy, Bach flower remedies, and several schools of crystal and magnetic therapy.

A medical doctor by training, Paracelsus objected to the inflexible and unscientific nature of medicine in his day. Physicians were trained to quote ancient authorities rather than pay attention to what was happening to the patient in front of them. The study of anatomy and experimentation was extremely limited and often illegal, as a result of the influence of the Roman Catholic Church in secular matters. Ignoring these conventions, Paracelsus made many enemies. He openly flaunted his disregard for the prevailing ignorance of the day—an ignorance born of the twins of superstition and rigid authoritarianism. Paracelsus disregarded the prescribed medical canon of the day—Avicenna and Galen—on the basis that they knew nothing of chemistry. In his book, *Das Buch Paragranum*, Paracelsus emphasizes that medicine must be based in alchemy, astronomy, ethics, and philosophy.

Paracelsus stated, "Marvelous virtues are inherent in the remedies. . . . For only a great artist is able to discover them, not one who is only versed in books, but only one who has acquired his ability and skill through the experience of his hands."

He routinely healed what were considered hopeless cases, and let it be known that he had done so. A perennial traveler due to his constant search for knowledge (and making of enemies), Paracelsus, like Agrippa, learned from anyone and everyone. Illiterate peasants, gypsies, herb wives, and folk healers, along with alchemists, magicians, and university lecturers, were all his teachers—both of what to do and what to avoid. His reputation grew, as did his list of admirers and opponents. Through it all, he managed to pass on to his students a massive body of learning deeply rooted in the Hermetic tradition. Paracelsus is said to have even confected the philosophers' stone and had quite the reputation as a sorcerer during his lifetime.

Weaving its way through all of this, however, is the fundamental premise of Hermeticism—or "As above, so Below" as it has come to be known. Integral to this in practical terms is the Doctrine of Signatures.

Just as there are four worlds in Qabala, each acting as a reflection of the other, in alchemy and Renaissance magic the existence of three worlds is positioned—the material, the astral, and the celestial. Each has its own distinct attributes, intelligences, and powers. In magic these are contacted through symbols, rituals, and gestures—which are all based upon an understanding of the Doctrine of Signatures. In alchemy there are three areas of work—plants, minerals, and animals. By understanding the fundamental process in the plant realm, or spagyrics, a term coined by Paracelsus meaning "to separate and recombine," we understand the process as it takes place in minerals, and even in humans.

Combined with the study of astrology or cycles, and symbols or magic, it is easy to see how the various worlds are interdependent on each other, and can be contacted through a variety of practices, and that to master one occult practice would lead to mastering all of them.

Paracelsus and Plant Medicine

Identifying the use of a plant for occult or practical terms has always been a challenge. During Paracelsus' age, the Doctrine of Signatures was often used to identify the nature and use of a plant. This doctrine states that the celestial forces make their mark in tangible and physical ways on all things. According to John Michael Greer's *The New Encyclopedia of the Occult*, the Doctrine of Signatures is "the belief that the medical and magical virtues of an herb may be found symbolized in some way in the herb's color, shape, or other qualities." Those things which are powerfully solar in nature, and pertain to the Sun, will have similar qualities to the physical Sun itself. They will be yellow, orange, bright, round, pleasant, warm, and fiery in nature. They will, in form, express the nature of the Sun, and in use, contain and project its energetic essence.

So if you wanted to increase the inner heat, strengthen the heart, or even improve the vision of a person—anything that falls under the domain of the Sun—a plant of a solar nature would be recommended. Or in the words of Paracelsus,

> Everything external in nature points to something internal; for nature is both inside man and outside. . . . That which comes from the heart of the macrocosm comforts the heart of man—gold, emerald, coral; that which comes from the liver of the macrocosm comforts the liver of man.

Over the centuries, several variations of the Doctrine of Signatures have developed: one which is strictly medical, another occult, and the third based on psychic or mystical experiences, such as those articulated by Boehme, Goethe, and several modern authorities. The Doctrine of Signatures is closely related to the Doctrine of Correspondences, and the latter term is often used to encompass the meaning of the former. However, the Doctrine of Signatures is distinct in that it is used exclusively in reference to herbal and plant lore, whereas the Doctrine of Correspondences encompasses the entire symbolic and energetic relationship of the magical cosmos.

Everything that exists in the material world has its seed and roots in an invisible reality. The physical is the fruit, not the tree or the branch of existence. Paracelsus also directs us to observe the form as being molded to express the inner essence of a thing, be it a plant, stone, or person:

> Behold the Satyrion root, is it not formed like the male privy parts? . . . Accordingly magic discovered it and revealed that it can restore a man's virility and passion. And then we have the thistle; do not its leaves prickle like needles? . . . There is no better herb against internal

prickling. The Siegwurz root is wrapped in an envelope like armour . . . it gives protection against weapons. And the Syderica bears the image of a snake on each of its leaves, and thus . . . it gives protection against any kind of poisoning. The chicory stands under a special influence of the Sun; this is seen in its leaves while the Sun is shining . . . as the Sun sets, the power of the chicory dwindles.

With nature always as the tapestry upon which the forces of life are expressed, we see little distinction between the ideals of science, art, magic, and alchemy, each expressing through its own particular method an aspect of the wisdom of experience.

Alchemists call themselves the handmaids of nature, stating that they imitate nature in their work of creating medicines for the body, psyche, and soul. One of the "fathers of the Italian Renaissance" and of the rejuvenation of Western culture, Pico della Mirandola, wrote, "Nature performs in a natural way the things the magician achieves by his art."

Science is not concerned with the cosmological questions of the mystic, but rather an understanding of how nature works in the physical world. This can be likened to a dream state upon awakening, when it is not always clear when one has passed from one domain into another. Even without ritual or consecrations, artists who are fired by the desire to express what is deep inside can create a talisman composed of symbols and images drawn from their own psyche, and unleash it upon the world, for good or ill. Correspondences are all around and within us. We are a composition of correspondences existing in a series of worlds of similar symbolic relationships.

Whether they recognize it or not, modern alchemy, herbalism, and holistic medicine owe a great deal of their theory and practice to the writings and techniques advanced by Paracelsus and his later followers, many of whom are held in as high esteem as "the Master" himself. Modern allopathic medicine, despite its hostility to things "occult," is also deeply rooted in Paracelsus' experimental view. It was Paracelsus who used laudanum as a tranquilizer and ether as an anesthetic, traced goiter to mineral content in drinking water, and described silicosis. His insistence on observation, research, science, and chemistry in medicine was heresy in his day, but is the basis for its modern practice.

For Further Reading

Jacobi, Jolande, ed. *Paracelsus: Selected Writings*. Bollingen Series XXVIII. Princeton: Princeton University Press, 1951.

The Herbal Alchemist

⤞ by Lynn Smythe ⤝

. . . the whole point of alchemy is to not be a slave to any book or formula, but to meditate, experiment and analyze, and come to one's own conclusion.
— Phillip Hurley, *Herbal Alchemy*

Alchemy was an ancient chemical philosophy primarily concerned with the transmutation of base metals into gold. Alchemy included elements of philosophy, religious mysticism, mythology, astrology, botany, zoology, and mineralogy.

Herbal alchemy is used for healing. The herbal alchemist mixes together a variety of herb-based tinctures, salves, and ointments in the pursuit of creating the elixir of immortality, also known as the philosophers' stone. Herbal alchemists make a variety of both simples (medicines made from a single herb) and compounds (two or more herbs).

When creating your own herbal formulas, try to find a location in your home where you can focus on creating your preparation without too many disturbances. A pantry or table top next to a kitchen is ideal. Historically, the stillroom was where the woman of the household prepared and stored the herbal remedies dispensed to the members of her family. The stillroom was situated as near to the kitchen as possible. This gave her easy access to all the equipment and supplies needed to make a variety of lotions, unguents, and other herbal treatments.

Storing Your Creations

The best containers for storing your herbal beauty creations are green, cobalt, or amber-colored glass bottles with screw-on lids. These are perfect for storing your liquid cosmetics and herbal medicines such as toners, tonics, and tinctures. For more solid creations, such as balms and ointments, use 1- to 4-ounce widemouthed opaque glass or plastic jars with screw-on lids.

Make sure to label each bottle, as most of these items will look very similar once they are placed into the bottles. They don't have to be elaborate—just list the contents, ingredients used, and the date it was created. Blank, self-adhesive labels can be purchased at office supply stores and stationery stores.

The Formulas

But one who has a small area of rough skin should pound this thyme with fresh lard and make an unguent from it. When he anoints himself with it, he will have good health.

—Hildegard von Bingen, *Physica*

This article focuses on creating your own natural botanical beauty preparations. Herbal beauty treatments can be used to impart a youthful glow to one's skin. Creating your own formulas ensures that they don't contain any harmful chemicals or preservatives, as might be found in many commercial beauty preparations.

These formulas can be concocted with a variety of herbs, essential oils, and base ingredients. Make these alchemical beauty potions in small batches as you have need for them. Most of the formulas that follow can be stored for up to one month at room temperature. Alcohol and vitamin E oil both have preservative qualities, and storing your creations in a cool location away from sunlight will also prolong their shelf life. For extended shelf life, try storing the formulas in your refrigerator.

Balms

Commercially made balms, such as Badger Balm and Tiger Balm, are available at health food stores. Here is a recipe for a wonderful homemade lip balm. Since a little goes a long way, this recipe makes enough to share with friends or give away as gifts.

Peppermint Lip Balm

This recipe is quite easy to follow. Peppermint essential oil is used in this recipe, but other essential oils, such as rose geranium or orange, can be used depending upon your own personal preference. If you like a creamier consistency for your lip balm, use a little bit less beeswax or add a bit more almond oil.

½   cup sweet almond oil

2   tablespoons jojoba oil

2   tablespoons beeswax pellets

2   tablespoons honey

5   vitamin E capsules

25   drops peppermint essential oil

A quart-size glass canning jar works as a good container in which to make this lip balm. Place the jar into a pan half filled with water and turn the heat to medium. Then carefully add the sweet almond oil, jojoba oil, and beeswax into the canning jar. Use a potholder to hold the top of the canning jar while stirring it around until the beeswax is completely melted. Stir in the honey and vitamin E and mix until the honey has been thoroughly incorporated. Remove the container from the pan of hot water and turn off your stove.

Stir in the essential oil, then pour the balm into containers and let them cool to room temperature before covering them with the lids. Empty plastic lip gloss containers, which hold approximately ¼ ounce, can be purchased from a variety of vendors. I prefer to use flat ½ ounce round aluminum containers to store my balm in. This recipe makes almost one cup (8 ounces) of balm.

Baths

Herbal Bath

Place a handful of dried or fresh herbs, such as calming and relaxing chamomile, lemon balm, or lavender, inside a muslin bag or tie them up in a double layer of cheesecloth. Place the bundle of herbs in your bathtub. Fill your tub with very warm water, which will release the essential oils of the herbs into the water. After approximately 10 minutes, the bundle of herbs can be rubbed all over your body as a sort of body scrub. Discard the herbs at the end of the bath.

Facials

A facial refers to any type of cosmetic treatment meant to be used on the face such as a facial steam or scrub. Facials help improve the appearance of your skin by removing dirt and debris from your pores.

Steam Facial

Fill a large bowl with boiling water. Add 2 to 4 drops of an appropriate essential oil to the water. For oily skin, lemon peppermint, rose, geranium, rosemary, tea tree, and ylang ylang oils work well. If you have dry skin, try lemon, orange, rosemary, lavender, rose, or sandalwood.

Place your face a few inches above the water, then cover your head with a towel to keep the steam from escaping. If you get too hot, lift the towel to get some fresh air. Place the towel back over your head and continue steaming and venting until the water cools down and has stopped steaming. At the end of the facial, splash your face with cool water and pat dry with a soft towel. You may want to apply a toner to your face at the conclusion of the facial to help close the pores of your skin.

Floral Facial Scrub

2 tablespoons dried lavender petals

2 tablespoons dried rose petals

2 tablespoons dried chamomile flowers

½ cup oatmeal

⅓ cup uncooked brown rice

Place the flowers and oatmeal into a coffee grinder and grind to a medium-fine consistency, then pour out into a bowl. Add the rice to the coffee grinder and grind to a fine consistency. Pour the ground rice into the ground oatmeal and herb mixture and stir until well blended. To store this mixture, pour it into a container with a tight-fitting lid.

To use as a facial, place 2 tablespoons of the scrub in a small muslin bag. Tie the bag closed with a piece of string. Briefly soak the bag in warm water to thoroughly wet the mixture, then use it to scrub all over your face. Rinse your face a final time with cool water, then pat dry with a soft cloth. This is a great way to help slough off dead, dry skin cells, and will impart a more radiant and youthful glow to your complexion. This recipe may also be used as a body scrub while taking a bath or shower.

Gels

Gels can be used as a general facial tonic to help moisturize and soothe your skin. Gels are gentle enough to be used on the delicate skin around your neck and chest area.

Moisturizing Gel

1 tablespoon slippery elm powder

5 ounces rose water or plain water

10 drops rose geranium essential oil

Mix the slippery elm powder with the rose water or plain water and place the mixture in an enamel or glass pan. Bring it to a boil, reduce the heat to low, and simmer for 5 minutes, stirring continuously while the gel thickens. Remove the pan from the heat and pour the gel into a glass bowl. Let the gel cool down to room temperature, which will take about 30 minutes, then stir in the essential oil. Apply the gel to your face and neck area. Let the gel remain in place for 5 to 10 minutes, then rinse off with water and a soft washcloth. Store any leftover gel in the refrigerator for up to a week.

Infusions

An infusion is the steeping of leafy herbs and flowers in hot water in order to extract their aromatic and medicinal properties. Infusions can be used externally in a compress or added to your bathtub for an enjoyable herbal bath.

A compress is a soft pad or cloth, often made of flannel, that is applied to a part of the body to reduce pain or control bleeding. Herbal compresses are first soaked in a warm herbal infusion, then wrung out before being applied to the body. When the compress has cooled down, you can remove it and re-soak it in the warm infusion if a second or third application is necessary.

Any leftover infusion can be stored in a bottle in the refrigerator for a few days. It's best to make small, frequent batches of these infusions, as they may begin to grow mold after one week.

Rose Infusion

¼ ounce (approximately ½ cup) dried rosebuds

4 cups water

Place the rosebuds in a glass bowl or large glass measuring cup. Bring the water to a boil and pour it over the rosebuds. Stir well, then cover the bowl with a towel. Let this mixture steep until the water has cooled down to room temperature. Strain out and discard the roses. Pour the infusion into a container and store it in the refrigerator until ready to use. This floral-scented infusion will have a pale rose color and can be used to make a variety of herbal cosmetics such as lotions and toners.

Liniments

A liniment is a liquid ointment with medicinal properties that is rubbed into the skin. It is meant for external use only. Liniments are often prepared with oil or isopropyl alcohol. Isopropyl alcohol, which is also called rubbing alcohol, can be found in 1-pint bottles in drug stores. Peppermint, eucalyptus, and wintergreen are three common herbs to use for making liniments. These herbs help to relieve basic aches and pains and work as a general muscle relaxant.

Basic Oil-Based Liniment

Add 1 cup of dried herbs to a pint-size canning jar. Fill the jar with grape-seed oil, then place the lid on the jar and shake well. Store the jar away from sunlight and shake once a day. At the end of 14 days strain out and discard the herbs. Mix in 1 tablespoon of liquid glycerin to act as a preservative.

You can massage the liniment into sore muscles as needed. Grape-seed oil works best for normal to oily skin. Other types of oil, such as olive and almond, can be used according to your personal preference.

Basic Alcohol-Based Liniment

If you prefer, you can make liniments with an alcohol base. Follow the same instructions as above, but substitute isopropyl alcohol for an oil. However, you do not need to add glycerin, because the alcohol in this liniment acts as its own preservative.

Lotions

Lotions are a medicine or cosmetic applied externally to a part of the body. They have the consistency of a thick and creamy liquid, and are an emulsion made of a blend of ingredients such as oil, beeswax, lanolin, glycerin, and essential oils.

If you want to make your own lotions but don't have the time or inclination to make them from scratch, you can purchase unscented, dye-free base lotions from a variety of cosmetic supply vendors. I have used a shea-butter base lotion to create my own lotion blends with wonderful results. To make your own lotion, add 6 to 8 drops of essential oil to every 2 ounces of the base lotion. To store them safely, I like to decant my lotions into 2-ounce plastic bottles with flip-top lids.

Here are a few suggestions for essential oils to use along with the unscented base lotion:

Essential Oil	Quality
lavender	calming
lemon and clove	invigorating
peppermint	refreshing
rosemary and patchouli	sensual

Oils

Herb-infused oils can be used to create a variety of balms, creams, lotions, and ointments. Herb-infused oils can be made with cosmetic-grade oils such as cold-pressed olive, hazelnut, grape-seed, or sweet almond. Healing herbs to use for creating oils include arnica flowers, calendula flowers, and comfrey leaves. Arnica is a terrific all-purpose healing herb for use on minor cuts, scrapes, sprains, and bruises.

Basic Healing Oil

¼ cup dried comfrey leaves

¼ cup dried calendula petals

Olive Oil

Place the herbs into a pint-size glass canning jar or similar container. Fill the jar with olive oil, making sure that the herbs are completely covered with oil. Place the lid on the jar and shake well. Store the jar at room temperature away from sunlight. Shake the jar once a day for four weeks. Decant the herb-infused oil into another jar and discard the herbs. Store the oil in the refrigerator until ready to use. Keep an eye out for any mold that may form. If mold is present you must discard the oil.

Ointments

Ointments are meant for external use only. They are similar to a liniment, but have a thicker consistency. With the addition of beeswax and other ingredients, an ointment can become as solid as a balm or as creamy as a lotion.

Cuticle Ointment

¼   cup basic healing oil

2   tablespoons beeswax pellets

¼   cup shea butter

⅓   cup rose infusion

    Contents of 3 vitamin E capsules

20   drops sweet orange essential oil

20   drops rosemary essential oil

Place the healing oil in a small glass or stainless-steel bowl, then place the bowl over a pan that is half filled with water. Turn the heat to medium and heat the mixture until the beeswax and shea butter have completely melted. Remove the bowl from the stove and turn off the heat. Stir in the rose infusion, vitamin E, and essential oils. Place the bowl into a larger bowl that has been filled halfway with ice cubes. Use a wire whisk or glass stirring rod to continuously beat and stir the mixture until it is thick and creamy. Pour or spoon the ointment into wide-mouth containers. Let the balm cool completely to room temperature before adding the lids.

This ointment helps moisturize dry and damaged skin especially on the knees, elbows, heels, and cuticles. It can also be used to help heal minor cuts and scrapes.

Toners

Toners are meant for external use only, and have the consistency of water. Witch hazel is a common ingredient to use when making your own toners. It can be found in pharmacies in pint bottles; this mixture of 86 percent witch hazel extract and 14 percent alcohol is for external use only. Use witch hazel as a skin astringent, facial cleanser, and for the relief of minor skin irritations due to insect bites, minor cuts, and minor scrapes.

Floral Toner

½ cup rose infusion

½ cup witch hazel

5 drops lavender essential oil

Mix all the ingredients together and pour the liquid into a glass or plastic bottle. Apply the toner to your face using a cotton ball. Toners can be used to help remove makeup and gently cleanse the skin of your face.

Cooling Toner

Mix ½ cup of a strong peppermint infusion with ½ cup of witch hazel. Place the resulting liquid into a small spray bottle. Place this toner in the refrigerator and use it to spray all over your body to help cool you down whenever you come inside after being in the hot summer sun. Shake the bottle well before using and be sure to avoid spraying near your eyes.

Herbs of the Mabinogion

≫ by Sorita D'Este ≪

The *Mabinogion* is the primary source work for Welsh mythology, introducing us to the family of Welsh deities such as Rhiannon, Arianrhod, Ceridwen, Lleu, Bran, and Branwen. Within the tales contained in *The Mabinogion* there are references to a number of herbs and trees, including the broom blossom, meadowsweet, and oak used to fashion the body of the Flower Maiden Blodeuwedd; the white clovers that appear wherever the maiden goddess Olwen walks; the unnamed herbs that the goddess Ceridwen added to her cauldron of wisdom; the fungus used by the magic god Gwydion, which he transformed into gilded shields to fool Pryderi; and many more.

The Mabinogion draws its stories from two old Welsh sources, the *White Book of Rhydderch* (c. 1325 AD) and the *Red Book of Hergest* (late fourteenth

century AD). These books were recorded by Christian monks, who had a tendency to belittle the Pagan themes within them, treating the old gods as mortal figures. While we should thank the monks for preserving the tales, we must keep their perceptions in mind. This is particularly true for the two stories that contain the most references to herbs—"Math the son of Mathonwy" and "Killwch and Olwen"—which are featured in this article.

Math the Son of Mathonwy

The tale of "Math the son of Mathonwy" (also known as "The Fourth Branch") introduces us to the Gods of Magic—Math and Gwydion—as well as to the Lord of Light, Lleu Llew Gyffes, the Stellar Goddess Arianrhod, and the Flower Maiden Blodeuwedd. Lleu is the illegitimate child of Arianrhod, raised by Gwydion after Arianrhod has cursed him never to have a name, bear weapons, or have a human wife. Through trickery Gwydion fools Arianrhod into giving him his name and weapons, but cannot get him a wife, so Math and Gwydion combine their talents to create a wife for Lleu Llew Gyffes. They make Blodeuwedd out of the blossoms of broom, meadowsweet, and oak.

Unfortunately their efforts lead to tragedy. Blodeuwedd, their creation, falls in love with the hunter Gronw. With Gronw she schemes to kill Lleu, her husband, but this fails and Lleu is only wounded and kills Gronw. The battle of Lleu and Gronw is the story of the battle between the Lord of Light (Lleu) and Lord of Dark (Gronw) for the hand of the earth goddess (Blodeuwedd), often celebrated in Pagan ceremonies.

In another part of the story, Gwydion tricks the hero Pryderi out of his magical pigs. The pigs were no ordinary animals, for they had been given to Pryderi by Arawn, lord of the otherworld. Gwydion works illusions to encourage Pryderi to swap, only for the illusory gifts to return to their true nature twenty-four hours later. This causes a mighty battle in which Gwydion kills Pryderi using his magic, much to the disgust of Math, who subsequently punishes him for his treachery.

Broom

Broom is one of the flowers used to create Blodeuwedd. Its early blossoming in spring, together with its color, hints at a bright blond and golden appearance for this goddess. Broom has a long history of use for its ability to impart fertility and fortune. This is best illustrated by the besom decorated with yellow broom flowers often used in traditional handfasting ceremonies. In Welsh folklore it was said that if the bride's skirt touched the broom she was already pregnant, and if the man's trousers touched the broom he would be unfaithful.

As might be expected of a yellow flower, according to the old *Doctrine of Signatures*, in which plants are given properties according to their appearance, the broom flower was sometimes used as a diuretic and to treat liver and kidney disorders. It was also used as a sedative, as farmers noticed that sheep first became excited, then dramatically calmed down, after eating the flowers. It is now known that this is due to the effect this herb has on the heart of mammals, first stimulating it and then calming it down.

Fungus

In the tale of Math the Son of Mathonwy, Gwydion works his magic and transforms an unnamed fungus into twelve gilded shields. Although we cannot be certain what type of fungus he used, it is likely to have been Birch Bracket fungus, which grows on the bark of birch trees. This fungus was used to sharpen blades and also as a canvas for painting. Symbolically (with the birch, tree of beginnings) and magically, as a blank canvas to work his spell on, Bracket fungus would have been ideal for Gwydion. Another old use for Birch Bracket fungus was to make torches, as it burns very well and may have been used in Imbolc celebrations. It is curious to note that two of the plant types that Gwydion transforms with his magic are also plants used as torches in sabbat celebrations.

Laver

At one point in the tale, Gwydion makes a boat out of seaweed and sedge. Although the seaweed is not named, it is almost certainly laver, a purple or red edible seaweed found on parts of the Welsh coast. Laver bread, as it is known, is made by collecting laver at low tide, washing it repeatedly, and cooking it mixed with oats to make a delicious delicacy. It has been eaten for many centuries in Wales, and is still popular today.

Meadowsweet

The meadowsweet blossom is the second of the ingredients used to make the Flower Maiden Blodeuwedd. The sweetening flavor of meadowsweet indicates the positive side of Blodeuwedd's character, her charm and beauty. Meadowsweet flowers were used externally to treat infections. When bound to wounds, their astringent and alexipharmic (anti-infection) qualities would help treat inflammation and reduce the chance of infection. They were also made into infusions in white wine to drink for fevers, being sudorific (sweat-inducing) and diuretic.

Although it was not known in ancient times, meadowsweet also contains salicylic acid, the active ingredient in aspirin (which takes its name from the old botanical name for meadowsweet, *Spirea ulmaria*). It is also found in white willow bark. More pleasurably, meadowsweet was also used to flavor mead and beer.

Oak

The blossoms of the oak are the third ingredient used to make Blodeuwedd. The oak was of course a very sacred tree to the Celts and the Druids, and Blodeuwedd's importance is emphasized through the use of oak blossoms in her creation.

The oak also appears as the tree in which Lleu, severely wounded and in eagle form, rests. When Gwydion (Lleu's uncle) tracks him down, he charms him down from the oak by reciting three englyns (short Welsh poetic verses). Gwydion speaks the englyns to the oak itself, indicating both a connection between

Gwydion's magic and the oak tree, and between the eagle (Lleu) and the oak. Gwydion uses the magic of the oak to help persuade Lleu to descend and receive healing.

The oak was arguably the most sacred of the Druid trees, as it was the home of the mistletoe and revered throughout the ancient world. The endurance of oak made it a good protector; the legendary Merlin was said to have planted an oak at Carmarthen and pronounced, "When Merlin's oak shall tumble down, then shall fall Carmarthen town." Many centuries later, the tree is still standing and the town safe.

Sedges

Gwydion works his magic to transform sedges and dry sticks into cordovan leather to make the finest shoes. He also makes a boat out of sedge and seaweed to transport the leather goods to Arianrhod's castle. Sedges are grasses found in wet or marshy ground, and dried sedge bundles were often used as torches in Beltane celebrations in Wales. This fits symbolically with their use to aid Lleu, the Lord of Light.

Although the specific type of sedge is not named, the type most commonly used is calamus, the root of which is aromatic and stimulatory. Calamus root was used to aid digestion and ease fevers, being either chewed or made into a tea. Calamus root was also powdered and used as a substitute for other spices like ginger and cinnamon due to its lovely spicy flavor.

Nettle

Nettle flowers are described as another one of the ingredients used to make the Flower Maiden Blodeuwedd in *Cad Goddeu* (The Battle of the Trees). There is a piece in the poem where Blodeuwedd is clearly speaking, when she says, "Of the flower of nettles, of the water of the ninth wave. I was enchanted by Math, before I became immortal, I was enchanted by Gwydion the great purifier of the Brython." That she should claim the venomous nettle as part of her make-up seems appropriate, considering the role she plays in betraying her husband Lleu.

Nettles have much in common with flax, and have been widely used to make fibers for fabric used to make sacks, sails, and cords. Nettles are best known for their stings, which, as is widely known, can be treated with dock leaves. The stings can also be treated with the leaves of sage, mint, or rosemary.

Nettles were traditionally used as a "pot-herb," the fresh green tops gathered in spring and boiled for use in soups and salads. They were also made into a pudding, and used to make beer. Nettle tea was also drunk as a blood purifier and is believed to alleviate rheumatic discomfort. An old charm using nettle was to pull up a whole plant by the roots, naming the sick person and their parents as you did so, and thus dispelling their fever.

Kilhwch and Olwen

Kilhwch and Olwen is a love story thought to date back to the tenth century AD. It tells of the heroic Kilhwch and his almost impossible quest to win the hand of Olwen, whom he falls in love with upon hearing her name. Her giant father sets a series of quests and a steep price for his daughter's hand as obstacles to the courtship and wedding. Kilhwch turns to his royal relative King Arthur for help, gaining the aid of Arthur and many of his heroes, as well as help from a number of the gods who turn up in other stories: Amaethon (the agriculture god), Govannon (the smith god), Gwyn ap Nudd (lord of the otherworld), Mabon (the divine child), and Manawyddan (the sea god).

Broom

Broom also occurs in the love story of Kilhwch and Olwen. Olwen's hair is likened to broom flower: "More yellow was her hair than the flowers of the broom, and her skin was whiter than the foam of the wave." The detailed imagery of Olwen's beauty makes it clear that she is no ordinary heroine.

Flax

Flax also occurs in the tale of Kilhwch and Olwen, when Olwen's father, the giant Yspaddaden, demands nine bushels of flax from Kilhwch to make the wimple for Olwen for her wedding. It is significant that he demands white flax as it produces superior fibers to that of the blue flowering variety when used to make cloth. The spinning of flax is a popular theme in Welsh folklore. Many tales tell of women who had to guess the name of a faery in exchange for the spinning of huge amounts of flax. Flax flowers are believed to protect the bearer from sorcery and magic, which may be how the women always manage to outwit the faeries in these tales.

Besides their nutritional value, linseeds (flaxseeds) are also very useful medicinally. They were crushed into poultices to treat inflammations and ulcerations, calming irritation and pain. Made into a tea, linseeds were used as a cough and cold remedy, and linseed oil (called carron oil) mixed with limewater was an efficacious treatment for burns and scalds. Linseed oil can also be rubbed into handmade wooden wands to seal the wood, give it a nice golden color, and of course provide extra protection!

Hawthorn

Hawthorn occurs indirectly in the tale as part of the meaning of the name Yspaddaden Penkawr, Olwen's father. It cannot be coincidental that hawthorn produces a white blossom, which matches the white flowers produced by Olwen, and is also the tree of chastity. By killing Yspaddaden, Kilhwch wins Olwen's hand, and then marries her, "killing" her chastity.

Hawthorn is also known as the faery tree and was believed to be one of the favorite meeting places for these beings. Perhaps because of this, hawthorn branches were hung over the doors of houses and stables to protect the residents from witches and faeries. But it was considered terrible luck to bring hawthorn into the house. This is expressed in the old rhyme "Hawthorn bloom and elder flower, fill the house with evil power."

Hawthorn flowers and berries are both astringent and diuretic, and were used in cough remedies. Hawthorn berries were used to make a liqueur by adding them to brandy, and the leaves were used to make a tea.

White Clover

White clovers sprang forth wherever Olwen walked, which befits her name, which means "white track." White clovers were considered to be protective against evil, and particularly effective if they had four leaves rather than three, with the added bonus of bringing good luck and the ability to see faeries. An extremely rare five-leaf clover was said to bring riches for life.

Considering the happy marriage of Olwen to Kilhwch, it is not surprising to see marriage folk charms connected with the white clover. Putting a four-leaf clover in your lover's shoe was said to ensure fidelity. Dreaming of clover meant a happy marriage if the girl could find a two-leaved clover afterwards—and recite the following charm whilst picking it:

A clover, a clover of two,
Put it in your right shoe.
The first young man you meet
In field, street, or lane,
You'll have him or one of his name!

Farmers always sought fields where clovers grew, as it was believed they would produce better milk and butter, and also that the flowers would protect the cows and their produce from enchantment by faeries or Witches.

Wood Anemone

Olwen's hands are likened to the wood anemone: "Fairer were her hands and fingers than the blossoms of the wood anemone amidst the spray of the meadow fountain." Wood anemone is one of the first flowers to bloom in spring, appearing from late February through May. It has six white petals that are rosy-pink nearer the base of the petal, hence the comparison to Olwen's hands. These flowers are mildly poisonous and should not be used in healing. The plant's association with faeries is partially due to the way the wood anemone closes its petals at night to protect them from morning dew or before rain, which has been described as the faeries "pulling the curtains" around themselves.

Other Arthurian Tales

Some stories included in *The Mabinogion* from the earlier sources have a distinctly Arthurian flavor, with a continental (European) influence. References to King Arthur and his knights can be either as major or minor characters. These tales include "Geraint the Son of Erbin" and "The Dream of Rhonabwy."

Apple

The apple tree appears in the tale "Geraint the Son of Erbin." Geraint, one of King Arthur's knights, goes through many adventures demonstrating his chivalrous nature, including defeating Ederyn ap Nudd, the Sparrowhawk Knight, who is the brother of Gwyn ap Nudd. Edeyrn is described as wearing a blue scarf with a golden apple on each corner, reminiscent of the widespread symbolism of the golden apples of immortality eaten by the gods, and hinting that he too was perhaps once seen as a god.

The apple was one of the most important plants to the Celts, as seen in the description of the apple tree in *Cad Goddeu* (The Battle of the Trees) as "the blessed wild apple, laughing in pride." Apple was the only other tree, apart from the oak, on which mistletoe would grow, and was seen as one of the most important trees of the Celts. It was known as the Silver Bough, as opposed the Golden Bough (oak), showing the lunar associations of the apple against the solar ones of the oak.

The popular folk saying "An apple a day keeps the doctor away" originates in Wales. It used to be said as "Eat an apple on going to bed, and you'll keep the doctor from earning his bread!" Apple blossoms were also placed on coffins prior to burial to ensure eternal youth in the Summerlands for the deceased.

The Welsh also had a curious remedy to encourage barren apple trees to bear fruit. Trees that bore little or no fruit were thought to be male. These trees would be dressed with petticoats and other female attire in an effort to convince the tree that it was really female, encouraging it to be more fruitful!

Holly

Holly boughs are spread on the floor of the hall where Rhonabwy has his dream in "The Dream of Rhonabwy." Rhonabwy and his companions stay in a hall ruled by a hag, and he sleeps on the floor and dreams of a chess game between Owain, son of the goddess Modron, and King Arthur. During the game, Arthur's men initially slay Owain's ravens, but then a raven banner is raised and the ravens kill many of Arthur's men. The dream's symbolism is very much about conflict, perhaps a warning of the troubles that would afflict Arthur and result in the decline of Camelot.

The dream occurring on a holly floor intimates the problems to come in the dream, as in Wales holly is another plant that was not usually brought into the home. In what may be a remnant of old Pagan lore, holly must be cut on Christmas Eve and only removed on Twelfth Night. They believed that doing it in any other combination would bring bad luck to all in the house and also result in heated arguments!

Holly leaves were used in infusions to treat fevers and rheumatism, since they possess tonic and febrifugal (antifever) qualities. By contrast, the berries are violently emetic and should be avoided, as they cause violent vomiting.

The Ogham

It is also interesting to note that four out of the twelve plants mentioned in these tales also form part of the Ogham alphabet. The four—hawthorn, oak, holly, and apple—all form part of the second set (group of five) of the Ogham letters. Thus *huathe* (hawthorn) is the sixth Ogham, *duir* (oak) is the seventh, *tinne* (holly) is the eighth, and *quert* (apple) is the tenth.

Nutty Tales for a Pagan's Hearth

by Nancy Bennett

Nuts, those delicious tree-borne offerings. We roast them, bake them in pies, grind them into flour, and feed them to our livestock. But in the past, Pagans have also used them to foretell the future, to seek knowledge, and to make wishes come true. Our myths abound with stories about nuts and how they came to be, and even about the spirits that protect them! Here are a few "nutty" offerings for you to savor.

Hazelnut/Filbert

Around a magical pool in Ireland there grew nine hazel trees. Their nuts were said to contain great wisdom. When these nuts dropped into the water, they were eaten by a salmon and spots on its skin sprung up for every nut eaten (nine).

This salmon became the Salmon of Knowledge, and it was said that the first person to eat him would turn into the wisest man in the world. The poet Finegas caught him, but, after a long battle, he was too tired to eat him just yet. He set him on a fire and bid his companion Fion (or Finn) to cook him, but not to eat him. Then he lay down. Fion accidently burned his fingers on the fire the salmon was cooking in and licked his thumb to ease the pain. Drops of the salmon's oil had fallen on the fire, and Fion became the wisest of men.

The name filbert comes from the feast day of St. Philbert during late August, when the nuts are harvested. Both filbert and hazelnut are names for the same nut.

An interesting custom comes from the Druids, who would make wishing caps by weaving twigs from the hazel tree into their hair, and then making a wish. They chewed the nuts as well, and inspiration was supposed to come from the consumption of the hazelnut. Halloween also had its relationship with the nut, for it is then, on "nutcrack night," that the hazelnut was used to divine the future.

Pecans

Found only in North America, pecans were known by the tribes who ate them as "paccan," meaning "a nut so hard you must crack it with a stone." In a Caddo Indian legend, two magical pecan nuts were given by the Great Squirrel to the Two Twins. The first twin planted one nut and overnight a tall pecan tree grew. He climbed his tree to receive his vision, instructing his brother not to be afraid.

His bones fell to the ground, but he was not dead. Instead, covered with a buffalo hide and pierced with a magical arrow, he returned, gifted by the Great Spirit. Once he finished the vision, he became thunder. The second boy also climbed the tree for his vision and he became lightning.

They then planted the second magical seed, which grew overnight, and they were able to enter the Land of the Ogres.

The ogres had killed many over the years, including their own mother. Now with their special powers, the twins were able to defeat the ogres and raise the dead from the sacred bones cast aside over the years.

Thomas Jefferson and George Washington planted pecans. Texans love them (butter pecan ice cream is sold in large quantities in that state). However, they are hard to grow, needing about 80 square feet of land per tree and taking a long time to produce a good crop. Is it worth the wait?

Shirley Skidmore, author of the historical novel *Coffin Ship Legacy* thinks so, and sent me this tasty recipe.

"The following has now been handed down to the third generation—maybe it is even older. I have used almonds or walnuts in it when I didn't have pecans—but the pecans are really the best."

Pecan Dreams

½   cup butter
2   tablespoons granulated sugar
1   teaspoon vanilla
1   cup flour
1   cup chopped pecans
     Icing sugar

Cream the sugar and butter. Add the vanilla, flour, and pecans. Roll it into balls and bake at 300 to 325 degrees F in a preheated oven for 25 minutes. While still warm, roll them in icing sugar.

Coconut

Coconut milk for drinking, meat for eating, and husks to make into ropes—the coconut is extremely versatile in its gifts. So important is the coconut to some parts of the world that cultures have associated it with taboos. In Bali, women are not allowed to touch the coconut trees because the fertility of the tree may drain into the female. Among the Maoris, the coconut was associated with the eel-god Tuna. This precious nut sprang from his head after he had been sacrificed. Mourners in the New Hebrides will eat coconut at the funeral of loved ones so they may contact them in the afterlife.

Farmers in Samoa employ the help of a Tapui spirit, who only allows the owner of the tree to collect the nut, while striking down would-be coconut thieves with lightning. The penalty is harsher in the Wanika tribe in Africa—cutting down a coconut tree is a crime equivalent to killing your own mother or father! Mysteriously, the origins of this nut are unknown, for the nuts have floated on oceans and taken root in many distant lands.

Cashews

The cashew nut is, according to Indian legend, a source of super power and strength. Anyone who has watched a harvest can see why! The people of Belize believe that the cashew tree was the only tree invented by the devil, as the devil in his haste left the seeds outside the fruit.

Botanists in the sixteenth century named the cashew "elephant lause" for the nut's resemblance to the trunk of an elephant. Ganesh, the Elephant God, is celebrated in India with large idols decorated with coins, pearls, flowers, almonds, and cashew nuts.

Though the cashew is grown in some of the world's poorest regions, North Americans pay the heftiest cost and consume more than 90 percent of the yearly crop. Great care must be taken in preparing the cashew after harvest, for between its two shells is a toxic inner membrane. Cashews are an indulgent, sweet-tasting nut high in iron and vitamins D and B1. Check out this great nutburger recipe (below), c/o Jessica North O'Connell of the Equinox Cafe and Catering, 79 Station St., B.C.

Nutburger

A vegetarian delight. For the burger mix, you'll need: 1 cup raw cashews, 1⅔ cup large flake oats, and 1 teaspoon turmeric. Salt and pepper to taste.

Put the ingredients into a food processor and blend until you have a medium-fine meal. You can store this in an air-tight container until you want to make a burger. When ready to cook, take ⅔ cup of mix and add to it 1 egg, ¼ onion chopped fine, and enough oil to shape the mixure into a patty. Fry until it's browned on both sides—it doesn't take long at all. Serve it on your favorite bun or bread with homemade mayo, Dijon mustard, lettuce, tomato, zucchini relish, or chutney and a nice baby greens salad on the side. Absolutely delicious! Turmeric is an anticancer agent and gives the burger a nice color. You can also add a bit of cumin to it to enhance the flavor.

Walnuts

The Romans thought this nut was associated with the brain because of its wrinkly and round appearance. Caryon was the name the Greeks gave it, from the word *kara*, which meant head. The name Carya also is associated with the walnut.

In Greek myth, the god Dionysus fell in love with a king's daughter named Carya. Her sisters tried to keep her away from him, but Dionysus cursed them with madness. When Carya died, Dionysus changed her into a walnut tree as a sign of their love. Earlier in history, the walnut was also apparently part of the culture. Fossils of walnuts have been found in the Swiss lake homes of neolithic man, dating back over 8,000 years.

People have found a wide range of mystical, ritualistic uses of the walnut over the course of time. If you wanted to avoid fever, you could always carry a spider in a walnut shell for protection. Walnuts can also mark you. If you lived among the ancient Goths and committed a crime, you could be condemned to have your hair dyed black from walnut shells. On Midsummer Eve, if you journey to Bologna, you might find Witches meeting under walnut trees, as they were reported to do long ago, feasting, no doubt, on this brainy nut.

Almonds

The Greeks tell of the princess Phyllis, whose wedding day was not successful when her intended, Demophon, did not show. It was not his fault, as his boat had been damaged on the way home from the Trojan War. Phyllis did not know this and waited a long time for him to return, finally dying of a broken heart. The gods, seeing her sacrifice, turned her into an almond tree.

When Demonphon finally returned, he heard the story and, with a remorseful heart, embraced the tree. Suddenly the tree burst into white flowers as a symbol of love. Almonds ever since have had a place at weddings and christenings as tokens of good luck. The Portugese believe that almonds first came to their land when a Scandinavian princess was pining for her snow-covered homeland. Her husband, a Moor, had the land planted with almond trees whose white flowers in the spring looked like the snow-covered fields of her homeland. Egyptians used it for oil (still do today), as did the Chinese. The oil is so fine, watch repairmen use it to lubricate delicate workings.

A New Year's tradition involves baking a cake with a single whole almond in it. Whoever is served the slice with the almond is blessed with good fortune for the whole year.

However you serve them up, nuts remain a delicious part of our culinary history. Next time you crack one open, ponder a bit on our nutty past, and maybe you will grow as wise as Fion!

A History of Winter Herbs

≈ by Sally McSweeney ≈

As the great wheel of the year turns toward the long, dark time of winter, the days grow shorter as we move toward the Winter Solstice, the fields lie still around us, and in the garden, everything sleeps. Not so within the house as we prepare for the festivals of the season, the highlight of this otherwise bleak and seemingly endless time that caused our ancestors to fear that the Sun may not return.

As a child, it seemed that the air was heavy with aromas: spicy puddings, sweet cookies, and the sharp pine of the decorative greenery. Remembered too are the scents of the medicine cabinet, especially the eucalyptus and camphor used to relieve stuffy noses and congested chests. These traditional herbs of winter all have fascinating histories and many uses.

Eucalyptus

Eucalyptus (*E. globulus*) was first written about in 1642 by the explorer Abel Janszoon Tasman after he he observed gum oozing from some tree trunks on the island of Tasmania (named after him). In 1770, Captain James Cook arrived in Botany Bay and referred to similar trees as "Gum Dragon." The name eucalyptus was given by botanist Charles Louis L'Heritier de Brutelle in the 1790s: "eu" meaning "well" and "kalyptos" meaning "I cover." The word *cover* refers to the lidlike structure that covers the flower until it blooms. Baron von Mueller, the German botanist for Queen Victoria from 1879 to 1884, published *Eucalyptographia*. Von Mueller's huge 10-volume work identifying 100 eucalyptus species was the first work about eucalyptus read by the public. There are now more than 500 species of eucalyptus growing in Australia, and it has been grown on every other continent (aside from Antarctica). Huge groves of eucalyptus were planted by Ellwood Cooper in California in the 1870s; his book *Forest Culture and Eucalyptus Trees* provided information on how to promote its growth in the state. Over the next 100 years, the California Board of Forestry and private landowners planted hundreds more acres.

Eucalyptus is also known as "blue gum," "curly mallee," and "stringy bark." The leaves are most famous as the staple for the lovable koala bear, while the gum provides a natural protection against harmful insects, which get stuck in it and drown. The fast-growing hardwood tree has been used for buildings, as windbreaks, and as fuel, while its oil has been used for medicines and body products. It corresponds to the Moon and is used for protection, purification, and health. Add leaves to sachets or sprinkle around your home for protection; sprinkle around a blue candle in healing rituals. Place a few drops of oil in a pan of water and simmer gently on the stove to purify the home both physically and spiritually. Fresh eucalyptus makes wonderfully scented wreaths and swags, which are especially striking when hung with tiny oranges and strings of fresh cranberries.

Bayberry

"A bayberry candle burned to the socket, puts food on the table and gold in the pocket," claims an early Germanic poem. True or not, bayberry (*Myrica cerifera*) certainly does lend itself to making aromatic and virtually smokeless candles. Because of this, it is also known as "wax myrtle," "tallow shrub," and "candleberry." When the berries are boiled, the wax floats to the top and can be skimmed off. On the eve of the Winter Solstice, inscribe a bayberry candle with dollar signs, light it, and say the poem to bring prosperity in the coming year.

This evergreen shrub is found in Japan, South America, the West Indies, along the east coast of North America, and in the Great Lakes. In the United States, the leaves of native species were boiled into a decoction against fevers by the Choctaw Indians. When crushed, the leaves give off a pleasant scent, but taste very bitter. Myrtle wax was first used in Louisiana in the 1600s. The berries were boiled and the waxy water taken to treat severe cases of dysentery. In 1722, bayberry was first documented for medicinal use, which included recipes for making shaving soap, as it was gentler on the skin than lye soap.

Mistletoe

At the Roman winter feast of Saturnalia, couples would pluck a berry and kiss; when the berries were gone, the kissing ended. In Scandinavia, mistletoe was used to denote peace; warring enemies could declare a truce and quarreling couples could kiss and make up. Elsewhere, mistletoe was used to welcome in the new year, ward off evil, and promote peace. A sprig hung over a baby's cradle could stop fairies from taking the child. Similarly, hanging sprigs above stalls protected animals and prevented house fires. A ring made of mistletoe stems warded off illness. The venerable Pliny claimed it was a cure for epilepsy; as it grew on a tree and did not touch the ground, neither would a sufferer fall to the ground in a fit if he carried some with him or drank an infusion.

Cloves and Cinnamon

Winter is synonymous with cozy kitchens and enticing smells, none more inviting than that of cloves and cinnamon. It's almost unheard of to make seasonal favorites without these spices—cookies, cakes, apple pies, stewed fruits, and of course the ubiquitous cup of hot chocolate. Tie bunches of cinnamon sticks together with raffia and add them to garlands and wreaths, or stud oranges with cloves as pomanders. Cloves (genus *Eugenia*, species *E. caryophyllata*, *syzygium aromaticum*) are native to the Indonesian Molucca Islands, where a clove tree was once planted at the birth of every child. They are also cultivated in Zanzibar, Brazil, Madagascar, and Sri Lanka. The word clove is from the Latin clavus, meaning "nail" and reflects this shape. The first references to cloves are found in the Han Dynasty (207 BC to 220 AD) in China under the name "chicken-tongue spice." Court visitors to the emperor kept cloves in their mouths when speaking to him so he was not offended by bad breath. Cloves were very costly, and wars were fought to maintain rights to successful clove businesses.

Cloves are extremely aromatic; their scent is warm and sweet. Best bought whole, they can be powdered, but the flavor soon deteriorates. According to folklore, sucking on two whole cloves without chewing or swallowing them helps curb the desire for alcohol. They were thought to have magical properties such as banishing negativity, stopping gossip, and promoting love. Carry some cloves in your pocket and it will never be empty of money. Sew some into a heart-shaped sachet and your heart will never want for love. Burned as incense, they produce positive spiritual vibrations and purify the area. Cloves are also well known for their culinary uses, and at this time of year they are added to mixes known as mulling spices. In medieval times, "mulling" was the heating and spicing of wine known as Ypocras or Hipocris, named after Hippocrates. The wine was heated in a pot over a fire or by plunging a hot poker into the filled cup. Make your own mulling spices by mixing cloves with cinnamon, dried apple, orange peel, star anise, allspice, nutmeg, and wild cherry bark. Whole cloves can also be used to stud meats such as pork, ham, and beef; stud an onion and add it to soups and stocks.

Cinnamon (*Cinnamomum zeylanicum*) is native to Sri Lanka and comes from the bark of an evergreen tree. Most cinnamon used in North America is from the cassia tree of Vietnam, China, Indonesia, and Central America and is inferior to "true" cinnamon. When the bark is harvested, it is tightly rolled into "quills." Like cloves, cinnamon has ancient roots, mentioned in Chinese writings from 2800 BC and used by the Egyptians in embalming. Empires were literally built on cinnamon trade and it was once accepted as currency; the Arabs kept it a closely guarded secret until they brought it to the West. It is mentioned several times in the Bible, as the Hebrews used it in holy anointing oils. Known as "sweet wood" to the Romans, who believed it sacred, Nero burnt a whole year's supply at his wife's funeral. When cinnamon came to the West, the trade was controlled by the Dutch until 1776 when it was finally cultivated. In folklore, it was used to raise spiritual vibrations and stimulate psychic powers. Sprinkle powdered cinnamon around your property for protection or carry some on you. Cinnamon has long been linked with prosperity; at the first New Moon after Yule, place a silver coin and a piece of citrine in a white pouch. Sprinkle a ring of cinnamon around a lit white candle, and say:

Glistening silver, coin of the Moon,
Shiny and round, bring me a boon.
Spice of fire, sacred sweet wood,
Bring to me, all that is good.

Frankincense and Myrrh

What winter season would be complete without frankincense and myrrh? Although they come in the form of resin, they are still considered herbs because they originate from small trees. Frankincense (*sp Boswellia*) is collected from an incision made in the bark, from which the oleo-resin flows and hardens. It is scraped off in the form of yellow pieces known as "tears." Mostly known to us from the story of the gifts of the Magi to Jesus, it has a history far before this time. The Boswellia species is found in limited areas of Africa; because of this, early demand exceeded output and so the price of frankincense rose higher than gold. Increased trade routes in 1100 BC enabled frankincense to be traded further afield, to places such as Egypt, India, China, Greece, and Rome, and by 200 AD, 3,000 tons were shipped per year. Herodotus, an Ionian traveler and storyteller of the fifth century BC, wrote that 1,000 talents (30,000 kg) were offered as a sacrifice to the god Bel every year. The Arabs called it al lubán, meaning "milk," which became olibanum, another name by which it is now known. Frankincense was popular in all areas as a temple incense, but was also burned in Greek and Roman homes on braziers. The Egyptians used it for embalming, and on the tomb of queen Hatshepsut (1500 BC) was inscribed how it was burned and the charred remains used to make kohl, the black eyeliner popular at the time.

Today in Oman, frankincense is used to show hospitality to guests. Burners are passed around so that the visitors can be enveloped in the sweet smoke. The people use every part of the tree for various purposes; they chew the tears or leaves to relieve heartburn and the bark for morning sickness, and the fruit and flowers are given to goats to strengthen them during lactation. As a beauty aid, the underbark is smoothed over dry skin (especially the hands) and the resin is burned to form a soot used in tattooing and cosmetics. As a purification incense, frankincense can be burned on charcoal as the new year approaches, banishing the old.

Myrrh (*Commiphora myrrha*) is also an oleo-gum resin from trees growing in Arabia and Somalia. It is red-brown in color when hardened and took its name from the Hebrew word murr, meaning "bitter." It too was one of the gifts of the Magi and used by many ancient cultures in religious ceremonies. When Greek soldiers went to war, they carried it with them as a healing agent; its antiseptic properties helped prevent infection of wounds. In Rome it was valued even more highly than frankincense, even though it was not as popular. The scent is not as sweet and can be overpowering, producing a heavy, sharp smoke—hence its use as a fumigator at funerals to mask the smell of the burning bodies! Due to this highly pungent aroma, myrrh was used to consecrate and purify ritual objects and to heighten spiritual awareness.

Pine ('Tis the Season)

The pine tree is not an herb but deserves mention, as this beloved evergreen perhaps embodies the spirit of winter most of all. In ancient Mesopotamia, beribboned branches were carried in procession in honor of the gods and goddesses of fertility and life. Pine trees were sacred to Zeus in Greek legend and the Celts called them "Bele Trees" or "Billy Glas," which meant evergreen or immortal. In Rome, boughs were hung with masks and flowers in honor of Bacchus, the god of wine. The first written record of a decorated pine tree is from Latvia in 1510. Adorned with paper flowers, it was set ablaze while the people danced around it. In 1747 in Bethlehem, Pennsylvania, a wooden frame covered with evergreen boughs was the first Christmas "tree" in the United States. Queen Victoria's husband, Albert, introduced the concept of glass-blown ornaments in 1841, but originally pine trees were decorated with fruits, nuts, and berries, all symbols of fertility as is the pine cone itself. Pine cones appeared on many ancient amulets and was often seen carved into bedposts! At the festival of Demeter in Greece, pine cones were offered "for the purpose of quickening the ground and the wombs of women." In Siberia, pine groves known as "shaman forests" were ridden through in silence so as not to offend the gods, and solitary pines were adorned with ribbons and sheepskins at midwinter. On the Epiphany (January 6), crosses were made over every door with the smoke of pine torchwood to protect houses and stables from evil spirits. Today some Russian Orthodox priests and house-wives use pine-scented tapers for this purpose.

As we bundle up in woolen coats and fur-lined boots, hats and knitted scarves to keep the biting wind and ice-laden snow at bay, we may find ourselves wishing that winter would soon pass. Yet if we take the time to enjoy these herbal gifts of the season in the ways of our ancestors, we are reminded of the magic of this dark time. At the traditional end of winter on February 1, Imbolc Eve, although the snow may still lie on the ground, take a pine bough to the front door and sweep out the last vestiges of winter, knowing that the wheel will bring the spring once more.

Literary Concoctions

⋙ by Cerridwen Iris Shea ⋘

There's rosemary, that's for remembrance.
Pray you, love, remember.
And there is pansies, that's for thoughts . . .
There's fennel for you, and columbines.
There's rue for you,
            and here's some for me.
We may call it herb of grace o' Sundays.
O, you must wear your rue
            with a difference.
There's a daisy.
I would give you some violets,
But they withered all when my
            father died.

—Ophelia, from *Hamlet*, act IV,
scene V

The above quote from Shakespeare's *Hamlet* immediately leaps to mind when the topic of herbs in literature comes up, but hundreds of books deal with them, both in mainstream and in "Wiccan fiction." Susan Wittig Albert, Diana Gabaldon, and even J.K. Rowling use herbs and references to herbs in their fiction.

It makes sense, especially in historical fiction. When the story is set in a time before modern medicine, or at the dawn of the brutality that turned into modern medicine, or if the lead character is a time traveler, people get sick and there are those who know how to alleviate some of the illness and suffering with herbs. The writer has to do the research to make sure the information is correct; the reader needs to believe it.

For instance, in Rowling's *Harry Potter and the Goblet of Fire*, Harry uses gillyweed in order to "grow" gills and breathe underwater for an hour to complete one of the tasks in the Triwizard Tournament. Gillyweed is a fictional herb, but is very real in the world of the Potter books. Rowling created a context for the fictional herb so it's rational and believable within that magical world. She uses young mandrakes as the antidote for the petrifying potion in *Harry Potter and the Chamber of Secrets*. Mandrake is an herb used in our reality, and, in some cases, it's considered to be fairly human-shaped and to scream when pulled from the ground. Rowling stayed with reality in the screaming and pushed the animated imagery of the root in the book. However, in her story, she uses it as an antidote, whereas its historical use is as an aphrodisiac. Here, she took the basis of an actual herb and transformed its meaning to fit her story.

Many books in Susan Wittig Albert's series featuring China Bayles are named for herbs (*Rueful Death, Rosemary Remembered, Mistletoe Man, Witches' Bane, Thyme of Death*). China Bayles is an ex-lawyer who opens an herbal shop in a small Texas town and solves crimes, often herb-related. In addition to writing interesting characters and strong plots and subplots, Albert's research is solid and the herbal information is good. In fact, it's so solid that Albert published (in October of 2006) *China Bayles's Book of Days: 365 Celebrations of the Mystery, Myth, and Magic of Herbs from the World of Pecan Springs*. She's expanded the website she shares with her husband and fellow author, Bill Albert, to include herbal lore and growing tips.

Diana Gabaldon, author of the *Outlander* series, finds one of the most useful sources of research to be *A Modern Herbal* by Mrs. M. Grieve (although she admits to owning fifty to sixty herbals she's gathered during the research of her books). She finds that the subtitle, "The Medicinal, Culinary, Cosmetic and Economic Properties, Cultivation and Folk-Lore of Herbs, Grasses, Fungi, Shrubs & Trees with Their Modern Scientific Uses," says it all. Gabaldon explained to me, "This contains vast amounts of historical information, chemical information on the active principles of each plant, and a fair amount of information on cultivation—which is important if you're writing historical fiction, because you have to make sure that when you mention a particular herb, it's possible for said herb to have been there (e.g., if it didn't naturally grow in, say, the American South at the time, but was found in China, you could still use it in Charleston, but would have to make a song-and-dance about a character getting it from an English importer, and how terrifically rare and expensive it was, etc.)."

We are a pill-dependent society. At the first sneeze, most people run to the doctor for a prescription. Most medications are chemically based (rather than naturally based) and often serve to cover or hide symptoms instead of working with the body's rhythms to heal. Sometimes this is necessary; however, as we become more and more aware of the need to eat organically and healthily, and rediscover the ways that herbal medicine can be used in tandem with Western medicine, interest in the old herbals flourishes.

Herbs are mysterious. They are living beings. As such, the use or misuse of their life force breeds fascination. When they were commonly used, there were "wise women"—"wise people" perhaps is a better term. Those with knowledge trained the younger generation. If a doctor was a three-day ride away and something happened, you'd better have a strong knowledge of local herbs and remedies to keep your family alive until medical care arrived. And you had better know the difference between something useful and something poisonous. There's a reason some remedies have been used for centuries—they work. The ignorant, then as now, were always fearful of the knowledgeable, which often led to false accusations of witchcraft. Little has changed through the centuries, although in modern times ignorance has become a choice.

For those who do not choose ignorance, reading fiction about herbs and their use is pleasurable—informative as well as entertaining. Of course, you don't simply brew up a concoction just because it's in a book. You have to double and triple check with a reliable health care professional or a reliable herbalist before you ingest anything. Agatha Christie used a great many poisons in her books. However, she was also a meticulous researcher, and the use of poisons in her work was authentic to the knowledge of the day. She worked as a nurse, and later in a hospital dispensary. Her very first novel, *The Mysterious Affair at Styles*, with its nurse character Evelyn Howard and three other characters, respectively a doctor, a dispensing chemist, and a toxicologist, uses Christie's working knowledge.

World-building authors can create herbs and uses natural to their worlds. But they have to be believable in context. Often, these herbs are inspired by plants with which we're familiar in our own world, but they're given a different name or a different usage (again, using the *Harry Potter* books as examples). Then there are authors who don't bother to research the actual properties of the herbs about which they write. If they need a quick way to do away with someone, they feed them an herb. If they want to scare the reader, they create a "Witch"—with no knowledge of working witchcraft or herbalism, or even basic botany. The stereotype is enough to get the effect, so why bother with research? They're writing fiction—they can make it up. They figure enough people don't know enough about herbs and they can get away with it. Of course, the publisher also puts a disclaimer in the book, basically stating "if you're dumb enough to eat this, it's not our fault," and everyone is home free. Do your own research and don't be stupid. Find out if it's actually ingestible. It is your responsibility.

But in fiction, which comes first? The herb or the story? In my own writing, I generally have my plot and subplot ideas worked out and then I go through my herbals to find the correct herbs to fit the plot. During research, I make note of interesting tangents and herbal lore that I think might come in handy later or in future stories. In my serial, *Angel Hunt*, when the two teenage boys come into the occult store looking for a poisonous herb that goes by more than one name—and they haven't done their research, only read about it in a book written by a charlatan—I wanted to point out the dangers of not knowing what you put in your potions. Lianna, the series' protagonist, gives them a stern talking-to and quite possibly saves their lives. Being teenaged boys, they still go out and get the poison from another source, but they know it's poisonous and handle it with more caution than they would have otherwise. And, when the spell goes awry, of course, they have to return to Lianna for help. When I wrote the outline of that arc of episodes, I knew I wanted to address the importance of not trusting a spell you don't understand—especially spells written by someone else or when you don't know the background—simply because it's written in a book. Only by digging deeper into the research of poisonous herbs did I realize the herb I wanted to use in this particular fictional spell went under two fairly well-known names. In that case, the development of the story happened somewhat in tandem.

Diana Gabaldon agrees. "For me, the research and the writing are done concurrently, and they sort of feed off each other. I'll begin by looking for something specific that I need—but in the process, I invariably discover all kinds of other things I wouldn't even have thought of looking for, which in turn either fit neatly into scenes and subplots I already have going, or which trigger new ones." Her novel *Dragonfly in Amber* comes most readily to mind, with both its use of black hellebore in one plot twist and madder-root in another. Furthermore, she adds, "There's also a continuing thread through several of the books which deals with penicillin (which is, or course, an herbal medicine, insofar as it is the natural extract of a bread mold—which technically belongs to the plant kingdom, or did, back when I was learning taxonomy, back in the Dark Ages), a (modern, time-traveling) character's knowledge of and need for it, her attempts to manufacture it under very primitive conditions, and the complications (such as the anaphylactic death of one of her patients) that ensue during her assorted uses of it."

The process in which the herbs create their place in the story is just as interesting as the final story. Hopefully, when a reader is enthralled and enticed by a good piece of "herbal fiction," interest is sparked enough that the reader will start researching and exploring the actual herbs—perhaps even putting some in the garden. Especially now, when the genetic greenhouse growers are in conflict with the organic heirloom growers, individual research and knowledge is important. I believe that emotional truth is often easier to communicate in fiction than in nonfiction. Stewardship of the planet can be just as easily provoked by a good story as by someone standing on a soapbox trying to guilt others into taking action. I started reading the China Bayles mysteries early in my training in the craft. On days when I felt as though I was never going to be able to remember all the herbal studies, taking a break to read those mysteries and seeing the use of herbs in context made it much easier for me to go back to my studies. When I discovered that Albert's usage was well-researched and correct, it made both the studies and the recreational reading even more enjoyable. They fed off each other.

The next time you pick up a novel, take notice of the usage of herbs, if any. Do you find the usage believable? Correct? Does it make you want to learn more? Enjoy this additional aspect to your reading—the experience of the "literary herb."

For Further Reading

Albert, Susan Wittig. *China Bayles' Book of Days*. New York: Penguin Group, 2006.

Beyerl, Paul. *The Master Book of Herbalism*. Custer, WA: Phoenix Publishing, 1984.

Christie, Agatha. *The Mysterious Affair at Styles*. New York: Berkley (reprint), 2004.

Gabaldon, Diana. www.dianagabaldon.com. Website for author, including information on the Outlander series, Lord John books, her anthologies, and non-fiction.

———*Dragonfly in Amber*. New York: Delacorte Press, 1992. Second book in the Outlander series.

———*The Outlandish Companion*. New York: Delacorte Press, 1999. A companion volume to the Outlander series, it has 600 or so of the books she used in researching the first four books.

Gill, Gillian. *Agatha Christie: The Woman and Her Mysteries*. New York: Free Press, 1990.

Grieve, M. *A Modern Herbal*. New York: Harcourt Brace,1931; reprinted by Dover, 1971.

www.mysterypartners.com. Website of Susan Wittig Albert and her husband Bill Albert, with links to her China Bayles series, herbal pages, and links to the new series featuring Beatrix Potter as detective, and the Victorian mystery series she and her husband write as Robin Paige.

Shakespeare, William. *Hamlet*. Various editions. Public domain.

The
Quarters and
Signs of the
Moon and
Moon
Tables

The Quarters and Signs
of the Moon

Everyone has seen the Moon wax and wane through a period of approximately twenty-nine-and-a-half days. This circuit from New Moon to Full Moon and back again is called the lunation cycle. The cycle is divided into parts called quarters or phases. There are several methods by which this can be done, and the system used in the *Herbal Almanac* may not correspond to those used in other almanacs.

The Quarters
First Quarter

The first quarter begins at the New Moon, when the Sun and Moon are in the same place, or conjunct. (This means that the Sun and Moon are in the same degree of the same sign.) The Moon is not visible at first, since it rises at the same time as the Sun. The New Moon is the time of new beginnings, beginnings of projects that favor growth, externalization of activities, and the growth of ideas. The first quarter is the time of germination, emergence, beginnings, and outwardly directed activity.

Second Quarter

The second quarter begins halfway between the New Moon and the Full Moon, when the Sun and Moon are at right angles, or a ninety-degree square to each other. This half Moon rises around noon and sets around midnight, so it can be seen in the western sky during the first half of the night. The second quarter is the time of growth and articulation of things that already exist.

Third Quarter

The third quarter begins at the Full Moon, when the Sun and Moon are opposite one another and the full light of the Sun can shine on the full sphere of the Moon. The round Moon can be seen rising in the east at sunset, and then rising a little later each evening. The Full Moon stands for illumination, fulfillment, culmination, completion, drawing inward, unrest, emotional expressions, and hasty actions leading to failure. The third quarter is a time of maturity, fruition, and the assumption of the full form of expression.

Fourth Quarter

The fourth quarter begins about halfway between the Full Moon and New Moon, when the Sun and Moon are again at ninety degrees, or square. This decreasing Moon rises at midnight and can be seen in the east during the last half of the night, reaching the overhead position just about as the Sun rises. The fourth quarter is a time of disintegration and drawing back for reorganization and reflection.

The Signs

Moon in Aries

Moon in Aries is good for starting things, but lacking in staying power. Things occur rapidly, but also quickly pass.

Moon in Taurus

With Moon in Taurus, things begun during this sign last the longest and tend to increase in value. Things begun now become habitual and hard to alter.

Moon in Gemini

Moon in Gemini is an inconsistent position for the Moon, characterized by a lot of talk. Things begun now are easily changed by outside influences.

Moon in Cancer

Moon in Cancer stimulates emotional rapport between people. It pinpoints need and supports growth and nurturance.

Moon in Leo

Moon in Leo accents showmanship, being seen, drama, recreation, and happy pursuits. It may be concerned with praise and subject to flattery.

Moon in Virgo

Moon in Virgo favors accomplishment of details and commands from higher up, while discouraging independent thinking.

Moon in Libra

Moon in Libra increases self-awareness. It favors self-examination and interaction with others, but discourages spontaneous initiative.

Moon in Scorpio

Moon in Scorpio increases awareness of psychic power. It precipitates psychic crises and ends connections thoroughly.

Moon in Sagittarius

Moon in Sagittarius encourages expansionary flights of imagination and confidence in the flow of life.

Moon in Capricorn

Moon in Capricorn increases awareness of the need for structure, discipline, and organization. Institutional activities are favored.

Moon in Aquarius

Moon in Aquarius favors activities that are unique and individualistic, concern for humanitarian needs and society as a whole, and improvements that can be made.

Moon in Pisces

During Moon in Pisces, energy withdraws from the surface of life and hibernates within, secretly reorganizing and realigning.

January Moon Table

Date	Sign	Element	Nature	Phase
1 Tue 8:32 pm	Scorpio	Water	Fruitful	4th
2 Wed	Scorpio	Water	Fruitful	4th
3 Thu	Scorpio	Water	Fruitful	4th
4 Fri 9:13 am	Sagittarius	Fire	Barren	4th
5 Sat	Sagittarius	Fire	Barren	4th
6 Sun 8:43 pm	Capricorn	Earth	Semi-fruitful	4th
7 Mon	Capricorn	Earth	Semi-fruitful	4th
8 Tue	Capricorn	Earth	Semi-fruitful	New 6:37 am
9 Wed 6:13 am	Aquarius	Air	Barren	1st
10 Thu	Aquarius	Air	Barren	1st
11 Fri 1:44 pm	Pisces	Water	Fruitful	1st
12 Sat	Pisces	Water	Fruitful	1st
13 Sun 7:23 pm	Aries	Fire	Barren	1st
14 Mon	Aries	Fire	Barren	1st
15 Tue 11:13 pm	Taurus	Earth	Semi-fruitful	2nd 2:46 pm
16 Wed	Taurus	Earth	Semi-fruitful	2nd
17 Thu	Taurus	Earth	Semi-fruitful	2nd
18 Fri 1:30 am	Gemini	Air	Barren	2nd
19 Sat	Gemini	Air	Barren	2nd
20 Sun 3:05 am	Cancer	Water	Fruitful	2nd
21 Mon	Cancer	Water	Fruitful	2nd
22 Tue 5:20 am	Leo	Fire	Barren	Full 8:35 am
23 Wed	Leo	Fire	Barren	3rd
24 Thu 9:48 am	Virgo	Earth	Barren	3rd
25 Fri	Virgo	Earth	Barren	3rd
26 Sat 5:35 pm	Libra	Air	Semi-fruitful	3rd
27 Sun	Libra	Air	Semi-fruitful	3rd
28 Mon	Libra	Air	Semi-fruitful	3rd
29 Tue 4:35 am	Scorpio	Water	Fruitful	3rd
30 Wed	Scorpio	Water	Fruitful	4th 12:03 am
31 Thu 5:08 pm	Sagittarius	Fire	Barren	4th

February Moon Table

Date	Sign	Element	Nature	Phase
1 Fri	Sagittarius	Fire	Barren	4th
2 Sat	Sagittarius	Fire	Barren	4th
3 Sun 4:52 am	Capricorn	Earth	Semi-fruitful	4th
4 Mon	Capricorn	Earth	Semi-fruitful	4th
5 Tue 2:10 pm	Aquarius	Air	Barren	4th
6 Wed	Aquarius	Air	Barren	New 10:44 pm
7 Thu 8:46 pm	Pisces	Water	Fruitful	1st
8 Fri	Pisces	Water	Fruitful	1st
9 Sat	Pisces	Water	Fruitful	1st
10 Sun 1:17 am	Aries	Fire	Barren	1st
11 Mon	Aries	Fire	Barren	1st
12 Tue 4:34 am	Taurus	Earth	Semi-fruitful	1st
13 Wed	Taurus	Earth	Semi-fruitful	2nd 10:33 pm
14 Thu 7:19 am	Gemini	Air	Barren	2nd
15 Fri	Gemini	Air	Barren	2nd
16 Sat 10:12 am	Cancer	Water	Fruitful	2nd
17 Sun	Cancer	Water	Fruitful	2nd
18 Mon 1:51 pm	Leo	Fire	Barren	2nd
19 Tue	Leo	Fire	Barren	2nd
20 Wed 7:06 pm	Virgo	Earth	Barren	Full 10:30 pm
21 Thu	Virgo	Earth	Barren	3rd
22 Fri	Virgo	Earth	Barren	3rd
23 Sat 2:44 am	Libra	Air	Semi-fruitful	3rd
24 Sun	Libra	Air	Semi-fruitful	3rd
25 Mon 1:05 pm	Scorpio	Water	Fruitful	3rd
26 Tue	Scorpio	Water	Fruitful	3rd
27 Wed	Scorpio	Water	Fruitful	3rd
28 Thu 1:22 am	Sagittarius	Fire	Barren	4th 9:18 pm
29 Fri	Sagittarius	Fire	Barren	4th

March Moon Table

Date	Sign	Element	Nature	Phase
1 Sat 1:33 pm	Capricorn	Earth	Semi-fruitful	4th
2 Sun	Capricorn	Earth	Semi-fruitful	4th
3 Mon 11:24 pm	Aquarius	Air	Barren	4th
4 Tue	Aquarius	Air	Barren	4th
5 Wed	Aquarius	Air	Barren	4th
6 Thu 5:53 am	Pisces	Water	Fruitful	4th
7 Fri	Pisces	Water	Fruitful	New 12:14 pm
8 Sat 9:23 am	Aries	Fire	Barren	1st
9 Sun	Aries	Fire	Barren	1st
10 Mon 12:13 pm	Taurus	Earth	Semi-fruitful	1st
11 Tue	Taurus	Earth	Semi-fruitful	1st
12 Wed 1:54 pm	Gemini	Air	Barren	1st
13 Thu	Gemini	Air	Barren	1st
14 Fri 4:37 pm	Cancer	Water	Fruitful	2nd 6:45 am
15 Sat	Cancer	Water	Fruitful	2nd
16 Sun 9:04 pm	Leo	Fire	Barren	2nd
17 Mon	Leo	Fire	Barren	2nd
18 Tue	Leo	Fire	Barren	2nd
19 Wed 3:25 am	Virgo	Earth	Barren	2nd
20 Thu	Virgo	Earth	Barren	2nd
21 Fri 11:45 am	Libra	Air	Semi-fruitful	Full 2:40 pm
22 Sat	Libra	Air	Semi-fruitful	3rd
23 Sun 10:06 pm	Scorpio	Water	Fruitful	3rd
24 Mon	Scorpio	Water	Fruitful	3rd
25 Tue	Scorpio	Water	Fruitful	3rd
26 Wed 10:11 am	Sagittarius	Fire	Barren	3rd
27 Thu	Sagittarius	Fire	Barren	3rd
28 Fri 10:43 pm	Capricorn	Earth	Semi-fruitful	3rd
29 Sat	Capricorn	Earth	Semi-fruitful	4th 5:47 pm
30 Sun	Capricorn	Earth	Semi-fruitful	4th
31 Mon 9:34 am	Aquarius	Air	Barren	4th

April Moon Table

Date	Sign	Element	Nature	Phase
1 Tue	Aquarius	Air	Barren	4th
2 Wed 4:55 pm	Pisces	Water	Fruitful	4th
3 Thu	Pisces	Water	Fruitful	4th
4 Fri 8:27 pm	Aries	Fire	Barren	4th
5 Sat	Aries	Fire	Barren	New 11:55 pm
6 Sun 9:19 pm	Taurus	Earth	Semi-fruitful	1st
7 Mon	Taurus	Earth	Semi-fruitful	1st
8 Tue 9:27 pm	Gemini	Air	Barren	1st
9 Wed	Gemini	Air	Barren	1st
10 Thu 10:43 pm	Cancer	Water	Fruitful	1st
11 Fri	Cancer	Water	Fruitful	1st
12 Sat	Cancer	Water	Fruitful	2nd 2:32 pm
13 Sun 2:29 am	Leo	Fire	Barren	2nd
14 Mon	Leo	Fire	Barren	2nd
15 Tue 9:06 am	Virgo	Earth	Barren	2nd
16 Wed	Virgo	Earth	Barren	2nd
17 Thu 6:10 pm	Libra	Air	Semi-fruitful	2nd
18 Fri	Libra	Air	Semi-fruitful	2nd
19 Sat	Libra	Air	Semi-fruitful	2nd
20 Sun 5:00 am	Scorpio	Water	Fruitful	Full 6:25 am
21 Mon	Scorpio	Water	Fruitful	3rd
22 Tue 5:07 pm	Sagittarius	Fire	Barren	3rd
23 Wed	Sagittarius	Fire	Barren	3rd
24 Thu	Sagittarius	Fire	Barren	3rd
25 Fri 5:47 am	Capricorn	Earth	Semi-fruitful	3rd
26 Sat	Capricorn	Earth	Semi-fruitful	3rd
27 Sun 5:27 pm	Aquarius	Air	Barren	3rd
28 Mon	Aquarius	Air	Barren	4th 10:12 am
29 Tue	Aquarius	Air	Barren	4th
30 Wed 2:11 am	Pisces	Water	Fruitful	4th

May Moon Table

Date	Sign	Element	Nature	Phase
1 Thu	Pisces	Water	Fruitful	4th
2 Fri 6:51 am	Aries	Fire	Barren	4th
3 Sat	Aries	Fire	Barren	4th
4 Sun 7:58 am	Taurus	Earth	Semi-fruitful	4th
5 Mon	Taurus	Earth	Semi-fruitful	New 8:18 am
6 Tue 7:17 am	Gemini	Air	Barren	1st
7 Wed	Gemini	Air	Barren	1st
8 Thu 7:02 am	Cancer	Water	Fruitful	1st
9 Fri	Cancer	Water	Fruitful	1st
10 Sat 9:10 am	Leo	Fire	Barren	1st
11 Sun	Leo	Fire	Barren	2nd 11:47 pm
12 Mon 2:48 pm	Virgo	Earth	Barren	2nd
13 Tue	Virgo	Earth	Barren	2nd
14 Wed 11:46 pm	Libra	Air	Semi-fruitful	2nd
15 Thu	Libra	Air	Semi-fruitful	2nd
16 Fri	Libra	Air	Semi-fruitful	2nd
17 Sat 10:59 am	Scorpio	Water	Fruitful	2nd
18 Sun	Scorpio	Water	Fruitful	2nd
19 Mon 11:18 pm	Sagittarius	Fire	Barren	Full 10:11 pm
20 Tue	Sagittarius	Fire	Barren	3rd
21 Wed	Sagittarius	Fire	Barren	3rd
22 Thu 11:55 am	Capricorn	Earth	Semi-fruitful	3rd
23 Fri	Capricorn	Earth	Semi-fruitful	3rd
24 Sat 11:51 pm	Aquarius	Air	Barren	3rd
25 Sun	Aquarius	Air	Barren	3rd
26 Mon	Aquarius	Air	Barren	3rd
27 Tue 9:38 am	Pisces	Water	Fruitful	4th 10:56 pm
28 Wed	Pisces	Water	Fruitful	4th
29 Thu 3:52 pm	Aries	Fire	Barren	4th
30 Fri	Aries	Fire	Barren	4th
31 Sat 6:18 pm	Taurus	Earth	Semi-fruitful	4th

June Moon Table

Date	Sign	Element	Nature	Phase
1 Sun	Taurus	Earth	Semi-fruitful	4th
2 Mon 6:06 pm	Gemini	Air	Barren	4th
3 Tue	Gemini	Air	Barren	New 3:22 pm
4 Wed 5:16 pm	Cancer	Water	Fruitful	1st
5 Thu	Cancer	Water	Fruitful	1st
6 Fri 6:00 pm	Leo	Fire	Barren	1st
7 Sat	Leo	Fire	Barren	1st
8 Sun 10:01 pm	Virgo	Earth	Barren	1st
9 Mon	Virgo	Earth	Barren	1st
10 Tue	Virgo	Earth	Barren	2nd 11:03 am
11 Wed 5:55 am	Libra	Air	Semi-fruitful	2nd
12 Thu	Libra	Air	Semi-fruitful	2nd
13 Fri 4:53 pm	Scorpio	Water	Fruitful	2nd
14 Sat	Scorpio	Water	Fruitful	2nd
15 Sun	Scorpio	Water	Fruitful	2nd
16 Mon 5:19 am	Sagittarius	Fire	Barren	2nd
17 Tue	Sagittarius	Fire	Barren	2nd
18 Wed 5:51 pm	Capricorn	Earth	Semi-fruitful	Full 1:30 pm
19 Thu	Capricorn	Earth	Semi-fruitful	3rd
20 Fri	Capricorn	Earth	Semi-fruitful	3rd
21 Sat 5:33 am	Aquarius	Air	Barren	3rd
22 Sun	Aquarius	Air	Barren	3rd
23 Mon 3:32 pm	Pisces	Water	Fruitful	3rd
24 Tue	Pisces	Water	Fruitful	3rd
25 Wed 10:49 pm	Aries	Fire	Barren	3rd
26 Thu	Aries	Fire	Barren	4th 8:10 am
27 Fri	Aries	Fire	Barren	4th
28 Sat 2:50 am	Taurus	Earth	Semi-fruitful	4th
29 Sun	Taurus	Earth	Semi-fruitful	4th
30 Mon 4:03 am	Gemini	Air	Barren	4th

July Moon Table

Date	Sign	Element	Nature	Phase
1 Tue	Gemini	Air	Barren	4th
2 Wed 3:53 am	Cancer	Water	Fruitful	New 10:18 pm
3 Thu	Cancer	Water	Fruitful	1st
4 Fri 4:15 am	Leo	Fire	Barren	1st
5 Sat	Leo	Fire	Barren	1st
6 Sun 7:04 am	Virgo	Earth	Barren	1st
7 Mon	Virgo	Earth	Barren	1st
8 Tue 1:31 pm	Libra	Air	Semi-fruitful	1st
9 Wed	Libra	Air	Semi-fruitful	1st
10 Thu 11:35 pm	Scorpio	Water	Fruitful	2nd 12:35 am
11 Fri	Scorpio	Water	Fruitful	2nd
12 Sat	Scorpio	Water	Fruitful	2nd
13 Sun 11:50 am	Sagittarius	Fire	Barren	2nd
14 Mon	Sagittarius	Fire	Barren	2nd
15 Tue	Sagittarius	Fire	Barren	2nd
16 Wed 12:20 am	Capricorn	Earth	Semi-fruitful	2nd
17 Thu	Capricorn	Earth	Semi-fruitful	2nd
18 Fri 11:40 am	Aquarius	Air	Barren	Full 3:59 am
19 Sat	Aquarius	Air	Barren	3rd
20 Sun 9:07 pm	Pisces	Water	Fruitful	3rd
21 Mon	Pisces	Water	Fruitful	3rd
22 Tue	Pisces	Water	Fruitful	3rd
23 Wed 4:22 am	Aries	Fire	Barren	3rd
24 Thu	Aries	Fire	Barren	3rd
25 Fri 9:14 am	Taurus	Earth	Semi-fruitful	4th 2:41 pm
26 Sat	Taurus	Earth	Semi-fruitful	4th
27 Sun 11:55 am	Gemini	Air	Barren	4th
28 Mon	Gemini	Air	Barren	4th
29 Tue 1:11 pm	Cancer	Water	Fruitful	4th
30 Wed	Cancer	Water	Fruitful	4th
31 Thu 2:21 pm	Leo	Fire	Barren	4th

August Moon Table

Date	Sign	Element	Nature	Phase
1 Fri	Leo	Fire	Barren	New 6:12 am
2 Sat 4:59 pm	Virgo	Earth	Barren	1st
3 Sun	Virgo	Earth	Barren	1st
4 Mon 10:28 pm	Libra	Air	Semi-fruitful	1st
5 Tue	Libra	Air	Semi-fruitful	1st
6 Wed	Libra	Air	Semi-fruitful	1st
7 Thu 7:26 am	Scorpio	Water	Fruitful	1st
8 Fri	Scorpio	Water	Fruitful	2nd 4:20 pm
9 Sat 7:10 pm	Sagittarius	Fire	Barren	2nd
10 Sun	Sagittarius	Fire	Barren	2nd
11 Mon	Sagittarius	Fire	Barren	2nd
12 Tue 7:42 am	Capricorn	Earth	Semi-fruitful	2nd
13 Wed	Capricorn	Earth	Semi-fruitful	2nd
14 Thu 6:56 pm	Aquarius	Air	Barren	2nd
15 Fri	Aquarius	Air	Barren	2nd
16 Sat	Aquarius	Air	Barren	Full 5:16 pm
17 Sun 3:46 am	Pisces	Water	Fruitful	3rd
18 Mon	Pisces	Water	Fruitful	3rd
19 Tue 10:10 am	Aries	Fire	Barren	3rd
20 Wed	Aries	Fire	Barren	3rd
21 Thu 2:38 pm	Taurus	Earth	Semi-fruitful	3rd
22 Fri	Taurus	Earth	Semi-fruitful	3rd
23 Sat 5:48 pm	Gemini	Air	Barren	4th 7:49 pm
24 Sun	Gemini	Air	Barren	4th
25 Mon 8:18 pm	Cancer	Water	Fruitful	4th
26 Tue	Cancer	Water	Fruitful	4th
27 Wed 10:51 pm	Leo	Fire	Barren	4th
28 Thu	Leo	Fire	Barren	4th
29 Fri	Leo	Fire	Barren	4th
30 Sat 2:18 am	Virgo	Earth	Barren	New 3:58 pm
31 Sun	Virgo	Earth	Barren	1st

September Moon Table

Date	Sign	Element	Nature	Phase
1 Mon 7:44 am	Libra	Air	Semi-fruitful	1st
2 Tue	Libra	Air	Semi-fruitful	1st
3 Wed 4:02 pm	Scorpio	Water	Fruitful	1st
4 Thu	Scorpio	Water	Fruitful	1st
5 Fri	Scorpio	Water	Fruitful	1st
6 Sat 3:11 am	Sagittarius	Fire	Barren	1st
7 Sun	Sagittarius	Fire	Barren	2nd 10:04 am
8 Mon 3:45 pm	Capricorn	Earth	Semi-fruitful	2nd
9 Tue	Capricorn	Earth	Semi-fruitful	2nd
10 Wed	Capricorn	Earth	Semi-fruitful	2nd
11 Thu 3:19 am	Aquarius	Air	Barren	2nd
12 Fri	Aquarius	Air	Barren	2nd
13 Sat 12:04 pm	Pisces	Water	Fruitful	2nd
14 Sun	Pisces	Water	Fruitful	2nd
15 Mon 5:39 pm	Aries	Fire	Barren	Full 5:13 am
16 Tue	Aries	Fire	Barren	3rd
17 Wed 8:56 pm	Taurus	Earth	Semi-fruitful	3rd
18 Thu	Taurus	Earth	Semi-fruitful	3rd
19 Fri 11:17 pm	Gemini	Air	Barren	3rd
20 Sat	Gemini	Air	Barren	3rd
21 Sun	Gemini	Air	Barren	3rd
22 Mon 1:48 am	Cancer	Water	Fruitful	4th 1:04 am
23 Tue	Cancer	Water	Fruitful	4th
24 Wed 5:13 am	Leo	Fire	Barren	4th
25 Thu	Leo	Fire	Barren	4th
26 Fri 9:52 am	Virgo	Earth	Barren	4th
27 Sat	Virgo	Earth	Barren	4th
28 Sun 4:05 pm	Libra	Air	Semi-fruitful	4th
29 Mon	Libra	Air	Semi-fruitful	New 4:12 am
30 Tue	Libra	Air	Semi-fruitful	1st

October Moon Table

Date	Sign	Element	Nature	Phase
1 Wed 12:26 am	Scorpio	Water	Fruitful	1st
2 Thu	Scorpio	Water	Fruitful	1st
3 Fri 11:14 am	Sagittarius	Fire	Barren	1st
4 Sat	Sagittarius	Fire	Barren	1st
5 Sun 11:48 pm	Capricorn	Earth	Semi-fruitful	1st
6 Mon	Capricorn	Earth	Semi-fruitful	1st
7 Tue	Capricorn	Earth	Semi-fruitful	2nd 5:04 am
8 Wed 12:03 pm	Aquarius	Air	Barren	2nd
9 Thu	Aquarius	Air	Barren	2nd
10 Fri 9:31 pm	Pisces	Water	Fruitful	2nd
11 Sat	Pisces	Water	Fruitful	2nd
12 Sun	Pisces	Water	Fruitful	2nd
13 Mon 3:07 am	Aries	Fire	Barren	2nd
14 Tue	Aries	Fire	Barren	Full 4:02 pm
15 Wed 5:31 am	Taurus	Earth	Semi-fruitful	3rd
16 Thu	Taurus	Earth	Semi-fruitful	3rd
17 Fri 6:25 am	Gemini	Air	Barren	3rd
18 Sat	Gemini	Air	Barren	3rd
19 Sun 7:40 am	Cancer	Water	Fruitful	3rd
20 Mon	Cancer	Water	Fruitful	3rd
21 Tue 10:35 am	Leo	Fire	Barren	4th 7:54 am
22 Wed	Leo	Fire	Barren	4th
23 Thu 3:40 pm	Virgo	Earth	Barren	4th
24 Fri	Virgo	Earth	Barren	4th
25 Sat 10:47 pm	Libra	Air	Semi-fruitful	4th
26 Sun	Libra	Air	Semi-fruitful	4th
27 Mon	Libra	Air	Semi-fruitful	4th
28 Tue 7:47 am	Scorpio	Water	Fruitful	New 7:14 pm
29 Wed	Scorpio	Water	Fruitful	1st
30 Thu 6:41 pm	Sagittarius	Fire	Barren	1st
31 Fri	Sagittarius	Fire	Barren	1st

November Moon Table

Date	Sign	Element	Nature	Phase
1 Sat	Sagittarius	Fire	Barren	1st
2 Sun 6:13 am	Capricorn	Earth	Semi-fruitful	1st
3 Mon	Capricorn	Earth	Semi-fruitful	1st
4 Tue 7:01 pm	Aquarius	Air	Barren	1st
5 Wed	Aquarius	Air	Barren	2nd 11:03 pm
6 Thu	Aquarius	Air	Barren	2nd
7 Fri 5:43 am	Pisces	Water	Fruitful	2nd
8 Sat	Pisces	Water	Fruitful	2nd
9 Sun 12:26 pm	Aries	Fire	Barren	2nd
10 Mon	Aries	Fire	Barren	2nd
11 Tue 3:05 pm	Taurus	Earth	Semi-fruitful	2nd
12 Wed	Taurus	Earth	Semi-fruitful	2nd
13 Thu 3:11 pm	Gemini	Air	Barren	Full 1:17 am
14 Fri	Gemini	Air	Barren	3rd
15 Sat 2:52 pm	Cancer	Water	Fruitful	3rd
16 Sun	Cancer	Water	Fruitful	3rd
17 Mon 4:07 pm	Leo	Fire	Barren	3rd
18 Tue	Leo	Fire	Barren	3rd
19 Wed 8:12 pm	Virgo	Earth	Barren	4th 4:31 pm
20 Thu	Virgo	Earth	Barren	4th
21 Fri	Virgo	Earth	Barren	4th
22 Sat 3:20 am	Libra	Air	Semi-fruitful	4th
23 Sun	Libra	Air	Semi-fruitful	4th
24 Mon 12:54 pm	Scorpio	Water	Fruitful	4th
25 Tue	Scorpio	Water	Fruitful	4th
26 Wed	Scorpio	Water	Fruitful	4th
27 Thu 12:14 am	Sagittarius	Fire	Barren	New 11:54 am
28 Fri	Sagittarius	Fire	Barren	1st
29 Sat 12:48 pm	Capricorn	Earth	Semi-fruitful	1st
30 Sun	Capricorn	Earth	Semi-fruitful	1st

December Moon Table

Date	Sign	Element	Nature	Phase
1 Thu	Capricorn	Earth	Semi-fruitful	1st
2 Tue 1:44 am	Aquarius	Air	Barren	1st
3 Wed	Aquarius	Air	Barren	1st
4 Thu 1:23 pm	Pisces	Water	Fruitful	1st
5 Fri	Pisces	Water	Fruitful	2nd 4:25 pm
6 Sat 9:44 pm	Aries	Fire	Barren	2nd
7 Sun	Aries	Fire	Barren	2nd
8 Mon	Aries	Fire	Barren	2nd
9 Tue 1:52 am	Taurus	Earth	Semi-fruitful	2nd
10 Wed	Taurus	Earth	Semi-fruitful	2nd
11 Thu 2:33 am	Gemini	Air	Barren	2nd
12 Fri	Gemini	Air	Barren	Full 11:37 am
13 Sat 1:39 am	Cancer	Water	Fruitful	3rd
14 Sun	Cancer	Water	Fruitful	3rd
15 Mon 1:22 am	Leo	Fire	Barren	3rd
16 Tue	Leo	Fire	Barren	3rd
17 Wed 3:35 am	Virgo	Earth	Barren	3rd
18 Thu	Virgo	Earth	Barren	3rd
19 Fri 9:23 am	Libra	Air	Semi-fruitful	4th 5:29 am
20 Sat	Libra	Air	Semi-fruitful	4th
21 Sun 6:36 pm	Scorpio	Water	Fruitful	4th
22 Mon	Scorpio	Water	Fruitful	4th
23 Tue	Scorpio	Water	Fruitful	4th
24 Wed 6:13 am	Sagittarius	Fire	Barren	4th
25 Thu	Sagittarius	Fire	Barren	4th
26 Fri 6:56 pm	Capricorn	Earth	Semi-fruitful	4th
27 Sat	Capricorn	Earth	Semi-fruitful	New 7:22 am
28 Sun	Capricorn	Earth	Semi-fruitful	1st
29 Mon 7:42 am	Aquarius	Air	Barren	1st
30 Tue	Aquarius	Air	Barren	1st
31 Wed 7:27 pm	Pisces	Water	Fruitful	1st

About the Authors

ELIZABETH BARRETTE serves as the managing editor of *PanGaia*. The central Illinois resident has been involved with the Pagan community for more than seventeen years. Her other writing fields include speculative fiction and gender studies. Visit her website at www.worthlink.net/~ysabet/sitemap.html.

CHANDRA MOIRA BEAL is a freelance writer currently living in England. She has authored three books and published hundreds of articles, all inspired by her day-to-day life and adventures. She has been writing for Llewellyn since 1998. Chandra is also a massage therapist. To learn more, visit www.beal-net.com/laluna.

NANCY BENNETT has been published in Llewellyn's annuals, *We'moon*, *Circle Network*, and many mainstream publications. Her pet projects include reading and writing about history and creating ethnic dinners to test on her family.

KRYSTAL BOWDEN, who has been studying the magical and mundane properties of herbs and essential oils for over ten years, has written articles on herbalism, aromatherapy, and natural living for the past six years. She has been the coordinator of the Circle of Gaia Dreaming for three years and also presents workshops relating to Paganism. She lives in Ohio with her partner, young son, five cats, and a dog.

KAAREN CHRIST is a consultant providing research and writing services to social service organizations. She also writes children's stories and crafts poetry. She lives in Prince Edward County, Ontario, with two beautiful children (Indigo and Challian), a Super-Dog called Lukki, and a magical boy-rabbit.

DALLAS JENNIFER COBB lives in an enchanted waterfront village where she focuses on what she loves: family, gardens, fitness, and fabulous food. Her essays are in Llewellyn's almanacs and recent Seal Press anthologies *Three Ring Circus* and *Far From Home*. Her video documentary, *Disparate Places*, appeared on TV Ontario's Planet Parent. Contact her at Jennifer.Cobb@Sympatico.ca.

SALLY CRAGIN writes the astrological forecast, "Moon Signs," for the *Boston Phoenix* and other papers. A regular arts reviewer and feature writer for the *Boston Globe*, she also edits *Button, New England's Tiniest Magazine of Poetry, Fiction, and Gracious Living*. For more, including your personal forecast, see moonsigns.net.

KAREN CREEL is a nurse by profession whose attendance at an herb conference five years ago resulted in starting her online business, GardenChick. Future plans include more herb gardens on her four-acre property in Georgia and opening a retail herb business with display gardens and room for teaching classes. Visit her site, www.GardenChick.com.

SORITA D'ESTE is an author, researcher, and Priestess. She is the author of *Artemis: Virgin Goddess of the Sun & Moon* and coauthor of *Circle of Fire* and *The Guises of the Morrigan*. She regularly contributes to MBS publications and community magazines. She spends most of her time in London (UK), where she writes. For more information, please visit www.avalonia.co.uk.

ALICE DEVILLE has presented more than 150 workshops and seminars related to astrological, feng shui, metaphysical, motivational, and business themes. In her northern Virginia practice, Alice specializes in relationships, health, healing, real estate, government affairs, career and change management, and spiritual development. Contact Alice at DeVilleAA@aol.com.

MAGENTA GRIFFITH, a Witch for nearly thirty years, was in 1980 a founding member of the coven Prodea. She has been a member of the Covenant of the Goddess, CUUPs, Church of All Worlds, and several other Pagan organizations. She presents workshops and classes at festivals and gatherings around the Midwest.

SALLY MCSWEENEY has been "digging in the dirt" since childhood. Many plants later, she is a master herbalist specializing in aromatherapy and creating blended teas. She also owns Triple Aspect Herbs, a metaphysical herbal apothecary in Oregon. She is working on a book about healing with the energies of the Moon. She lives in Oregon with her husband and her two cats.

LEEDA ALLEYN PACOTTI is a naturopathic doctor, specializing in sleep and dream rehabilitation. Her authorship includes texts on natural cure for both professionals and nonprofessionals, although her publishing ventures are wide-ranging and eclectic. Some of her works are available at ultradiancreative.com.

SUZANNE RESS has been writing nonfiction and fiction for an eclectic array of publications for twenty-five years. She is an accomplished self-taught gardener and silversmith/mosaicist. She lives in the woods at the foot of the alps in northern Italy with her husband, two teenage daughters, wolf dog, and two horses.

LAUREL REUFNER has been a solitary Pagan for more than a decade. She is active in the Circle of Gaia Dreaming and is often attracted to bright and shiny ideas. She lives in Athens County (Ohio) with her husband and two adorable heathens, er, daughters. Her website is www.spiritrealm.com/Melinda/paganism.html.

ANNE SALA is a freelance journalist based in Minnesota. She has been interested in herbs ever since she was a toddler and her mother let her gather dill weed from the pot on the windowsill.

MICHELLE SKYE has been a practicing Witch for nine years. A founding member of the Sisterhood of the Crescent Moon, she is active in the southeastern Massachusetts Pagan community, presenting various workshops, classes, and apprenticeship programs. An ordained minister (Universal Life Church), she performs legal handfastings, weddings, and other spiritual rites of passage.

CERRIDWEN IRIS SHEA is a writer, teacher, and tarot reader who loves ice hockey and horse racing. Visit her website at www.cerridwenscottage.com; visit her blog Kemmyrk, which discusses working with tarot and oracles, at kemmyrk.wordpress.com.

LYNN SMYTHE is a freelance writer living in south Florida with her husband, son, and daughter. She has written articles for publications such as *The Herb Quarterly*, *Back Home*, and Llewellyn's annual *Herbal Almanac*. Lynn founded and is the manager of the online community Herb Witch, groups.msn.com/herbwitch.

MARK STAVISH is a practicing alchemist and the director of studies for the Institute for Hermetic Studies in Wyoming, PA. His work has been widely published in academic, specialty, and mass-market publications. His new book, *The Path of Alchemy*, is a useful, comprehensive guide for students of alchemy, Qabala, elemental witchcraft, and herbalism.

AARTIANA has worked with herbs and natural healing since the early 1990s and became a certified Master Herbalist in 2007. She lives in Western Montana with her husband, her two teenage children, and an old black tomcat with white whiskers named Chuckles. Find out more at www.myspace.com/aartiana.

SUSUN WEED began studying herbal medicine in 1965. Today, her work appears in peer-reviewed journals and magazines like *Sagewoman*. Her first book, *Wise Woman Herbal for the Childbearing Year*, was published in 1985. Her worldwide teaching schedule includes herbal medicine, the psychology of healing, nutrition, and women's health. Learn more at www.susunweed.com.

PATTI WIGINGTON is a staff writer for a central Ohio newspaper and a contributing editor for *Garden and Hearth*. Her articles have appeared in *Gaea's Cauldron*, *Twinshelp*, *Pediatrics for Parents*, and *The Witches Tutorial*. She is also the author of a historical adventure novel, a children's book, and *Summer's Ashes*, the first book in a series about teen Witches.

ZAEDA YIN is three-quarters Chinese, a tad Irish, and a lifelong solitary eclectic Pagan. She has lived, studied, and traveled extensively in India, Nepal, Japan, Hong Kong, Taiwan, Singapore, Malaysia, Thailand, and Borneo. Now based in Australia, her time is divided between writing and teaching the use of crystals, holy beads, and sacred objects from India and the Himalayas.